Cultural Policies in East Asia

Also by Lorraine Lim

CULTURAL POLICY IN EAST ASIA: Contemporary Issues and Trends (*editor*)

Cultural Policies in East Asia

Dynamics between the State, Arts and Creative Industries

Edited by

Hye-Kyung Lee
King's College London, UK

and

Lorraine Lim
Birkbeck College, University of London, UK

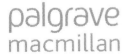

First published 2014 by
PALGRAVE MACMILLAN

Palgrave Macmillan in the UK is an imprint of Macmillan Publishers Limited,
registered in England, company number 785998, of Houndmills, Basingstoke,
Hampshire RG21 6XS.

Palgrave Macmillan in the US is a division of St Martin's Press LLC,
175 Fifth Avenue, New York, NY 10010.

Palgrave Macmillan is the global academic imprint of the above companies
and has companies and representatives throughout the world.

Palgrave® and Macmillan® are registered trademarks in the United States,
the United Kingdom, Europe and other countries

ISBN 978-1-349-46019-9   ISBN 978-1-137-32777-2 (eBook)
DOI 10.1057/9781137327772

A catalogue record for this book is available from the British Library.

Library of Congress Cataloging-in-Publication Data

Cultural policies in East Asia : dynamics between the state, arts and creative
industries / edited by Hye-Kyung Lee (King's College London, UK), Lorraine Lim
(Birkbeck University of London, UK).
      pages cm
   Includes bibliographical references.
   ISBN 978-1-349-46019-9
   1. East Asia – Cultural policy. 2. Art and state – East Asia. 3. Cultural
industries – Government policy – East Asia. 4. Politics and culture – East Asia.
5. Group identity – East Asia. 6. Social change – East Asia. 7. East Asia – Politics
and government. 8. East Asia – Economic conditions. I. Lee, Hye-Kyung, 1968–
II. Lim, Lorraine, 1980–

DS509.3.C86 2014
700.1′03095—dc23   2014020548.

Transferred to Digital Printing in 2014

Contents

Part III   The Rise of Creative Industries Policy

List of Illustrations

Figures

Tables

Notes on Contributors

Terence Chong is Senior Fellow and coordinator of the Regional Social and Cultural Studies Programme at the Institute of Southeast Asian Studies. His research interests include Christianity in Southeast Asia, heritage, cultural policies and politics in Singapore, new Chinese immigrants in CLMV countries, and the sociology of religion. He has published in *Journal of Contemporary Asia, Critical Asian Studies, Modern Asian Studies* and *Asian Studies Review*. He is the author of *The Theatre and the State in Singapore: Orthodoxy and Resistance* (2010) and co-author of *Different Under God: A Survey of Church-going Protestants in Singapore* (2013)

Hsiao-Ling Chung is Assistant Professor within the Institute of Creative Industries Design at National Cheng Kung University, Taiwan. She completed her masters in Creative and Media Enterprise and PhD in Creative Industries at the University of Warwick, UK. She has held managerial positions with various cultural and creative enterprises in Taipei. Her research interests lie in the application of cross-disciplinary theoretical perspectives and cross-context analytical approaches on the network ecology of the creative sector. Her current research examines the talent networks of the creative audio-visual industries between Taiwan and Mainland China.

Anthony Y.H. Fung has been the director of the School of Journalism and Communications at the Chinese University of Hong Kong since 2011. He is a veteran scholar with more than 15 years of research experience in the fields of identity studies, popular culture and creative industries. He has many publications on Asian pop culture, including his latest work, *Asian Popular Culture: The Global (Dis)continuity*. He also serves on the editorial board of *Popular Communication* and founded Interasia Pop Music Group, a platform for over 100 scholars and researchers to promote the study of popular culture.

Xin Gu is Research Fellow in the School of Culture and Communication and a member of the Research Unit in Public Culture at the University of Melbourne. Xin has been prominent in the attempt to contextualize contemporary western debates around cultural economy, creative cities and cultural policy in the Chinese context. Her main focus has been on developing a sociological understanding of 'cultural entrepreneurship' based on small-scale local creative industries; developing new theoretical and methodological approaches to understanding urban 'creative clusters' based on case studies in China and Australia; and a cross-cultural understanding of 'Chinese urban modernities.'

Kiwon Hong is Professor in Arts and Cultural Administration at Sookmyung Women's University, Korea. Based on her research in Aesthetics and Public Administration, she worked as a chief researcher at the Korea Culture and Tourism Institute (KCTI), a policy research body to the Korean Ministry of Culture, Sports, and Tourism. She has been involved in cultural diversity and international cultural exchange issues through legislative process and policy evaluation. Her main research area includes the historical development of Korean cultural policy, cultural diversity policy and policy evaluation. She is also the author of the Korea profile for World Cultural Policy website.

Nobuko Kawashima received her PhD in Cultural Policy from the University of Warwick in England and is currently Professor at the Faculty of Economics, Doshisha University in Kyoto, Japan. From 1995 to 1999, she was a research fellow at the Centre for Cultural Policy Studies, University of Warwick. Her areas of interest include cultural policy, cultural economics, copyright law and the creative industries. Her recent publications include *The Creative Industries: From Economic, Legal and Managerial Perspectives* (2009, in Japanese) and 'Corporate Support for the Arts in Japan: Beyond Emulation of the Western Models,' *International Journal of Cultural Policy* (2012).

Michael Keane is Principal Research fellow at the ARC Centre Fellow at the Australian Research Council Centre of Excellence for Creative Industries and Innovation (CCI), Queensland University of Technology, Brisbane. Keane's research interests include China's cultural and media policy, creative industries in China and East Asia, and East Asian cultural exports. He is author or editor of numerous books on Chinese and East Asian media and creative industries and is Director of the Asian Creative Transformations research cluster at http://www.creativetransformations.asia.

Mari Kobayashi is Associate Professor at the University of Tokyo in Cultural Resources Studies in the Graduate School of Humanities and Sociology. She graduated from Waseda University before undertaking her PhD at Waseda in Human Sciences. Before starting in her present position, she was a lecturer at Shizuoka University of Arts and Culture in the Department of Cultural Policy. Since 2013, she is the chairperson of the board of directors of the Japan Association for Cultural Policy Research. She also advises many local governments in Japan about their local cultural policy.

Hye-Kyung Lee is Lecturer in Cultural and Creative Industries at King's College London. She researches cultural policy, cultural industries and cultural consumption within both global and East Asian contexts. She has published research papers in major journals in the field including the *International Journal of Cultural Policy, Poetics* and *Media, Culture & Society*, and has guest-edited special issues for *Creative Industries Journal* and *Arts Marketing: An International Journal*. She is currently undertaking a knowledge-transfer project on public culture and online consumption and is writing *Cultural Policy in South Korea* (2016). She has been awarded the Korea Foundation's field research fellowship (2012/2013) and the Academy of Korean Studies' competitive research grant (2014/2015).

Lorraine Lim is Lecturer in Arts Management at Birkbeck College, University of London. Her research interests focus on cultural strategies utilized by cities in Asia to transform themselves into capitals of culture. She has edited a special issue for the *International Journal of Cultural Policy* on cultural policy in Asia, which will be published as a book in 2014, and has co-authored the chapter 'Beyond Conventional Western Views of Creativity and Innovation' for *The Handbook of Management and Creativity* (2014). She is currently working on a funded research project examining unpaid internships in the arts in the UK.

Jerry C.Y. Liu is Associate Professor of the Graduate School of Arts Management and Cultural Policy at the National Taiwan University of Arts. He teaches cultural policy studies at the postgraduate and doctoral levels. Since 2011, LIU has been a consultant member for *Culture Basic Law* and *Culture and Arts Reward Act* in Taiwan. He is a board member of the Taiwan Association of Culture Law and the author/editor of *Global Cities, Cultural Governance and Cultural Strategies* (2013). His current research focuses on the ReOrienting of cultural governance and cultural policy, and the interactivity between culture and the political economy.

Li-Jung Wang is Professor and Chief of the MA course in Hakka Social and Cultural Studies, National Central University, Taiwan. She has a PhD in Cultural Policy Studies from the University of Warwick (1999–2003). Wang's academic interests are related to cultural policy, Hakka studies, cultural identity, cultural citizenship, transnational community and media uses. Her works include *The Development of Hakka Ethnicity* *and Cultural Policy in Taiwan* (2012, book in Chinese), 'Towards Cultural Citizenship? Cultural Rights and Cultural Policy in Taiwan,' *Citizenship Studies* (2013), 'Diaspora, Identity and Cultural Citizenship: the Hakkas in Multicultural Taiwan,' *Ethnic and Racial Studies* (2007).

Elaine Jing Zhao is Lecturer in the School of the Arts and Media, Faculty of Arts and Social Sciences at the University of New South Wales (UNSW), Australia. Elaine has been researching and publishing on digital media, cultural economy, user co-creation, informal media economies, and their social, cultural and economic implications. Her publications on these and other topics include contributions to *International Journal of Cultural Studies, Media, Culture & Society, Global Media and Communication,* and *Convergence: The International Journal of Research into New Media Technologies.* Elaine also acts as Deputy Director of the Asian Creative Transformations research cluster at http://www.creativetransformations. asia/. Before joining UNSW, Elaine was a postdoctoral research fellow at the ARC CCI Centre for Excellence for Creative Industries & Innovation based at Queensland University of Technology.

Cultural Policies in East Asia: An Introduction

Hye-Kyung Lee and Lorraine Lim

Why study East Asian cultural policies?

Cultural policy is an emerging field of research that attracts scholars in many disciplines ranging from cultural studies, cultural sociology, public policy studies, and media studies to cultural economics. More recently, with a growing interest from policy makers and academics on the creative industries and creative economy, the scope of and themes within cultural policy research have been broadened further. As a new and interdisciplinary field, the research makes use of conceptual and theoretical tools drawn from various disciplines. The difficulty in clearly defining key subject knowledge and theoretical frameworks, however, indicates that perhaps cultural policy is closer to a theme shared by those disciplines than a discrete area of study (Kawashima forthcoming). This implies that there are multiple, sometimes independent, sets of keywords and analytical approaches to studying this area. For instance, cultural economists (Peacock and Rizzo 1994) and critical cultural theorists (McGuigan 2004) provide two very different ways of understanding culture-state relations. As cultural policy research advances and matures, we expect that there will be more calls for it to develop its own language and theoretical perspectives.

Another visible attribute of current research is its orientation toward issues embedded in Anglophone and European societies. The nature of and dynamics in cultural policies elsewhere seldom draw the research community's serious attention and tend to be viewed mostly as one-off case studies. One reason for this might be that scholarly consciousness and investigation of cultural policy emerged and advanced earlier in Western Europe and North America than other parts of the world. Another reason might be the language barriers that deter researchers from accessing cultural policy debates 'out there' and sharing key research findings by local scholars unless they are communicated in English. The uneven distribution of research outputs across different linguistic territories is likely to skew the research community's attention towards contexts and experiences of Anglophone and European democracies. For example, culture's autonomy and its role as a civil sector is somewhat taken for granted, though it is a product of a lengthy historical process that has not yet taken place or is still ongoing in societies beyond Western democracies. There is also an existing preoccupation in current cultural policy research with exploring culture itself and its critical and reflexive faculties at the expense of a more focused discussion on other key constituents of cultural policy such as the state, politics and bureaucracy. While the available writings are often inclined to perceive culture and the state as differentiated realms, cultural policies in many parts of the world show that this relationship is far more complicated. It may be impossible to separate one from the other in societies under authoritarian regimes, and the relationship might be unstable and unfixed in some societies where there exist serious discrepancies between the boundary of the nation state and that of cultural and linguistic communities.

This book aims to enhance our understanding of cultural policy by looking *beyond* the Anglophone and European contexts and bringing in East Asian perspectives. East Asia, a region encompassing Japan to Singapore, is a geographical area known for its rapid economic modernization and growth (As of 2012, China, Japan and South Korea are the world's second, third and fifteenth largest economies respectively, according to the World Bank, 2013) and dynamic political and social transformations during the past decades. With the rise of their economic and political significance, countries in the region now possess the capacity to actively partake in the global cultural economy as both producers and consumers (Iwabuchi 2002; Kim 2013). This process has broadly corresponded with a series of cultural policy developments, though Japan is relatively reserved about state intervention in culture. Yet there has been little attempt to draw an overall outlook of cultural policies in the region, and the current cultural policy research within the region itself shows a tendency to look westward to find both theoretical tools for policy analysis and practical strategies for policy development.

The lack of academic research in East Asian cultural policies contrasts the remarkable growth in volume of scholarly writings in East Asian popular culture during the last couple of decades. Witnessing the expansion of the region's cultural industries and the unprecedented regional sharing of Japanese and then Korean pop culture, an increasing number of scholars have explored inter-Asian culture and cultural connections by looking into popular cultural texts and idols, their appropriation in the region, their transnational fandom mediated by online and digital technologies, and the issue of national and cultural identities (Chua and Iwabuchi 2008; Iwabuchi 2002). The literature in this area occasionally comments on the roles pop culture play in nation building and nation branding, but scant attention has been paid to national and regional implications of state policies in cultural production, distribution and consumption. Meanwhile, Asian studies are a huge area of research with varying foci from culture and language to politics and defense. While the knowledge of Asian culture or cultures of individual countries in both broader and narrow senses has advanced in this discipline, state policies on culture still remains a niche area that is in need of more attention.

With this book, we attempt to fill some of those gaps and unpack the dynamics between the state, arts and creative industries in East Asian countries. This book acknowledges multiple meanings of culture, from the arts and media to a way of life. This broad scope therefore accommodates multiple goals, orientations and functions of cultural policy, from support for and control of the arts and media, to the formation and modification of national cultural identity and people's way of life. Cultural policy operates at multiple levels – from the state discourse of culture, policy implementation at governmental levels, the cultural sector's own understanding of cultural practices, cultural discourse in the media and intellectual circles, cultural organizations' interaction with citizens, and citizens' own creation of their everyday cultural life. This implies that the scope of cultural policy is far bigger than the remit of formal institutions for cultural policy such as cultural ministries, cultural budgets and related laws. Some of above activities operate as 'explicit' or 'implicit' cultural policies, while this distinction is not always clear (Ahearne 2009). This book's primary aim is to provide a broad historical, social and political outlook of such cultural policies in East Asian countries, rather than giving a complete map of cultural policy in each country or carrying out a cross-national comparative analysis. Corresponding with cultural policy research's interdisciplinary nature, the book combines different disciplinary approaches from cultural history and cultural theories to nation branding. It goes beyond presenting the region's cultural policies as a collection of individual case studies that represent cultural policy in each country and intends to draw attention to key factors that have determined the orientation, structure and organization of cultural policies in the region. In doing so, we hope to help develop theoretical and analytical perspectives that are pertinent to cultural policies in East Asia, bringing new references and research agendas to the field of cultural policy research.

An overview of the region

East Asia within this book is defined not merely by geography but also by political, economic and cultural proximity. Geographically, this region 'extends from Japan and Korea in the north-east to Singapore and Hong Kong in the south' (Rozman 1991, p. 7). The selected countries – China, Japan, Singapore, South Korea and Taiwan – are hugely different in terms of population and territory size, ranging from nearly 1.36 billion Chinese living in an area of 9.6 million square kilometres to 5 million Singaporeans in a landmass of just 710 square kilometres (United Nations 2012; UNdata 2013). While China is the region's largest economy, followed by Japan and South Korea, GDP per capita tells a different story. Here Singapore and Japan are placed at the top of both East Asian and World leagues, while China lags far behind. There is, however, more than just the geographical closeness of these countries that allow for them to be discussed collectively; what we observe is noticeable economic, socio-cultural and historical proximities between countries, albeit to varying degrees.

The first commonality shared by these countries is that they have all experienced state-led industrial advancement and economic growth during the second half of the 20th century (Vogel 1991). Japan, South Korea, Singapore and Taiwan are often defined as 'developmental states' where the state prioritizes economic development over other policy goals and implements proactive industrial policies, maintaining a tight grip on market forces. Although China adopts a communist political system and was cut off from the capitalist market economy until 1978, the country's current approach to economic management indicates some similarity with the rest of the group. Secondly, it is also widely acknowledged that the countries share a Confucian cultural heritage that values loyalty, hard work, education and a sense of collective responsibility, which affects the way society is organized and coordinated (Rozman 1991). The Confucian heritage, which was once regarded as a barrier to modernization, is now seen as a crucial factor for the rapid economic progress achieved by the region. Its influence can be also seen in the common governance style in the region, which is responsive to the needs of the citizens through prioritizing the creation and maintenance of social order and harmony and the uses of moral persuasion (Tu 2000,

p. 205). Thirdly, the region has been subjected to complex historical and ideological tensions 'within,' a product of the history of colonization, ideological conflicts and the Cold War. The relationships between countries in question have been shaped heavily by such factors: for example the historical atrocity between Japan on the one hand and South Korea and China on the other hand, the ideological rivalry between China and Taiwan during the Cold War period, the diehard political and military tension between South and North Korea, and the territorial disputes between the countries. It is not surprising that those regional factors have been important variables that have determined the region's cultural policies. The East Asian countries have achieved political democracy at different times in the 20th century, with China being an exception, but all have witnessed a flourishing consumer society in accordance with their economic growth. In addition, it is now possible to see an increasing influence of neoliberalism on the politics and economies of these countries, with China accommodating neoliberal approaches selectively on its economy.

With the growing political and economic roles they are playing within the global economy, the countries in the region are now showing an increasing interest in the 'creative industries' and are endeavoring to expand them. In spite of the unceasing debate around the definition and boundary of these industries, they are seen not only as a crucial source of wealth generation but also an effective means for raising the country's international profile and harness their soft power. With these changing socio-economic and political backdrops, it is imperative to examine the evolving dynamics between the state and culture in these countries through an investigation of both the continuity and reformulation of their cultural policies.

What are the emerging themes?

The chapters in this book address three key themes that are emerging from the region's cultural policies: cultural identity formation and nation building; the negotiation between culture and the state; and the rise of creative industries policy. These three aspects of cultural policy are interlinked and overlap with one another. For example, cultural identity construction and nation building necessarily involves negotiations between culture and the state, and both aspects are clearly reflected in the current development of creative industries policy. Thus we would like to present these themes not as separate areas of cultural policy but as three connected dimensions of the policy. While cultural policy discourse in these countries has shifted its focus over time from cultural identity formation towards the agenda of creative industries, the concerns with the former shape the latter, while their relations are mediated via culture-state negotiations.

The first common theme cutting across East Asian cultural policies is that they have been moulded significantly by regional – historical and geopolitical – factors as well as domestic politics. This explains why the countries have seen a tight entanglement between culture, identity formation and nation building. Japan appears as an odd case here. Its past as a colonizer, its overt abuses of culture for patriotic and imperial purposes during its colonial and the Second World War periods, and America's influence on the country during the occupation period have led the country to adopt a non-statist cultural policy. The laissez-faire attitude in cultural policy is also in accordance with the country's relaxed attitude to Western cultural influences. Japanese society's open reception of Western aesthetics and art forms might have been a reflection of its confidence in the continuity of its traditional culture and heritage without large-scale interruptions by external forces (Tomooka et al. 2002). The country's stable democracy and the organic growth of the cultural sector have also legitimized the non-statist cultural policy. Meanwhile, South Korea, Taiwan, Singapore and China share the experience of being occupied/colonized by either Japanese and/or Western forces, with their independence or building of a new nation only occurring between the 1940s and 1960s. Hence, the decolonization and the reconstruction of national identity would become an essential part of these countries' initial cultural policies. This process took place with the overall Westernization of society, and cultural policy was called upon to preserve traditional and indigenous cultural forms while cultivating the society's competency to produce and enjoy Western (high) culture. The ideological tensions and rivalries in claiming the ownership of 'national culture' within the Korean peninsula and between China and Taiwan have also left significant marks on the countries' politics and society. Within such context, governments in these countries developed highly interventionist cultural policies that involved top-down constructions of ideological consensus and national identity.

In Singapore and Taiwan, cultural policy needed to manage internal ethnic and linguistic diversity, colonial legacies and cultural influences from the West. While the former regarded multiculturalism as a state mission and adopted an international outlook from early on, the latter initially prioritized *Han* culture brought over by Chinese mainlanders and normalized via its cultural policy. Terence Chong and Li-jung Wang address these issues via their chapters. Chong's chapter points out that elite bureaucrats have been key actors in the formation of cultural identity in Singapore, generating and imposing their bureaucratic imaginations on the nation. He argues that the arts were imagined as a sign of cosmopolitan sophistication and a means for promoting the country as a global city in the 1990s. More recently, the government has attempted to develop new imaginations where the interests of the national and the global are to be reconciled, bringing together ideas of Singapore as both 'home' (and community) and a 'global city.' Wang's chapter interrogates the links between national identity and cultural policy in Taiwan, highlighting how the formation and evolution of Taiwanese cultural identity has occurred under the complex cultural and ethnic dynamics within the island, as well as its changing relationship with China. She shows how state policy for performing arts has been both a catalyst for this process and a response to it.

For South Korea and China, which possess largely mono-cultural populations, the formation of cultural identity and nation building were driven more by the need for political and ideological unity. For South Korea, potential threats from North Korea, coupled with the colonial legacies and rapid influx of Western culture, defined the government's early cultural policy to promote anti-communism and a coherent system of ideas onto society and to protect the country's 'national (traditional) culture.' Meanwhile, in China, communist ideologies shaped national identity with little room for diverse cultures and traditions to be equally recognized. During the recent two decades, however, the dynamics between cultural policy, nation building and cultural identity have noticeably changed. In line with the dissolution of the Cold War, China's transformation into a communist market economy and the rise of neoliberalizing forces in the region, governments have taken more open attitudes to bottom-up cultural initiatives and market-driven approaches. All five countries in the region now view culture as an effective tool for nation branding and soft power, and both Anthony Fung's and Kiwon Hong's work highlights the uses of culture to achieve these goals. Fung's chapter on Chinese online games examines the intricate interaction between nationalism, a market-driven cultural economy, and cultural globalization. It demonstrates that the Chinese online games industry has achieved multiple goals of conforming to state control, maximizing commercial gains in the domestic market and increased its global competitiveness by capitalizing on the country's cultural specificity and developing nationalistic content. Meanwhile, Hong sees South Korea's nation branding policy as the country's response to economic globalization and the rise of a global cultural economy. Yet, she pinpoints the ambiguity of such a policy by finding that state bureaucrats tend to fuse market-driven agendas of nation branding with their continuing concerns on the promotion of the country's traditional culture. To sum up, these chapters indicate that the process of cultural identity formation and nation building in the region is increasingly taking place across borders between the national and the global and between governmental and market domains. This seems to imply that the scope of cultural policy is continually being stretched as it tries to take account of and reach audiences and markets beyond the territory of the nation state.

The second theme that emerges from this collection is the close coupling of culture and the state in the East Asian region, with Japan, again, as the only exception. The roles played by the state in these nations are too dominant to be simply defined as 'mediating' between culture and the market or 'correcting' market failures (Peacock and Rizzo 1994). Similarly, a cultural sociological understanding that sees the field of cultural production as autonomous from the state (Bourdieu 1993; McGuigan 2004) has limited explanatory power when it comes to East Asian countries. Existing conceptual tools for comparative cultural studies, for examples, those based on Western welfare regimes (Toepler and Zimmer 2002) also do not fit well here. The intertwined relationships between culture and the state in East Asia have multiple dimensions, and these relationships were produced and sustained by authoritarian regimes that aimed to maintain ideological and moral control over culture. In spite of the political democracy the countries have achieved, their current cultural policies are still bounded by such political legacies.

Here, the chapters by Hye-Kyung Lee and Lorraine Lim examine past and current state intervention into the arts sector in Korea and Singapore respectively and argue for greater negotiation between the state and the arts sector if the arts are to continue to flourish in both of these countries. Lee's chapter argues that the developmental state, social legitimation of the arts, and the arts sector's internal conditions are key determinants of the Korean style of arts policy, where the state (still) functions as a main resource provider and coordinator of different interests in the arts sector. It calls for reflexivity on the parts of both the state and the arts sector and the latter's strengthened capacity as a civil society. These findings resonate with Lim's chapter on Singaporean arts policy, where the theatre sector demonstrates its ability to challenge the state discourse on Singaporean society by creating a new space for the discussion of politically and socially contentious issues, subverting the limited roles of 'civic' societies imposed by the government.

The governments in these countries have demonstrated a noticeable capacity to mobilize resources and implement ambitious cultural planning. In spite of the overall marketizing trends, the countries' cultural policies are still characterized by a strong state. Cultural policy and the management of major cultural institutions in the region are carried out more or less by state bureaucrats. Reflecting the Confucian cultural heritage and political ideology in the region, bureaucrats in these countries tend to be recruited via rigorous meritocratic selection processes. What is problematic is that they do not necessarily possess cultural knowledge and aptitude and have a tendency to manage culture through the same bureaucratic reasoning and procedures as those typically applied to economic or social policies. The supremacy of generalist bureaucrats in cultural policy making in East Asia can be compared with Anglophone and European cultural policies where cultural experts themselves often take the role of bureaucrats or are recruited to manage cultural facilities and programs. Jerry Liu's chapter is an attempt to find a language and perspective that would be more relevant to cultural policies in the region. Liu adopts 'cultural governance' as a framework that better captures an 'East Asian' or a 'Confucian' way of making and developing cultural policy, where state governance has been mediated by culture, and state bureaucrats themselves have also been subjected to this form of governance. Through examples drawn from Taiwan and China, the chapter shows cultural governance's continuity over history and also highlights recent attempts by Taiwanese civil society to reformulate it. Meanwhile, Mari Kobayashi's chapter demonstrates how cultural policy in Japanese local authorities, which has counterbalanced the central government's non-statist cultural policy, has been transformed in the last ten years as part of the country's public sector reforms. She argues that this change has opened up a new avenue where local cultural policy making accommodates not only market-driven approaches but also bottom-up initiatives from civil societies.

The final core theme that this book addresses is the dynamics between the state and the creative economy in East Asia. There has been an increase in the accommodation of neoliberal and market-driven perspectives in the region's cultural policies. The countries began paying attention to the potential economic values of culture in the 1990s, and the emergence of this new wave of cultural policy was attributed to their increasing embrace of the discourse of the knowledge economy, post-industrial society and globalization. The Asian economic crises in 1997 also resulted in these countries seriously questioning the sustainability of their economies, which until then had been fuelled by manufacturing industries. While China was making attempts to modernize and marketize its cultural sector in line with the overall transformation of the economy, the rest of the region believed that it was now necessary to foster an economy led by knowledge and skills, which would be less affected by rising competition from manufacturing-led developing economies.

It is within this context that Singapore, South Korea and Taiwan began actively formulating policies for creative industries that broadly included arts, media and digital cultural industries, under slightly different names: from 'content industries' to 'cultural and creative industries.' The Singaporean government recognized culture's economic potentials in the early 1990s and aspired to develop the city state to a hub of creative industries. This was followed by the substantial development of policies in the 2000s with an emphasis on the 'Renaissance City' (focusing on cultural and arts sector), design, and media (Cunningham 2009; Kong et al. 2006). In South Korea, the notion of content industries became part of the cultural policy lexicon in early 2000s, and the central government took a proactive approach to planning and funding in this area. Like arts policy in the past, this new policy area has been led by new legislations, the creation of new funding bodies and strong leadership of the cultural ministry. Taiwan embraced the idea of the creative industries around the early 2000s, with the view that these industries would be the source for the country's next economic boom (Kong et al. 2006). The importance of the creative industries has also been recognized by the Chinese government. Since the mid-2000s, creative industries policy at both central and local levels has addressed issues of innovation, clustering and soft power. All four countries' cultural and creative industries policies show historical and political embeddedness: while they have developed a new policy area with economic- and market-orientation, the way policies are made resembles the way culture and cultural policy used to be organized in the country in question. This explains why, while the market begins to play crucial roles in defining, directing and guiding cultural production and consumption in China, the country's cultural and creative sectors still needs to respond to political imperatives (Tong and Hung 2012). Similarly, we can detect strong social concern in the Singaporean government's creative industries policy. It is found that these countries are taking a top-down and hands-on approach to the development of their creative economy; regardless how much bottom up entrepreneurialism is emphasized in the (Western) theory of creative industries.

Here, Michael Keane and Elaine Zhao's chapter provides a succinct overview of the historical trajectory of cultural policy in China since

1978 and locates the current discourse of creative industries within a historical context. For China, the process of developing cultural and creative industries is a complex one where the state tries to embrace a new understanding of culture, both as an economic activity and as a nation branding tool, while keeping it under its ideological parameters. The inherent tension between regulating and marketizing forces has intensified with the rise of convergence culture and bottom-up initiatives of active consumers. Such new developments seem to present both potential schisms and opportunities for the cultural sector. Xin Gu's chapter explores such tensions in more detail via her case study of creative industries policy in Shanghai. Locating the discrepancy between the Western formulation of the creative industries theory and their reality in China, her analysis perceives China's approach to these industries as a conflicted cultural policy, ridden with much ambiguity that is in line with the country's complicated political economy. Hsiao-Ling Chung's chapter provides an examination of the conception and implementation of cultural and creative industries policy from the perspectives of five municipal governments in Taiwan. It is found that the policy has been localized and reformulated, corresponding to local environments and needs, and this process is heavily dependent on the mediating roles played by local cultural bureaucrats.

Finally, Nobuko Kawashima's article problematizes the relationship between the state and creative economy from a slightly different angle. Her chapter examines the growth of the Japanese film industry under the overall absence of state cultural policy and questions if this growth can be sustained without direct state support in the future. Highlighting the changing demographics of the country, the underperformance of Japanese feature films in overseas markets, the industry's overt commercialism, and the lack of international co-production, Kawashima argues that it might now be necessary for the Japanese government to reconsider its hands-off approach to film policy, if not its cultural policy in general.

Reflecting on and reimagining the region's cultural policies

The three themes in this book provide a snapshot of the current state of cultural policy research within East Asia today. The cultural policies of these five countries are developing rapidly but, at the same time, show strong path dependency: while being continuously reformulated with new goals, mechanism and resources, the way they are managed and implemented is guided by their historical and political legacies. The issues faced by individual countries, such as the bureaucratic management of culture and the lack of civil forces within cultural policy making, are also shared across the region. The chapters in this book demonstrate how quickly the governments in East Asia have embraced culture to support and promote various goals, ranging from the formation of identity, to developing their economies, and to boosting their international profile and soft power.

In the next few years, it is very likely that the investment in culture within these countries will not only be maintained but also increase. With growing policy attention to the creative industries and creative economy, the remit of cultural policy is expanding and its structure is becoming more complicated. What remains to be seen with the government's rising interest in culture in these countries would be the nature of the relationship between the state and culture itself. There are calls for greater deregulation from countries such as Singapore, South Korea and Taiwan, yet, at the same time, there is a growing recognition that Japan's minimal state intervention might not be the way forward. In the meantime, cultural policy in China might find it too difficult to maintain the thin lines between the conflicting forces of politics, markets and bottom-up initiatives. As pointed out by many of the contributors in this book, there needs to be greater reflection, both from the state and from the cultural sector, about the ways in which culture can or should be managed within East Asian societies. Many of the ways in which culture has been supported in what were then newly formed East Asian nation states were meant to bolster and create a coherent cultural identity or ideological consensus. As these countries mature both politically and economically, and increasingly recognize diverse voices in society, what roles should culture then play in relation to these changes? In addition, increasingly affluent societies in these five nations have afforded a younger generation the opportunity to access culture from all over the world and experience living, working or studying abroad. This generation's exposure to global culture and their transnational lifestyle would make obsolete a prefixed and top-down concept of national or cultural identity. This has the potential to have an impact on the types of work that the state and cultural practitioners would support or develop in the future. The surge in convergence culture – where cultural consumers and audiences take on roles as creators – poses another serious question to the region's cultural policies, challenging not only the policies' existing frameworks for aesthetic consideration and resource distribution but also their bureaucratic management of culture. Will cultural globalization and convergence culture give rise to new forms of cultural policy that involve civil societies as key actors? Or will it result in the strengthening of market forces in the region's cultural sphere? As the countries are constructing creative clusters and expanding their cultural infrastructure in an attempt to harness their creative economy, there is an urgent need for a crucial consideration about the roles of culture in society and the ways it is governed and managed. Perhaps it might be time for researchers within the region to work with each other, taking into account their shared historical, political and cultural contexts, in order to reflect on culture-state relations in the region and reimagine its cultural policies. It is hoped for, too, that an increase in the number of bilingual scholars working in Anglophone and European cultural policy research might also see the creation of new international collaborations that explore common cultural policy issues across different regions, leading to new understandings and interpretations of key issues in cultural policy.

The experience of East Asia broadens cultural policy research's perspectives of culture-state relations and their dynamics: in this region, we have witnessed that the contemporary development of cultural policies occurred in parallel with the countries' economic expansion, and that the development was both led by and suffered from the state's bureaucratic imagination and management of culture. Within the continuation of policies' initial orientation and structure and the efforts to redefine them, we observe an increasing schism between the state and culture, and the rise of alternative approaches which are driven sometimes by bottom-up and civil initiatives, and at other times by the reformulation of the existing ideologies of cultural policy. The characteristics of East Asian cultural policies this book has observed – ideological coupling between the state and culture, developmental approach to culture, supremacy of cultural bureaucrats, the Confucian ideal of cultural governance and the rising effort to define culture as a civil sector – propose a new set of references current cultural policy research can further advance.

References

Ahearne, J. (2009) 'Cultural Policy Explicit and Implicit: A Distinction and Some Uses', *International Journal of Cultural Policy*, 15(2), 141–153.

Bourdieu, P. (1993) *The Field of Cultural Production* (Cambridge: Polity).

Chua, B. and Iwabuchi, K. (2008) *East Asian Pop Culture: Analysing the Korean Wave* (Hong Kong: Hong Kong University Press).

Cunningham, S. (2009) 'Trojan Horse or Rorschach Blot? Creative Industries Discourse around the World', *International Journal of Cultural Policy*, 15(4), 375–386.

Iwabuchi, K. (2002) *Recentering Globalization: Popular Culture and Japanese Transnationalism* (London: Duke University Press).

Kawashima, N. (forthcoming) 'An Overview of Cultural Policies in East Asia', in J.D. Wright (ed.), *International Encyclopaedia of Social and Behavioral Sciences* (2nd edition) (Oxford: Elsevier).

Kim, Y. (ed.) (2013) *The Korean Wave: Korean Media Go Global* (London: Routledge).

Kong, L., Gibson, C., Khoo, L.-M. and Semple, A.-L. (2006) 'Knowledges of the Creative Economy: Towards a Rational Geography of Diffusion and Adaptation in Asia', *Asia Pacific Viewpoint*, 47(2), 173–194.

McGuigan, J. (2004) *Rethinking Cultural Policy* (Maidenhead: Open University Press).

Peacock, A. and Rizzo, I. (eds) (1994) *Cultural Economic and Cultural Policies* (London: Kluwer Academic Publishers).

Rozman, G. (ed.) (1991) *The East Asian Region Confucian Heritage and Its Modern Adaptation* (Princeton: Princeton University Press).

Toepler, S. and Zimmer, A. (2002) 'Subsidizing the Arts: Government and the Arts in Western Europe and the United States', in D. Crane, N. Kawashima and K. Kawasaki (eds), *Global Culture: Media, Arts, Policy and Globalization* (London: Routledge), 29–48.

Tomooka, K., Kanno, S. and Kobayashi, M. (2002) 'Building National Prestige: Japanese Cultural Policy and the Influence of Western Institutions', in D. Crane, N. Kawashima and K. Kawasaki (eds), *Global Culture: Media, Arts, Policy and Globalization* (London: Routledge), 49–62.

Tong, Q.S. and Hung, R. (2012) 'Cultural Policy between the State and the Market: Regulation, Creativity and Contradiction', *International Journal of Cultural Policy*, 18(3), 265–278.

Tu, W. (2000) 'Implications of the Rise of "Confucian" East Asia', *Daedalus*, 129(1), 195–218.

The World Bank (2013) GDP ranking, http://data.worldbank.org/data-catalog/GDP-ranking-table, data accessed October 10, 2013.

UNdata (2013) Surface Area, http://data.un.org/Data.aspx?d=WDI&f=Indicator_Code%3AAG.SRF.TOTL.K2, data accessed October 10, 2013.

Vogel, Ezra F. (1991) *The Four Little Dragons: The Spread of Industrialization in East Asia* (Cambridge: Massachusetts: Harvard University Press).

Part I

Cultural Identity Formation and Nation Building

1
Bureaucratic Imaginations in the Global City: Arts and Culture in Singapore

Terence Chong[1]

Among the many tensions in Singapore, there are few as pervasive as that between the economic desire to be a global city and the primordial need to be a nation. The island's history as a colonial *entrepôt* and its unexpected independence in 1965 have been discursively synthesized by the postcolonial ruling People's Action Party (PAP) into a durable narrative of a country that cannot survive should it ever flounder as a city open to the world. Being a global city is therefore no mere expression of state vanity but a deep-seated belief among the ruling elite that the little nation, bereft of natural resources, can only thrive if it is plugged into the international market. Speaking in 1972 to the Foreign Press Club, S. Rajaratnam, who first used the term 'global city' about the country, explained, 'once you see Singapore as a Global City the problem of hinterland becomes unimportant because as a Global City, the world is its hinterland' (Chan and Ul Haq 2007, p. 217).

During the early industrializing years, this tension was, to a large extent, cushioned by rapid economic growth, material affluence, and the visible expansion of the middle class. In the last decade, however, it has bubbled to the surface of public debates with increasing frequency. The widening wage gap, uneven distribution of wealth, and stagnant income of the working class have animated this tension in a variety of ways. From apparently disparate issues such as liberal immigration, the overwhelming presence of global capital, citizens playing second fiddle to foreigners, to the loss of cultural heritage, the interests of the nation are often quickly and starkly brought into diametric opposition to those of the global city. This is because the nation is perceived as exclusive, reserved for citizens who have deep attachment to the land and community while the global city, necessarily inclusive by nature, is cosmopolitan, fluid and dynamic. Here the nation is only deemed 'authentic' if it is successfully constructed as 'timeless' and 'pure,' stable and constant, in contrast to the impersonal and capricious nature of neo-capitalism and modernity (Duara 1998). This timelessness is where citizens can find security in the collective memory and go on to form emotional bonds. In short, the nation is where citizens' lives find meaning, while the city is where they make a living. There are few places where the Singapore state's attempts to reconcile these tensions are more apparent than in the arts and culture.

Unlike today, the arts and culture had a straightforward role during the early years of independence. A host of pressing national priorities such as unemployment, housing and infrastructural needs, as well as defense and healthcare development occupied the postcolonial government. Consequently, the arts and culture were relegated primarily to the ideological task of nation building. Whether to create a 'civilized' citizenry or to play out official fantasies of multiracialism, the arts and culture were tasked in the early years to visualize and perform a distinct national identity for the masses of a young nation (Chong 2010). It became *de rigueur* to use the arts to idealize racial harmony, with ethnic costume dances performed by students in schools or in the national day parades. As the then Minister of State for Culture, LEE Khoon Choy, declared just a year after independence, 'The days of Art for Art's sake are over. Artists should play an integral part in our effort to build a multiracial, multi-lingual, and multi-religious society where every citizen has a place under the sun.' (Lee 1966) More vividly, JEK Yeun Tong, Minister of Culture, observed in 1972,

> Our national culture should therefore not only reflect the culture of our forbearers but should also express and embody the new character and personality of Singapore's modern society – its dynamism, its industrialism, its multiracialism and its ceaseless endeavours to create a better milieu for all. A modern Singapore should portray this hope and optimism of the people, whether these be expressed in dance or song, art, literature or drama. (Jek 1972)

This nation-building agenda continues to shape national policies on arts and culture to this day.

Since the 1990s, however, these policies have become increasingly layered with economic objectives in order to achieve global city status. In practical terms, this meant developing the city-state into an international base for multinational companies in manufacture and service, as well as establishing its credentials as a regional, if not global, centre for education, medical services and finance. To achieve this vision, the ruling elite began to actively compare and contrast the city-state with top-tier cities like London and New York, and second-tier ones like Sydney, Hong Kong, Edinburgh and Melbourne. As the national economy reached the limits of cheap labor and low-skilled manufacturing, the ruling elite's desire for greater cultural sophistication grew to complement the economic imperative to move up the international division of labor.

Tailing these broad economic efforts was the arts and culture. A relatively new area in Singapore's globalizing thrust is the arts, culture and entertainment. In this area the government envisions Singapore as a 'Renaissance City,' a place where local, regional and international arts and culture are displayed and consumed and a 'cosmopolitan city plugged into the international network where the world's talents and ideas can converge and multiply' (Chang 2000, p. 818). This marked a profound shift in the way bureaucrats viewed arts and culture in Singapore.

This chapter looks at the bureaucratic imagination of art through the lenses of various arts reports. It defines the bureaucratic imagination as the application of art and its imagined qualities as a solution to economic or socio-political challenges thrown up by the global city-nation binary and demonstrates the evolving mechanisms of imagination over the years. It proceeds to examine the *Advisory Council on Culture and the Arts Report* (1989) and *Renaissance City Report* (2000) as key documents. As documents of bureaucratic imagination, they reveal the ideological role assigned to arts and culture and the romantic interpretations that bureaucrats held to, both of which were ultimately limiting. The chapter goes on to examine the *Arts and Culture Strategic Review Report* (2012), and demonstrates how it has conjured up imaginations of 'community.' It will conclude with examples of challenges to this imagination from the artistic community.

The bureaucrat and the bureaucratic imagination

The Singaporean bureaucrat is the most important art critic in the country. Perhaps more than any other cultural intermediary, the bureaucrat has been the most powerful and influential when it comes to defining art and circumscribing its role. In light of the relatively small pool of artists and public intellectuals, as well as the particularities of the power structure across the arts and cultural landscape, the bureaucrat has emerged as the nation's chief visionary for the arts. This is not surprising in light of the city's characterization as an 'administrative state' (Chan 1975) where 'a skilled, efficient bureaucracy with an emphasis on scientific management' (Ortmann 2010, p. 64), steeped in developmentalist values, has its hands on the levels of power. Indeed, the intimacy between the bureaucrat and the politician stems from the PAP's concerted effort to change and shape the values of the bureaucrats during the early years of independence in order to establish a close working relationship when the threat of communism was tangible (Chan 1975). The result of this close working relationship is 'a cohesive power elite which is made up of the political elite, the bureaucrats and the select professional elite' (Chen 1978, p. 9).

The state's elitist selection process has ensured the convergence of well-educated individuals in the higher ranks of the bureaucracy, many of whom have rotating portfolios. Arts-related portfolios include regulatory bodies like the Media Development Authority (MDA), arts funding agencies like the National Arts Council (NAC), and the Ministry of Culture, Community and Youth, the senior management of which consist of well qualified and highly competent career civil servants, many of whom are government scholarship recipients who may or may not have an interest in the arts. Very often, the absence of artists or academics is compensated through the co-option process, where the latter are invited to sit on committees or resource panels for their domain expertise.

Consequently, the history of arts and culture in Singapore has been less defined by artistic periods or philosophical movements than it has by policy announcements, government reports, and key speeches by top bureaucrats and politicians (see Chong 2010). As a result, bureaucratic slogans like 'global city for the arts' and 'renaissance city,' and state documents like *Report of the Censorship Review Committee* (1992) have become more efficient signposts in the nation's cultural history than artistic styles and movements. Collectively, these have served as the platform for the bureaucratic imagination of arts and culture.

The bureaucratic imagination is defined as the selective and rudimentary application of art and its imagined qualities as a creative solution to perceived economic or socio-political challenges in order to reconcile the interests of the global city and nation. It is an imagination conjured up from the deeply ingrained conventions of the bureaucrat, such as problem-identification and problem-solving, the harnessing of resources for maximum gain within the frame of scientific management guided by a developmentalist logic. While open to external challenge, the bureaucratic imagination may reflect some sort of elitist triumph in the bureaucrats' ability to temporarily transcend their field, or in corporate lingo, 'think outside the box,' in order to engage with so-called 'stake-holders' – usually taken to mean artists. After all, the narrow focus of the bureaucracy and its commitment toward specific outcomes (see Weber 1991) may raise its consciousness of its own limitations, prompting the co-option of experts and practitioners into its fold when preparing major arts reports or policy consultation, thus enabling bureaucrats to unlearn the stiffness of 'bureaucratese' and to pick up the softer patois of arts and artists.

The bureaucrat has imagined art in several different ways through the decades. Art may be imagined as a *social unifier*. Here, art is seen to possess the ability to bring different people together, and this is most obvious in its exploitation as a vehicle to promote racial or social harmony through cultural performances. Art may also be imagined as a *great ennobler* where moral aesthetics are called forth to nurture a more gracious and cultured society. In other words, 'Music, painting, drama, literature and a concern for beauty generally are what transforms a prosperous society into a civilized society.' (*The Mirror* 28 December 1972) Art is also imagined to be a *national anchor* that keeps Singaporeans emotionally rooted to the country: 'Culture and the arts are important to us because they enhance our quality of life, contribute to our sense of national identity, and add to the attractiveness of our country' (*Renaissance City Report* 2000, p. 4). It is believed to be a medium from which national identity and culture can be explored and expressed, resulting in a more anchored citizenry in an age of globalization. National culture and identity are presumed to be inclusive and unproblematic experiences without the messy cultural politics that arise from tensions between ethnic majority and minorities.

Art can be imagined as offering *creative solutions* to economic challenges. Whether in the service of creative and design industries or the knowledge-based economy, the promotion of art and culture has become synonymous with the promotion of creativity, inventiveness or innovation: 'A thriving arts scene also generates the economic benefit of engendering a more creative people and a more attractive global city. These economic imperatives add impetus for greater state support for the arts.' (*Renaissance City Report* 2000, p. 47) Finally, art is imagined as a *cosmopolitan lens* that allows the parochial citizen to rise above local and immediate interests in order to be endowed with a global perspective on various issues. Art here is believed to imbue citizens with a global sensitivity that embraces the values of inclusivity and diversity, both of which are key for global city ambitions.

The bureaucratic imagination of art occupies a privileged position for three reasons. Broadly and historically speaking, the calculated move to form a nation from disparate immigrant identities led the young post-colonial government to practice 'selective amnesia' in order to exorcize 'ancestral ghosts' (Hong and Huang 2010). This meant that the civilizations of China and India, from which the two main immigrant groups came, were deemed unsuitable as cultural or artistic resources by the postcolonial elite, for fear they would undermine the multicultural nation building project. Without these civilizations to tap on, art and culture in Singapore were more readily re-directed and co-opted by the state.

Another reason was the way very few public intellectuals or artists challenged state definitions of art and culture. The pace of industrialization during the early years, the crackdown on political dissidents, and the efficient delivery of public services all combined to offer little room for intellectual or ideological challenge, whether in the form of aesthetics or politics, to the ruling PAP. This often left the PAP ruling elite as arbiters of taste and morality. The postcolonial government invariably gravitated toward politically conservative art. Master bureaucrat GOH Keng Swee, at the opening of the Japanese Gardens in 1973, lamented:

> I refer to the widespread popularity of the barbarous form of music produced by the steel guitar linked to the ear shattering system of sound amplification. Voice accompaniment takes the form of inane tasteless wailing. It is barbarous music of this kind that is mainly responsible for attracting the mindless young of Singapore to the cult of the permissive of the western world. It is hardly a coincidence that the problem of drug addiction has become serious where performers and audience foregather. I trust the Ministry of Home Affairs will take stern action against this menace. (Goh 1973)

Finally, in practical terms, the state remains the biggest funder of arts and culture. As the gatekeeper of public funds, the bureaucrat's power over the arts is often justified as good governance. The bureaucrat, in needing to justify expenditure, becomes the de facto connoisseur and patron of art in Singapore. This ability to define art and to fund it makes the bureaucrat more powerful than any individual in the arts and culture.

Nevertheless, bureaucratic imagination of art, while generally instrumentalist in character, may be also be a powerful and progressive force. French Cultural Minister Andre Malraux's drive to fulfill the ideals of *droit à la culture* (the right to culture) saw a cultural democratization process which resulted in concrete infrastructure changes such as the establishment of regional cultural centers around the country. Such forms of cultural democracy were not alien to Singapore either. The 'Art for Everyone' exhibitions, launched in 1971, encouraged ordinary citizens to partake in the art production process (see below). Indeed, these examples demonstrate the possibilities of progressive regimes and structures that may emerge from bureaucratic imaginations.

The mechanisms of bureaucratic imaginations

Bureaucratic imaginations are more than mere visions of art. They are accompanied by the power to materialize these visions in light of the state mechanisms at the bureaucrat's disposal. Naturally, such mechanisms have evolved and have been refined over the years. From the crude censorship interventions from the police under the Public Entertainment Licence Unit in the early years, to more subtle forms of influence through the co-option of cultural practitioners into government committees, such mechanisms, sometimes visible, sometimes hidden, help normalize the bureaucrat's imagination. In other words, such mechanisms misrecognize specific views of art and inflict symbolic violence forms of art that do not conform to orthodoxy (see Bourdieu 1993).

One tried and tested mechanism is the withholding of state funds. Take for example Drama Box – an established Mandarin-language theatre group – staging *Vaginalogues* in 2000. The play, inspired by American playwright Eve Ensler's *The Vagina Monologues*, was in Mandarin. NAC objected to a featured slide that showed a black and white picture of a vagina and wanted it removed from the play. The playwright and actor LI Xie, together with Drama Box, refused to do so, and NAC responded by withdrawing its grant of S$8000 (*Straits Times* Oct 8, 2007). More recently, in 2010, Wild Rice's annual funding was cut by NAC 'because its productions promoted alternative lifestyles, were critical of government policies and satirized political leaders' (*Straits Times* May 5, 2010).

Other more subtle mechanisms include the formation of various 'advisory' panels or committees on different levels of the bureaucratic hierarchy. Such panels are usually made up of non-bureaucratic personnel and may comprise cultural practitioners themselves who offer non-binding advice and feedback to bureaucrats. NAC, for example, has prominent artists serving on its Arts Resource Panels who advise the council on the various disciplines of theatre, dance, music, fine art, and literature. Similarly it also has prominent practitioners and laypersons serving as Arts Advisors. The purpose, ostensibly, is to ensure as broad a cross-section of the public representation as possible when it comes to issues of censorship or aesthetic morality.

In the case of film, the Board of Film Censors, whose task is to classify films, may seek feedback from the Films Consultative Panel, which is comprised of 'individuals from different sectors of society including housewives, educationists, psychologists and business professionals' (Media Development Authority website). Such advisory panels not only allow bureaucrats to interact and benefit from the views of practitioners and laypersons, they are also able to negotiate more contentious issues like censorship or fund distribution by pointing to the presence of non-bureaucrats in such committees.

Perhaps the most influential and sustainable form of bureaucratic imagination is its manifestation in documents like state-commissioned arts and cultural reports. These reports carry the rhetoric of the day as shaped by contemporary state interests and perspectives. They often identify the types of challenges faced by the nation – be it shifting up the international division of labor, needing more global capital and talent, retaining globally mobile Singaporeans, or participating in the creative economy – and proceed to prescribe the arts and culture as instrumental in meeting them. It is in the prescriptive discourse that the bureaucratic imagination of the arts is fully fleshed out. It is here that the contradictions between the interests of the global and the needs of the local are magically resolved.

The Renaissance City Report

The economic potential of arts and culture received its first serious official expression in the 1989 *Advisory Council on Culture and the Arts Report* (ACCA). Headed by ONG Teng Cheong, then-Second Deputy Prime Minister, the ACCA Report may be read as part of the greater national effort to shift the domestic economy from low-skill to higher-value manufacturing as the country sought to move up the international division of labor. The 1985 recession had painfully underlined the need for high value industries and R&D, both of which required attracting skilled individuals to the national economy. Before this, the overseas reach of the arts and culture extended to luring tourists in search of an exotic and romanticized orientalist world. Instead, the ACCA Report made clear that 'Good [arts] facilities and [cultural] activities help to attract world class performances and exhibitions, thus creating a more congenial environment for investors and professionals to stay and tourists to visit Singapore.' (ACCA Report 1989, p. no number)

This marked the first time that the arts and culture were bureaucratically desired as sign of cosmopolitan sophistication. No longer mere crude signifiers of racial harmony or the exotic East, the arts and culture were tasked to lend the city-state a cultural polish and refinement to attract global capital. In duly efficient form, recommendations were put forth for the National Arts Council (established in 1991) and the Esplanade (opened in 2002). With these developments, the art and culture were imagined as solutions to the real challenges posed by intensifying global competition for capital and talent.

In 1992, bureaucrats presented Singapore as a 'Global City for the Arts.' Two reports, both entitled *Singapore: Global City for the Arts*, were published – the first jointly by the Economic Development Board (EDB) and MITA, and the second, also jointly, by the then- Singapore Tourist Promotion Board (STPB) and MITA. Under the 'Global City for the Arts' project, the relationship between the arts and economics was brought to its logical conclusion – while the government would fund the arts, it would be the market that would be the ultimate judge of what flourished or wilted. Then-Acting Minister for Information and the Arts, George YEO, declared:

> Let me summarize the argument: To be competitive in the next phase of our national development, we need to promote the arts. This involves not just a few individuals but large numbers of Singaporeans and foreigners living in Singapore as producers, consumers and benefactors of the arts. But the arts span a wide field. Which segments should we promote? Which will succeed? No one knows for sure. Because no one knows for sure, we have to build a market test. (Yeo 1990)

A decade later, the *Renaissance City Report* (RC Report) was released in 2000. At the heart of the report was the bureaucrats' romanticization of the Italian Renaissance transposed unproblematically onto the cultural histories of broader Asia. The economic rise of China and, to some extent, India, prompted international commentators and regional policymakers to conclude that global power would gradually but surely gravitate toward Asia. Or as observed by Yeo, 'There is every likelihood that the centre of world economy will shift to the Asia-Pacific in the next century. The economic growth will be accompanied by a cultural renaissance of historical importance. In response to this, art dealers and galleries in the West have set up shop in East Asia ... It is our hope that Singapore will be a centre of culture in East Asia' (*Singapore: Global City for the Arts* 1992, p. 3).

From the glossy pages of the RC Report, the ideal Singaporean was birthed. The 'Renaissance Singaporean' was imagined to be an 'individual with an open, analytical and creative mind that is capable of acquiring, sharing, applying and creating new knowledge.' Imagined as male, naturally, this Renaissance Singaporean had 'a strong sense of identity and belonging to his community and nation' which 'gives him the confidence to pursue activities beyond our shores' (p. 39). And to address the government's concerns over globally mobile Singaporeans leaving the country, the Renaissance Singaporean was conveniently imagined as cosmopolitan in taste but 'attuned to his Asian roots and heritage' (ibid.). In addition, 'The Renaissance Singaporean is an individual with a strong passion for life...He dares to be different; he perseveres and is not afraid to fail.' (ibid.)

While the Renaissance Singaporean could be deconstructed as a catalogue of state insecurities and fantasises, as a piece of bureaucratic imagination, it was also disjointed from past imaginations. After all, the 'renaissance' trope was used in very different ways by the late HON Sui Sen, former Minister for Finance, and S. Dhanabalan, former Minister for Culture in 1980 and 1984, respectively (Chong 2010). For Dhanabalan in particular, the 'Renaissance' was contrasted against the 'Romantic Movement' in order to criticize artistic free-spiritedness and to privilege power and hierarchy. The Culture Minister observed that

> The Renaissance world was quite different. In the Renaissance world and for much of Western history, the artist was often considered a craftsman. The artist did not consider it demeaning to be working to meet the demands of his patron within the bounds set by his patron...This is not to say that he just did what he was told. But his inspiration and creativity could not run too far ahead of his patrons. (Dhanabalan 1984, p. 32–33)

Imagined as craftsman, the artist could and *should* work within the perimeters set by his patron or, in the Singapore case, the state. Bureaucratic imaginations are sometimes fractured, even conflicting, fuelled by contemporary needs and temporal conditions without commitment to the past. As a cultural artefact, the RC Report is an ahistorical document, an ideological site in which highpoints of Italian civilization were cherry-picked to address state concerns over a quickly globalizing world.

The Arts and Culture Strategic Review Report

Over a decade after the release of the RC Report, the social and political landscape had shifted yet again. The political fallout from accelerated immigration, a heated property market, and the rising cost of living had ratcheted tensions between the twin desires for a global city and nation to new heights. Public discontent over the pace of change had resulted in the lowest share of the popular vote ever garnered by the PAP in the 2011 General Elections. This was quickly followed up by the ruling party's decisive losses in two by-elections in 2012 and 2013. These electoral setbacks prompted the ruling party to rein in its global city urges by temporarily reducing the number of foreigners into the country. In short, citizens were reacting against the ruling elite's unbridled global city desires. It is against this changing backdrop that the 'Arts and Culture Strategic Review Report' (ACSR) was released in 2012. Headed by LEE Tzu Yang, Chairman for the School of the Arts, it can be viewed as one in a series of government commissioned reviews of the arts and cultural landscape over the decades. Coming after the aforementioned ACCA Report and the RC Report, the ASCR Report may be seen as part of the corporatist state's agenda of regularly updating and reassessing existing public policies.

The ACSR Report is ostensibly 'a review of existing arts and culture policies and programmes led by the private sector, the community, and the arts and culture sector' (ACSR Report 2012, p. 5). It observes that while the ACCA Report and RC Report 'emphasized arts and culture's role in nation building and economic growth respectively ... The ACSR shifts the focus for the next phase of our cultural development to our people and society' (ACSR Report 2012, p. 15). Of course there is no real substantial difference between the emphasis on 'arts and culture's role in nation-building' and the focus on 'cultural development [of] our people and society' given the state's history of ideologically appropriating arts and culture policies. Nevertheless, it is necessarily part of bureaucratic mastery to offer distinction and distance between policy documents because such distinctions and distance enable them to be presented as linear and progressive products where past achievements are defined and built upon. In this sense, bureaucratic mastery paradoxically demands both the wilful blindness to the substance of past policies and the self-conscious attempt to move beyond them.

Bureaucratic imagination is also able to reconcile the seemingly irreconcilable interests of the nation and global city. The ACSR Report contains visions such as 'A nation of cultured and gracious people, at home with our heritage, proud of our Singaporean identity' (ACSR Report 2012, p. 15). And with bureaucratic mastery, Singapore can be both 'Leading Global City and an Endearing Home' (ACSR Report 2012, p. 24), thus revealing the bureaucrat's power to instantaneously resolve the conflicting economic and political demands of either with the magic of neat slogans. This is down to the chimera-like vision that bureaucrats have of the arts. Whether art is believed to make a person more gracious, to encapsulate the best of civilization, to articulate deeply personal stories for universal empathy, or simply to provide entertainment products that command a premium from global travellers, it has become a mystical creature from which bureaucrats can summon forth varying definitions to suit policy agenda.

Bureaucratic mastery may, likewise, demand the re-imagination of historic cultural capitals. According to the ACSR Report (2012, p. 6),

> Throughout the history of the Western and Eastern world, several cities have stood out as the arts and cultural capital of their time. Chang'an in Tang Dynasty China, Baghdad in the 9th century, Renaissance Florence, British colonial Mumbai, Paris in the 19th century and post-World War II New York have all reigned as the arts and cultural capitals of their heyday.

Such comparisons not only belie the aspirations of bureaucrats but also reveal a misreading of the cultural success of these capitals. The report points to the shared characteristics of these historic capitals, such as being 'centres of trade,' sites of 'confluences of talent and ideas' and 'concentration of wealth and patronage' (ASCR Report 2012, p. 6). Equally important but left unsaid are the reasons that drive art production in these historic capitals.

For example, the strong religion-power nexus in many of these capitals provided the vital ingredients of finance, prestige and grand canvases for artists in Baghdad and Renaissance Italy. The struggle for political power among important families, as seen in Renaissance Italy, also helped to elevate art as a symbol of political status and economic strength. Finally, as a site for the avant-garde, in the cases of Paris and New York, the ability to speak the unspeakable and explore new exciting movements such as Impressionism, Dadaism, Cubism, psychoanalysis and abstract expressionism created a fertile environment for art to violate taboos and orthodoxy, leading to new developments. In Singapore, political power remains firmly concentrated, with the PAP state leaving no space art to be exploited as a symbol of political power or status. Religion is closely scrutinized, lest its leaders transgress the boundaries of the church, temple or mosque. Meanwhile the PAP state continues to demonstrate low tolerance for heterodoxy, especially in areas of politics, 'race' and religion, let alone the avant-garde.

Art is everywhere, the community is everyone, and everyone loves art

Coming in the aftermath of the divisive and polarizing 2011 General Elections, the role of 'community' took center stage in the ACSR Report. It summoned the power of arts and culture to build and strengthen the community, whether through 'community outreach,' 'community engagement,' 'community identities,' 'community-based arts,' 'community talents,' 'heart of the community,' 'community advocates,' 'community of passionate individuals,' or 'nation of networked communities' (see ACSR Report). 'Community' is bureaucratically imagined to be self-evidently good, worthy of support, unproblematic and irreducible. This is not surprising, since any attempt to imagine a community involves an unwitting homogenization process.

Committed to 'Bring arts and culture to everyone, everywhere, everyday,' community engagement was meant 'to promote creative expression and encourage participation and engagement of all Singaporeans in the artistic and cultural life of their communities' (ACSR Report 2012, p. 31). The national community is bureaucratically imagined as receptive to art, and if it is not, it is only because it has not yet been properly introduced to it. For the bureaucrat, it is elitist art and the self-indulgent artist that need to change, not the community. And for art to be free from elitism, the bureaucrat imagines art to be everywhere and everything: 'Yet the truth is, far from being elitist or inaccessible, arts and culture is in fact already everywhere: in the designs of our clothes and accessories, the graphics in magazines and billboards, the films in cinemas and on television, the music in bars and cafes.' (ACSR Report 2012, p. 17)

However, the bureaucratic imagination reveals its disjointedness again. It is a far cry from GOH Keng Swee's earlier distaste for the 'barbarous form of music produced by the steel guitar' and the 'inane tasteless wailing' of popular music. Such disjointed imaginations speak of the contemporary bureaucrat's ability to forget or disavow past imaginations, a necessary skill to negotiate contemporary objectives and agenda. Bureaucratic imaginations past and present cannot commune lest they unveil contradictions. It also speaks of the bureaucrat's power to define art without significant challenge.

While the ACSR Report sees art as a grassroots activity, this is not new. In a way, it is a return to the traditional nation building role of the arts. The Ministry of Culture, together with the People's Association, launched a series of grassroots exhibitions in May 1971 entitled 'Art for Everyone.' Foreign Affairs Parliamentary Secretary, ONG Soo Chuan, explained the rationale for the 'Art for Everyone' project thus:

> Unfortunately, some young people have adopted the decadent part of the western culture uncritically. Sporting long hair and clad in outlandish clothes, these people can be seen loafing in groups of three or five in the street all day long. They take drugs and have no desire to get ahead, pleasure-seeking being their only business in life. They have virtually become a hindrance to nation-building. How should young people spend their leisure? We should induce them to spend it on wholesome cultural and recreational activities or artistic pursuits. Such activities or pursuits will be conducive to their mental and physical well-being and career by keeping them away from drug addiction. (Ong 1973)

At these exhibitions there would 'be neither well known names nor artistic masterpieces – simply ordinary men and women from all walks of life who feel the urge for self-expressing. The themes are very ordinary ones – just those themes that are close to the lives of the people.' (Chan 1971) The exhibitions were popular. There were 15 exhibitions in 3 years – there were 8 exhibitions in 1973 alone – held in different community centers with a total of 524 art works by 83 artists exhibited. These exhibitions were inclusive and eclectic, with artwork emphasizing citizenry participation. It was not uncommon to see Chinese ink calligraphy, modernist oil paintings, and abstract and representational sculptures all under one roof. The exhibitions drew a respectable number of visitors, too, averaging about 700, not including tourists. By 1977, a total of 50 exhibitions had been held. After being displayed at community centres around Singapore, these art works would make their way to the Singapore Conference Hall for national display.

Nevertheless, how the ACSR Report imagines arts audiences as 'community' contains internal contradictions. In assuming that the 'community' is turned off by 'elitist' or 'inaccessible' art, it relies on superficial sociological observations over class-based notions of aesthetic taste. The logical conclusion then is to divide accessible arts for the lower-middle income 'heartlanders' and esoteric art for the elite, thus leading to the fracturing of the very coherent and unproblematic 'community' that the report imagines. In the meantime, it fails to account for how anyone, regardless of class, may have a subjective aesthetic experience with 'inaccessible art,' or the patterns of consumptive enjoyment of popular culture by the elite. In assuming that art is everywhere and everyone can enjoy art, the bureaucratic imagination is ultimately just as prescriptive and exacting as any rigid criteria for art.

Challenging the bureaucratic imagination

The bureaucratic imagination's influence on art orthodoxies has shaped the way art is expressed by the state and government discourse. Such imaginations are by no means merely discursive. They are self-sustaining and self-affirming in light of the public funds that are channelled toward artists who produce unproblematic work. Nevertheless, whilst this imagination has influenced official discourse on art, art's purpose, and the distribution of public funds, the field of arts and culture is one where heterodoxy enjoys a privileged position. The heterodox nature of art and artists ensures that such imaginations are occasionally resisted and challenged.

There have been art works and productions that have challenged bureaucratic imaginations of art as platform for social harmony and multiculturalism. One example is the 1999 play, *Talaq*, by Tamil playwright Elangovan. Focusing on marital rape and domestic violence suffered by Indian Muslim women, the play's second run in English was stopped by authorities because conservative members of the Indian community protested. Another of Elangovan's plays, *Smegma*, was again banned in 2006. The play was initially granted a license from the Media Development Authority (MDA), which was subsequently withdrawn. It was originally given an 'RA' rating, and the theatre company was obliged to announce that the play contained 'objectionable language' and 'adult theme' in its publicity materials. However, according to MDA, *Smegma* 'undermines the values underpinning Singapore's multi-racial, multi-religious society. The play portrays Muslims in a negative light.' (Media Development Authority, Aug 4, 2006) It noted that the Arts Consultative Panel 'found most of the content of the play insensitive and inappropriate for staging' and that 'The members were concerned that the play could create unhappiness and disaffection amongst Muslims.' (ibid.)

In October 2012, the film *Sex.Violence.Family.Values* by Ken KWEK had its 'M18' rating revoked just days before its premier. A member of the public, upon watching the trailers, complained to MDA about racist remarks against Indians in the film. A Film Consultative Panel was formed to review the film with the Board of Film Censors (BFC), subsequently issuing a 'not for classification' rating for the film, effectively banning it from local screens. The BFC remained unmoved despite explanations from the filmmaker and the Indian cast of the component story, *Malasa Porn*, that the 'racist remarks' were satire designed to, in fact, underscore racial stereotypes and prejudices. It was only after the filmmaker submitted an appeal to the Films Appeal Committee (*Straits Times* November 12, 2012) that the film's 'M18' rating was reinstated, but only after eight seconds of the film was censored. The film was finally screened on March 14, 2013.

Most recently, a group of artists and academics produced an 'arts manifesto' in order to contribute to the government's 'Our Singapore Conversation' (OSC) initiative. The OSC was launched in 2012 to glean public feedback in order to encourage greater citizenry stake in the country's future.[2] The arts manifesto offered several statements such as 'Do not attempt to define Art for others;' 'Art unifies and divides;' 'Art is about possibilities;' 'Art can be challenged but not censored;' and 'Art is political,' among others (*Straits Times* March 19, 2013). This manifesto represents a self-conscious attempt to offer alternative perspectives and roles for art.

Such examples challenge the supremacy of the bureaucratic imagination. By using their craft to interrogate, challenge and, in the case of Kwek, even satirize the taboo topic of 'race,' some artists are reclaiming a key function of art often ignored by bureaucrats – the power to unveil prejudices and give voice to the voiceless. This inherently political function of art is conspicuously missing from bureaucratic imaginations because it exposes structural and institutional asymmetries within society. While the bureaucratic imagination will continue to influence orthodox definitions of art and the nature of its audience for the foreseeable future, its dominance is no longer as assured as before. Younger artists, many of whom have trained overseas, are more resistant to orthodox art and are willing to rupture the discursive objectives of such art. Subversion and re-appropriation of ethnic cultural forms of art for alternative stories and narratives will become increasingly common.

Conclusion

There is little doubt that the bureaucrat remains one of the most influential figures in the arts and cultural landscape. Highly educated, competent and well informed, the bureaucrat's imagination has permeated and shaped much of Singaporean life. Within the bureaucratic imagination, arts and culture in Singapore have been used to reconcile often diametrically opposed interests of the global city and nation. Like magical enchantments, the arts and culture have been summoned by the bureaucratic imagination for a variety of contradictory purposes from attracting global capital to forging national identity, ignoring the socio-political tensions that may arise from these diametrical interests. Art, like magic, needs no explanation and can be conjured up to achieve the impossible. Much of this has been due to the strong authorship that the bureaucrat enjoys over definitions of art, an authorship afforded by the particular historical trajectories of nation-building, resulting in very few challenges to the bureaucratic imagination during the developing years.

Nevertheless, the bureaucratic imagination will face greater resistance from younger and more heterodox artists. Many of these artists and cultural producers, especially those less reliant on public funds, will use the arts as a vehicle for dissent, defiance or irreverence. This is also largely down to the deepening professionalization of the arts. As arts professionals become more highly trained, they develop greater domain literacy and jealousy over their chosen fields, and become less open to prescriptive interventions from non-art organizations like the state or non-arts trained individuals like the professional bureaucrat. All these point to the emergence of more tension and conflict between art and bureaucracy.

Notes

1. The author wishes to thank Sasitharan Thirunalan and Tan Tarn How for their comments on earlier drafts of this chapter.
2. The author of this paper was also jointly responsible for crafting the arts manifesto.

References

Arts and Culture Strategic Review Report (2012) Ministry of Information, Communication and the Arts: Singapore.

Bourdieu, P. (1993) *Sociology in Question*. trans. Richard Nice (London: Sage).

Chan, C-S. (1971) Speech by Mr. Chan Chee Seng, Parliamentary Secretary (Social Affairs) at the occasion of the opening of the 'Art for Everyone' exhibition at Maude Road Community Centre, on Friday, July 9 at 8pm. Singapore: Ministry of Culture.

Chan, H-C. (1975) 'Politics in an administrative State: Where has the politics gone?' in Seah Chee Meow (ed.), *Trends in Singapore: Proceedings and Background Paper* (Singapore: Singapore University Press).

Chan, H-C. and Ul Haq, O. (2007) *S. Rajaratnam: The Prophetic and the Political* (Institute of Southeast Asian Studies: Singapore).

Chang, T-C. (2000) 'Renaissance revisited: Singapore as a "Global City for the Arts"', *International Journal of Urban and Regional Research*, 24(4), 818–831.

Chen, P.S.J. (1978) 'The Power Elite in Singapore', in Ong Jin Hui, Tong Chee Kiong, and Tan Ern Ser (eds), *Understanding Singapore Society* (Singapore: Times Academic Press).

Chong, T. (2010) *The Theatre and the State in Singapore: Orthodoxy and Resistance* (London and New York: Routledge).

Dhanabalan, S. (1984) 'Artists have to depend on patronage', *Speeches: A Monthly Collection of Ministerial Speeches*, 8(1), Jan/Feb (Singapore: Ministry of Culture).

Duara, P. (1998) 'The Regime of Authenticity: Timelessness, Gender, and National History in Modern China', *History and Theory*, 37(3), 287–308.

Goh K-S. (1973) Minister of Defense, Speech at the Opening of SEIWAEN (Japanese Gardens), February 16 at 6pm.

Hong, L. and Huang, J. (2010) *The Scripting of a National History: Singapore and its Pasts* (NUS Press: Singapore).

Jek, Y-T. (1972) Speech by the Minister of Culture at the Opening of Tuju'ana Theatre, a contemporary dance performance by the Maureen Lim Dancers at the Cultural Centre, Fort Canning Rise, April 1 at 8.30pm (Singapore: Ministry of Culture).

Lee, K-C. (1966) Speech by Mr Lee Khoon Choy, Minister of State for Culture, at an art exhibition by the arts selection committee of the National Theatre Trust at the National Theatre, August 5 at 5.30pm (Ministry of Culture: Singapore).

Media Development Authority (Aug 4, 2006) MDA withdraws licence for the play SMEGMA. http://www.mda.gov.sg/wms.www/thenewsdesk.aspx?sid=727. Accessed: March 10, 2013.

Ong, S-C. (1973) Speech by Mr Ong Soo Chuan, Parliamentary Secretary to the Minister for Foreign Affairs and MP for Nee Soon, at the Opening of the 'Art For Everyone' exhibition organized by the Ministry for Culture and the People's Association at the Nee Soon Community Centre on Friday, 6 April at 8pm (Singapore: Ministry of Culture).

Ortmann, S. (2010) *Politics and Change in Singapore and Hong Kong* (London: Routledge).

Renaissance City Report (2000) (Singapore: Ministry of Information and the Arts).

Singapore: Global City for the Arts (1992) (Singapore: Economic Development Board and Ministry of Information and the Arts).

Singapore in Figures (2012) (Department of Statistics, Singapore: Singapore).

Straits Times (May 5, 2010) 'NAC Cuts Funds to Theatre Company Wild Rice'.

Tan, C. (2013) 'Big Names in Arts Community behind Plans to Put Out an Arts Manifesto', *Straits Times*, March 19.

The Mirror: A Weekly Almanac of Current Affairs (December 28, 1972), 'Prosperous Society into Civilized Society'.

Weber, M. (1991) [1948]. *From Max Weber: Essays in Sociology*, H.H. Gerth and C. Wright Mills (eds) (London: Routledge).

Yeo, G. Y-B (1990) Speech by BG (RES) George Yeo, AG Minister for Information and the Arts and Senior Minister of State for Foreign Affairs, at the 1990 Cultural Awards Presentation Ceremony, at the Marina Mandarin, March 22 at 8pm (Singapore: Ministry of Information and the Arts).

2

Cultural Difference, National Identity and Cultural Policy in Taiwan

Li-jung Wang

Few people share a common national identity in Taiwan because of its peculiar history. The strong tensions between the forces of cultural diversity (for example, ethnic differences, the rise of hybrid culture, and multiple identities) and homogenizing forces (the construction of a national identity) have continued through the various phases of Taiwanese history, affecting the Taiwanese version of multiculturalism. From the 1940s, the conflict between Chinese nationalism and Taiwanese consciousness led to a continuing crisis in Taiwanese society, where cultural policy was used to promote Chinese nationalism. The rise of Taiwanese consciousness challenged the dominance of Chinese nationalism in the 1970s, inevitably having an effect on the development of various cultural forms in the country. Since the 1990s, multiculturalism has been viewed as a new way to solve this conflict and to embrace the various cultural identities. This chapter addresses how cultural policy and its new emphasis on multiculturalism have influenced the formation of national identity in the case of performing arts in Taiwan.

National identity has an important role in the development and modification of cultural policy, and thus cultural policy always encounters a dilemma between the agenda of integrating identity and the need to respect differences in values. In addition, cultural policy efforts made to construct national identity in Taiwan are fraught with their own particular challenges, in particular related to the influence of globalization, such as the experience of migrant workers and the influence of China in Taiwan. This chapter is intended to address the relationship between national identity and cultural policy in Taiwan from a historical perspective.

The age of Chinese nationalism from 1949 to the 1970s

The 1940s to the early 1970s is characterized by the promotion of Chinese nationalism in Taiwan. The complex history of Taiwan and the Kuomindang (KMT)[1] government led to a particularly strong emphasis on national identity. The KMT government tried to be 'more Chinese than China,' with the exiles keeping alive the 'authentic' cultural traditions. Added to Taiwan's history of colonization and its pre-existing ethnic diversity, this stance created greater tension, which underscored the strong Chinese nationalism of the first phase.

For the KMT government, establishing a strong Chinese identity in Taiwan was crucial. As the threat from the Chinese Communist Party persisted, the KMT government sought two key goals to maintain its power: achieving strong international support and establishing the legitimacy of its rule in Taiwan. During the Cold War period, the US was eager to support the KMT government as the 'representative of China' in the United Nations, strengthening the KMT's international position. Furthermore, as a key strategy for consolidating its legitimacy, the KMT government was determined to compel the people in Taiwan to become 'Chinese,' which involved a rigorous program of 'thought censorship' and a fundamental change in the people's national identity. This priority underpinned the KMT's direction in cultural policy – 'sino-lisation' – from 1949 to 1971.

Before 1949, however, Taiwan had no clear common national identity for several reasons. First, the idea of nationalism did not exist in Chinese history; rather, it was a product of Western societies arising in the 18th century. The father of the Republic of China (ROC) – Dr. SUN Yat-Sen – 'pirated' (Anderson 1983) the ideal of Western nationalism to create a Chinese identity, but Taiwanese society was not affected by this Chinese nationalism. Secondly, at that time, the Japanese government ruled Taiwan. During the occupation, the people in Taiwan[2] were forced to learn Japanese as a common language, acquire Japanese names, and identify themselves as Japanese. Doing so established a Japanese identity in Taiwanese society. Hence, in 1949, when the KMT government came to Taiwan, the Taiwanese people did not have a strong Chinese identity. Accordingly, 1949 marked the beginning of the KMT government's effort to construct a new Chinese national identity, and most of Taiwan's cultural policies served this purpose until the late 1970s.

This chapter argues that Chinese nationalism in Taiwan was constructed by the state. It was originally conceived to reduce the

Japanese influence in Taiwan and to provide a new political legitimacy for the KMT rule. In addition, it was 'imagined' because most of the population in Taiwan, except for mainlanders, had never been to Mainland China. Most Taiwanese had no experience with the basic components of Chinese nationalism, such as Chinese history, geography, languages, customs, and culture. Thus, Chinese nationalism in Taiwan was simply 'imagined' by the KMT government and imposed through cultural policy. The KMT used various methods to create 'national culture.' Political leaders established guidelines for culture. They also established specialized institutions for cultural affairs in the government (within the Ministry of Defense and the Ministry of Education) and in the KMT party (for example, the Committee of Cultural Works). Thus, the KMT government could control cultural affairs at different levels. It also helped people who were close to the KMT party to establish artistic and cultural organizations that could influence the cultural development of the whole society. In practice, from 1950, the KMT government constructed a national culture according to some basic policies.

In 1953, CHIANG Kai-Shek promulgated the 'Two Papers on Education and Entertainment' in *The Three Principles of the People*, which established the direction of cultural policy. He sought to combine the Taiwanese and Chinese cultural traditions and emphasized the importance of maintaining Chinese culture. In contrast, the Chinese communists had tried to transplant Russian culture to Mainland China. This stance strengthened CHIANG's legitimacy as a protector of Chinese history and identity. In 1967, CHIANG announced the Chinese Culture Renaissance Movement (CCRM) to resist the Cultural Revolution in Mainland China. He considered this movement to be equivalent to an anti-communist strategy. The revival of Chinese culture was anti-communist, and all anti-communists should seek to revive Chinese culture (Xiao 1991, p. 92). Thus, all concepts of the CCRM were developed under this. Furthermore, the CCRM played a vital role in the construction of a national culture. The purpose of the CCRM was three-fold: to integrate Taiwanese culture with Chinese culture, to slow the Westernization of Taiwan, and to maintain the regime's legitimacy in the world (Kuo 1989, p. 58). The government and civil society promoted the CCRM.

In addition, the KMT government selected appropriate symbols of national culture in various artistic and cultural areas. For example, before the 1950s, the most popular traditional forms of theater were marionette plays and *Gezaxi* (traditional Hokkein theater), both of which had come from Mainland China with the Han immigration in the 18th century. In the period of Japanese rule, the government tried to destroy these theatrical forms, but because it could not do so, it sought to modify them through an injection of Japanese nationalist thinking and culture. In turn, the subsequent KMT government set up the Committee for the Guidance of Local Theatres to change and 'de-Japanize' these theatrical forms. However, language limitations meant that marionette plays and *Gezaxi* both declined, because they used the Hokkein dialect. Thus, the KMT government decided to promote the Ping Opera[3] as Taiwan's national opera. In 1953, the Ministry of Defense[4] took over the Gu Theater, one of the Ping Opera theaters in Taiwan, and changed its system to set up the Lu-Quang and Hai-Qaung theater schools. In 1966, the Ministry of Education took over the management of the Fu-Xing theater school – a school for training in Ping Opera. Hence, the Ministries of Defense and Education became the most important institutions for the promotion of Ping Opera, which the KMT government viewed as 'national opera' (Zhou 1995, pp. 56–59). They also made sure that the content of the Ping Opera followed the official ideology of strengthening nationalism, reinforcing the power of Chinese culture, and opposing Chinese communists (Zhou 1995, p. 58).

Hobsbawm and Ranger (1995) examine the construction of national identity through 'the invention of tradition,' including historical tradition, national language, and various kinds of national festivals. For Hobsbawm and Ranger, *invented tradition* means a set of practices normally governed by overtly or tacitly accepted rules and having a ritual or symbolic nature that seek to inculcate certain values and norms of behavior by repetition. This invention is an attempt to establish continuity with a suitable historic past and to respond to novel situations by referring to former situations. The main processes of inventing traditions are formalization and ritualization (Hobsbawm and Ranger 1995, p. 1). Hobsbawm and Ranger identify three overlapping types of invented tradition: Those establishing or symbolizing social cohesion or the membership of groups and real or artificial communities; those establishing or legitimizing institutions, status, or relations of authority; and those whose main purpose is socialization, the inculcation of beliefs, value systems, and conventions of behavior (Hobsbawm and Ranger 1995, p. 9).

With regard to Chinese nationalism, invented tradition also plays an important role in constructing the collective national identity, establishing the legitimacy of political power, and linking individuals and the state. These initiatives fall into two broad categories. First, through the invention of historical tradition, they improve the sense of identity with Chinese history; second, through the invention of national language, national music, national opera, and national painting,[5] they increase the common consciousness of the entire Taiwanese society. These developments fit with Hobsbawm and Ranger's (1995) description of national identity as an invention of tradition. In this manner, the KMT government successfully incorporated the development of traditional theater in its efforts to control cultural affairs. This direction in cultural policy led to significant change in the development of dance in Taiwan. Ballet and modern dance were developed very well during the colonial age of Japanese rule; however, they were replaced by traditional Chinese folk dances during KMT rule. The KMT government set up a committee and competitions and also provided funding, lessons, and TV programs and promoted Chinese folk dances in educational systems and mass media. Chinese folk dances became the most important dance form prior to the 1970s (Yang 2003, pp. 24–25). With the strong influence of Chinese nationalism, people were forced to share a common identity – that is, Chinese identity – and to give up their cultural and ethnic traditions. Many art forms and collective memories, which were not relative to Chinese culture, were exclusive to cultural policy; therefore, it was viewed as 'the age of homogenization.'

During this period, the KMT government maintained tight control over cultural policy, and policies were implemented directly by the KMT party and administrative institutions. They censored the media and all publications, and established cultural and arts associations under the control of KMT party. In addition, the president himself was the foremost and highest administrator of cultural affairs. He constructed and delivered cultural policy without soliciting any collaboration within the central government. The resulting cultural policies were explicit and dominated by political considerations, party interests and Chinese identity.

The rise of Taiwanese consciousness from the 1970s to the 1990s

In the 1970s, the KMT government faced new problems in Taiwanese society and international situations because of political and economic changes.[6] Even though KMT tried to maintain its authoritarian power, it had to face two major challenges. The first was increasing resistance to the autocratic rule of the government, the KMT party, and the army. The second was the rise of Taiwanese consciousness, which had been hitherto been suppressed. Taiwanese consciousness posed a challenge to the KMT government and its cultural policy based on Chinese nationalism.

On the one hand, Taiwanese consciousness disrupted 'the age of homogenization' and called for more cultural diversity in Taiwanese society. Its influences were present in music, arts, dance, films, literature, and the theater. On the other hand, the tension between diversity and unity was ongoing in the development of Taiwanese consciousness. Taiwanese consciousness became a new form of 'tyranny of the majority,' with genuine cultural diversity being subjugated to a homogenized idea of Taiwanese consciousness. Minority cultural differences were still marginal in the discourse of Taiwanese consciousness. For this reason, some minority groups rejected Taiwanese consciousness as a new common identity in Taiwan. Thus, reconciling unity and diversity in Taiwanese history is difficult.

What is important is that Taiwanese consciousness rejected KMT Chinese nationalism. The differences between Taiwanese consciousness and Chinese nationalism were the subject of constant debate. Those who supported Taiwanese consciousness stressed three main points. First, they emphasized that Taiwanese society had developed a 'common consciousness' different from that of Mainland China. They argued that this common consciousness arose from Taiwan's unique political, economic, and social systems that were historically and culturally isolated from Mainland China for about 100 years. Second, advocates of Taiwanese consciousness believed that it was quite separate from and not subordinate to Chinese consciousness. The two were seen as equal and parallel. Third, they challenged the Chinese nationalism created by the KMT through 'de-sinolization' or 'localization.' They rejected the discussion of Taiwanese history and literature as 'local' culture or 'local' literature.

After 1987, with the abolition of martial law, the arguments about independence, unification, and the relationship between Chinese identity and Taiwanese consciousness became very important arguments in Taiwan. Taiwanese consciousness, as a new Taiwanese nationalism, was constructed in several ways. First, it emphasized Taiwan's experience of being colonized since the 17th century by the Netherlands, Spain, China, Japan, and the KMT government, successively. It defined the latter as a colonial regime in Taiwan, and it looked to a future in which the Taiwanese people would be their own masters. It stressed that, if Taiwan unified with Mainland China, the Taiwanese people would be colonized by the Chinese people again. Moreover, the desire of the Taiwanese people to control their own destiny meant that Taiwanese independence would be a better choice than unification with the mainland. Second, Taiwanese consciousness constructed a Taiwanese nation, including the Han people and the aborigines, that would be different from the Chinese nation in terms of culture and ethnicity, highlighting the fact that the Taiwanese people had emerged through the experience of 400 years of colonization. Within Taiwanese consciousness, the Taiwanese nation was regarded as a unique entity, despite the fact that the Hokkein and Hakka people were immigrants from Mainland China, because the ethnic groups were from different cultures and social, political, and economic systems.

Taiwanese consciousness broke up the monoculture of Taiwan and forced the KMT to amend its cultural policy. Even though the KMT government still saw Chinese-ness as a core identity, it needed to respect Taiwanese culture in its policy to meet the demands of Taiwanese society. It was within this context that the KMT defined Chinese culture as 'central culture' and Taiwanese culture as 'local culture'; such a move implied that the government considered Chinese culture essential, but Taiwanese culture could not be ignored. The development of Taiwanese consciousness was also considered dependent on the development of Taiwanese cultural nationalism (Xiao 1999, pp. 4–50). With the development of Taiwanese consciousness, initially, traditional Chinese opera, music, and theater declined in popularity, and local or native cultures – such as Taiwanese opera, Taiwanese soap opera, folk culture, and Hokkein and aboriginal music – became more popular. Furthermore, Taiwanese consciousness – or native consciousness – influenced a variety of cultural forms, such as Taiwanese literature, Taiwanese New Films, the Folk Music Movement, and Taiwanese native painting. Artists used Taiwanese experience and culture as the inspiration for their work and created their own styles. Finally, the National Theatre and national academic institutions began to accept the performances of Taiwanese theater companies and Taiwanese opera. These national institutions set up the Traditional Cultural and Artistic Center to improve Taiwanese native culture at the national level.

Some new cultural policies were developed to respond to the development of Taiwanese consciousness. In 1977, President CHIANG Kuo Chiang presented 'Twelve Constructions,' and then the government decided to establish a cultural center in every city and county to improve local culture. In 1983, The Council of Cultural Affairs (CCA)[7] promulgated the 'Essential Points of Cultural Centers' to improve the functioning of cultural centers. In addition, the third chairman of the CCA, SHEN Xue-Yong, provided a new concept for cultural policy – a shift from 'central to local' in 1993. Thus, the CCA had two policies emphasizing the role of local cultural centers as 'local CCAs' on the one hand, and 'cultural communalism' on the other. The CCA hoped that the local cultural centers would not only be 'space[s] of cultural activities' but also serve as local CCAs to develop local culture. The purpose of 'cultural communalism' was to improve the power and ability of local cultural centers and to provide independence and autonomy in developing culture. Furthermore, the CCA stressed the importance of cultural and social reconstruction in Taiwan, a kind of community renaissance, because the development of the economy and society had led to a loss of social value and cohesion. There, the CCA used a new policy of communal renaissance to restructure communal identity and consciousness as the basis of a common identity in Taiwan. This effort has become the main basis for Taiwanese studies (Su 1999). These policies are a response to the need for a genuinely Taiwanese local culture. Furthermore, the KMT government has tried to regain the power to interpret Taiwanese culture; thus, it emphasizes the importance of 'community consciousness.' In its descriptions, the KMT government refers to 'community consciousness' but not 'Taiwanese consciousness' to avoid strengthening Taiwanese nationalism.

In performance arts, the birth in the 1970s of Cloud Gate Dance Theater is considered the most important example for the development of Taiwanese consciousness because the dancers and artists try to open dialogue with the entire society to consider self-definition, cultural identity, and collective memory in performing arts. A good example would be their dances, such as *Water Moon*, which represent the process of self-searching for Taiwanese cultural identity. Wu (2008) notes that Cloud Gate Dance Theater is the main cultural symbol of Taiwanese nationalism, and their dances always reconsider and respond to the changing meanings of Taiwanese cultural identity and the conflicts between these two identities (Wu 2008, p. 32). Wu discusses the importance of Cloud Gate Dance Theater, for example, in showing Taiwanese history in dance and trying to create 'our dance and culture' from Taiwanese society, which is different from Chinese and other cultural experiences. Thus, Cloud Gate Dance Theater has become a primary symbol of the cultural movement of Taiwanese localization (Wu 2008, p. 55). Influenced by this company, many dancers and artists try to create and define Taiwan's history and identity through dance, theater, and music, leading to a new cultural movement in performing arts.

In this age, the KMT government faced many challenges from civil society, which demanded more freedom and democracy, requiring the government to use more careful and implicit ways of managing cultural affairs. The government claimed that the establishment of CCA and local cultural centers was to provide better and more cultural services and art activities to people, rather than to control culture or promote Chinese identity. In responding to the demands for a greater recognition of Taiwanese ethnicity, the KMT government worked to shape public perception in order to reduce conflicts arising from difference between Chinese identity and Taiwanese identity. In addition, arts funding and financial support for cultural endeavors took the place of the censorship system as the main tools for cultural policy.

'The age of multicultural Taiwan and globalization' from the 1990s to the present

Multiculturalism is especially important in Taiwan. In 1997, Taiwan's government stated in the constitution that Taiwan is a multicultural country. It did so for two reasons. First, the conflict and confusion surrounding national identity – represented in the choice between unification with and independence from Mainland China – had led to a crisis. In Taiwan, differences concerning national identity are always related to ethnic differences. Thus, multiculturalism is viewed as a new way to achieve political integration. Second, inequality among various ethnic groups, seen especially in the subservient position of the Taiwanese aborigines, has become a major obstacle to the development of democracy in Taiwan. Multiculturalism is seen as a good way to protect the rights of ethnic groups, especially ethnic minorities. That is, it is used to confront the tension between political integration and separation. This explains the double purposes that exist in multicultural policy: the protection of minority rights and the construction of a common national identity, which leads to contradictions and challenges in cultural policy. On the one hand, minority groups rely on the resources and assistance of the government to practice cultural rights; on the other hand, their autonomy and circumstances remain under government control.

A cultural policy toward multiculturalism and 'Four Ethnic Groups'

The conflicts between Chinese nationalism and Taiwanese consciousness are based primarily on the positions of two ethnic groups: the mainlanders and the Hokkeins. The former, accounting for about 13% of Taiwan's total population, controlled the ruling power in the name of Chinese nationalism from the 1940s to the late 1980s. The latter was the majority group, accounting for about 65% of the population, and became the main proponents for Taiwanese consciousness. Other minority groups, such as the Hakkas and Taiwanese aborigines, felt isolated from their conflicts. However, the rise of new social movements in the 1980s and 1990s, in particular ethnic movements, such as those of the Taiwanese aborigines and the Hakkas, led people to search for a wider common identity. The concept of 'Four Ethnic Groups' became the core of the discourse of multicultural Taiwan – the Hokkeins, the Hakkas, the Mainlanders, and Taiwanese aborigines. The government hoped to provide public resources to promote these groups' cultures. For example, the government could set up various ethnic committees to develop multicultural policy based on the principle of Four Ethnic Groups.

In 1996, the Council of Indigenous Peoples (CIP) was established to take charge of aboriginal cultural policy. This event can be seen as the first step toward multiculturalism in Taiwan. In 1997, the amendment of the Tenth Article of the Constitution of the Republic of China claimed that the ROC recognized multiple cultures and supported multiculturalism. Later, the term *Multicultural Taiwan* was adopted to describe the national identity. In 2000, the newly elected Democratic Progressive Party (DPP) government listed ethnic cultural policy as its priority for the 2000s. The new chief of the CCA, CHEN Yu-Xiu, indicated that it was important to protect ethnic cultures, especially those of minority groups. Policies were planned to develop ethnic cultures, and local authorities were supported in implementing these policies (CCA 2001). In 2001, the establishment of the Hakka Affairs Council (HAC) represented the second step in the development of multicultural Taiwan.

The development of multiculturalism provided new concepts for multicultural citizenship and ethnic rights in Taiwan. First, the Constitution recognized collective rights, in particular those of Taiwanese indigenous peoples. According to the revised article in the constitution, new laws and regulations, such as The Act of Indigenous Education, The Act of Indigenous Development, and The Basic Act of Indigenous Peoples, as well as by the establishment of the CIP, protect many new indigenous rights. Second, the Taiwanese government protected many cultural rights with new laws and regulations. The Act for Indigenous Education (1998)[8] emphasized the importance of maintaining respect for indigenous peoples, and improving the common interests of all indigenous people.[9] The government highlighted the importance of multicultural education and the improvement of indigenous cultural identity by creating 'The Plans to Promote Indigenous Culture for Six Years.'[10]

The rise of multiculturalism in Taiwan has led to the recognition of many new rights based on liberal theory. Kymlicka (1995) suggests the term 'multicultural citizenship' and elaborates it in terms of three forms of group-differentiated rights: self-government rights, polyethnic rights, and special representation rights (Kymlicka 1995, pp. 26–33). Parekh (1991) emphasizes that 'a politics of citizenship which both promotes the rights of communities with regard to each other, as well as the obligations of communities to each other is an essential precondition of the pluralist vision' (Parekh 1991, p. 197). Parekh suggests ways of strengthening cultural difference in citizenship, such as giving cultural diversity public status and dignity, and enabling minorities to accept the obligations associated with citizenship of their home country at their own pace and in a direction of their own choosing. Parekh also believes that the government should promote conditions in which minorities can be sure that the wider society is not hostile to them, so they can participate fully in the decision-making at all levels (Parekh 1991, pp. 198–199).

Many new aboriginal and Hakka performances have been developed with the support of government ethnic cultural policy. Emerging generations of young Taiwanese aborigines try to create or represent their traditions, reproduce and strengthen their identity, and revive new meaning for traditional rituals in contemporary life. The Formosa Aboriginal Singing and Dance Troupe is the most important example. With the assistance of tribal elders and anthropologists, the troupe participated in a number of field studies to collect many slowly disappearing traditional aboriginal songs and dances. At the same time, tribal elders helped with the transcription in the oral histories of songs and dances. They designed their works to help the troupe portray the spirit of aboriginal memorial ceremonies as faithfully as possible. In turn, their vital performances have helped to promote wider understanding between different ethnic groups and developed a rich and varied theater culture (Liu 2002, p. 21). With the development of Hakka cultural policy, various Hakka arts have been created, such as performance arts – Hakka popular music, drama, theater, and dance – and visual arts – films, TV programs, documentaries, painting, and photography. These Hakka arts provide new perspectives on Hakka ethnic images, identity construction, and ethnic classification (Wang 2012). In particular, Hakka performance arts play an important role in exhibiting their collective memory, cultural tradition, nostalgia, and life experience, which help in understanding how Hakka define and redefine their culture and identity, changes and development.

The influence of migrant workers and transnational community

Since the late 1990s, Multicultural Taiwan has faced challenges from migrant workers and transnational communities.[11] These new problems, which directly affect the current and future identity of Taiwan, challenge society as a whole and will blur and destabilize the current boundaries that separate different internal ethnic groups and the identities separating Taiwan and other countries. Everyone in Taiwan will be challenged to live in a society characterized by an increasingly diverse and intertwined cultural landscape. At the same time, the Taiwan government faces many demands from NGOs to improve the rights of and establish equal treatment for migrant workers and foreign brides. Some new cultural policies have been implemented in response to these demands.

In 1995, the Council of Labour Affairs (CLA) began to sponsor broadcast radio programs for Thai, Indonesian, and Filipino workers (Chiou 1999, pp. 180–182). The CLA also began opening consulting centers for migrant workers at the local government level. These centers have evolved into the main institutions for providing legal advice and cultural activities for these workers. For example, the Taipei consulting center held the first cultural exchange party, 'We Are the World,' in 1996, indicating a new attitude toward migrant workers might possibly be developing in local governments.[12] The cultural activities for these workers sponsored by the Taipei City Council serve several purposes. Activities allow migrant workers to maintain their cultural experiences and traditions in Taiwan. Examples include the Christmas party at St. Christopher's Catholic Church (2000), the celebration of St. Cross Day (1998–2001), and the migrant worker carnival (2000), featuring music by bands from the Philippines and Thailand. Thus, migrant workers have been able to observe important cultural festivals in Taiwan. In addition, cultural activity programs try to improve the collective culture of migrant workers in Taiwan and raise its stature in Taiwanese society. An exhibition of photographs of the life of migrant workers in Taiwan (2000) and a migrant workers' poetry writing contest (2001) were held both to foster the development of cultural diversity in Taiwan and to provide greater opportunity for Taiwanese to understand migrant workers and their lives. Meanwhile, foreign brides represent a direct challenge to current policies promoting a 'multicultural Taiwan.' It is because, unlike migrant workers who are supposed to stay in Taiwan for a short term, foreign brides are permanent residents. The government protects the former's cultural rights based on the 'International Convention of the Protection of the Rights of All Migrant Workers and Members of Their Families'. However, it believes foreign brides should learn and adapt themselves to Taiwanese culture as soon as possible. Those brides are expected to assimilate into Taiwan's culture and abandon their own cultures.

Nevertheless, this new cultural policy highlights changing attitudes toward multiculturalism as a whole. Migrant workers, while not holding the status of citizens, deserve to have their rights protected in accordance with universal human rights. With the changing attitude toward migrant workers in Taiwan, multicultural policy and citizenship have already begun to expand beyond national boundaries to incorporate needs and concerns arising from the transnational influx of workers. The new cultural policy has led to an increase in performing arts for transnational communities in Taiwan. For example, in 2012, a dance related to the Vietnamese collective memory of the Vietnam War, 'Dry Rain,' was performed in south Taiwan, and many Vietnamese migrants were touched to experience their home culture.[13] Furthermore, some new performing art groups, such as The Theatre for Trans Asia Sisters, were set up in 2009 to encourage female migrants from Vietnam, Thailand, Malaysia and Indonesia to express their voices through dance, theater, and music based on their migration, life experiences, and interactions with Taiwanese society.[14]

The influence of Mainland China

From the 1980s, the economic development of Mainland China has had increasing influence in Taiwan. From the 1990s, the cultural and economic exchanges between Taiwan and China have become more frequent, and the number of Taiwanese living, working, and studying in China is increasing rapidly. Now, China is viewed as having a significant role in the formation of various political, economic, cultural, and social policies in Taiwan. In terms of cultural policy, the Taiwanese government faces some new challenges in dealing with the so-called 'China factor': the issue of national identity is becoming increasingly complex. Since the 1970s, the tension between the Chinese and the Taiwanese identity has grown, and a new, powerful China is intensifying this tension. The growing political, economic, and cultural exchanges with China have forced the Taiwanese to reconsider their identity.

One thing to note here is that China is viewed as a new market for Taiwan, in particular for performing arts. For example, since 1997, *The Peach Blossom Land*, by the famous theater company Performance Workshop in Taiwan, has been successfully performed 150 times in China. In addition, the company began to use Chinese actors. In 2001,

Millennium Teahouse was performed in Beijing and was reported on by Central TV in China. In 2008, Performance Workshop created a new show portraying the development of Chinese society over 30 years: *Watching TV with Me* is a completely Chinese production and experience that is now returning to Taiwan. Since 2011, six theatrical companies – some of them companies established by local governments and commercial organizations – have presented a series of plays in China.

Even Cloud Gate Dance Theater, which is very popular in Europe and the US, has begun moving into the Chinese market. In 2010, Cloud Gate Dance Theater appeared only twice in China, but in 2011, it had 13 performances. The emphasis on the Chinese market has had some influence on the content of performance. For example, in 2012, Performance Workshop modified some lines in its show out of political consideration, raising concerns about Chinese control over Taiwanese cultural content.

The idea of multicultural Taiwan is close to liberal multiculturalism. In liberal multiculturalism, multicultural citizenship is considered a significant new balance between unity and diversity. On the one hand, multicultural citizenship is related to the construction of a common public sphere and nation; on the other hand, multicultural citizenship is also concerned with respect for cultural diversity and minority communities.

Two kinds of rights are needed to practice multicultural citizenship. One kind includes the basic rights of all groups and individuals, while the other is group specific. Within this framework, Taiwanese aborigines have legitimized their demands for more multicultural citizenship. The Hakka have used the same rationale to gain political and financial support for expanding their cultural rights. At the same time, Multicultural Taiwan is challenged by the influences of globalization, such as the growth of transnational communities and the so-called China factors.

The development of multiculturalism shows the deepening tensions in Taiwanese society between diversity (respecting cultural differences) and unity (constructing a national identity), between separation (respecting special cultural rights) and integration (establishing a common political citizenship), and between hybridity (incorporating global cultures and identities) and homogeneity (recognizing the Four Ethnic Groups). These tensions have led to many contradictions and challenges in its cultural policy.

Currently, the cultural policies relative to national identity are becoming more implicit, indirect, and decentralized. First, the Council of Cultural Affairs (or Ministry of Culture) is not alone in establishing cultural policy. Rather, the Hakka Affairs Council (HAC), the Council of Indigenous Peoples (CIP), and the Council of Labor Affairs (CLA) all play major roles and have a strong influence on cultural policy relative to national identity. Secondly, the growing importance of economic interests has begun to surpass that of national identity as the primary driver of cultural policy. Finally, because the influences of transnational communities and the China factor make the issue of national identity more complex and contradictory, it is more difficult than ever for the government to develop explicit cultural policy.

Conclusion

This chapter' findings can be summed up as follows. First, national identity still has an important role in the development and modification of cultural policy. Cultural policy always encounters a dilemma between integrating identity and respecting different values. In the age of Chinese nationalism, the KMT government chose to ignore the differences between people and promoted a nationalism based on Mainland China. However, ultimately, Chinese nationalism failed. Afterwards, there was a period where 'Taiwanese consciousness' tried to be a 'common consciousness,' but the idea of its common experience was criticized and viewed as a kind of 'Hokkein centralism.' The subsequent new thinking – multiculturalism – promises to provide a good balance between political integration and ethnic differences.

Second, the representation of Multicultural Taiwan indicates a close relationship between the discourse of the Four Ethnic Groups and an emphasis on ethnic cultural differences; however, it ignores the cultural differences stemming from gender, class, and gay or lesbian identities. In addition, the issues of migrant workers and foreign brides present further difficulties because Multicultural Taiwan is based on the concept of a self-contained national identity inside Taiwan's borders. In this respect, the multicultural identity is expected to accommodate new forms of cultural difference, hybrid cultures, and multiple identities beyond national boundaries.

Therefore, the specificity of multiculturalism in the global age must be considered. With the increase of diasporas and transnational populations, all societies are multicultural. As Cornwell and Stoddard (2001) note, multicultural states are both temporal and spatial phenomena. To appreciate the extent to which all societies are multicultural, it is necessary to understand historically how peoples have shifted around the globe such that their self-identified cultural borders bear little relation to the state borders. At the same time, a spatial analysis of societies is crucial to recognizing the multicultural composition of most states (Cornwell and Stoddard 2001, p. 2).

In summary, the construction of a national identity in Taiwan encounters challenges in its cultural policy. The first challenge is that it is now more difficult to construct a homogeneous ethnic culture and identity. A second challenge is related to the influence of globalization, such as the experience of migrant workers and the influence of China in Taiwan. These factors make the relationship between national identity and cultural policy more complex and unstable.

Notes

1. The Kuomintang (KMT) nationalists established the 'Republic of China' in Taiwan in opposition to Mainland China's communist regime in 1945.
2. The Taiwanese people were referred to as the Hokkein people for a long time. This designation did not include other ethnic groups, especially the mainlanders and aborigines. Since the 1990s, 'the Taiwanese people' referred to all people who identified themselves as Taiwanese. However, the term 'people in Taiwan' means the people who live in Taiwan, including the Hokkein, the Hakka, and the aborigines, before the coming of the KMT government in 1949. Today, there are four main ethnic groups in Taiwan:
   1. Taiwanese aborigines are native to the island of Taiwan. They are Austronesian and of Malayo-Polynesian descent. They share a very close blood relationship and appearance with other aboriginal people in Malaysia, the Philippines, and some islands in the Pacific Ocean. Their population is about 2–3% of the whole population of Taiwan.
   2. The mainlanders are those people who came to Taiwan with the KMT government around 1945–1949. They include administrators of the KMT party, government members, military men and their families, and people who wanted to run away from war. Their population is 12–15 % of the whole population in Taiwan.
   3. The Hakka is a special ethnic group with a long history in Mainland China. Most people believe the Hakka came from the northern part of Mainland China and moved on more than five occasions on a large scale to the south. During the Ching Dynasty, many Hakka lived in Canton Province. Later, some Hakka moved to Taiwan, some moved to Southeast Asia (for example, Hong Kong, Singapore, Indonesia and Malaysia), and some continued to live in Mainland China. The Hakka arrived in Taiwan about 300 years ago, later than the Fulos. Their population is 15–18% of Taiwan, making it the second largest group.
   4. The Hokkein are the largest ethnic group in Taiwan, comprising about 65% of the total population. Their ancestors emigrated from Fujian province in the southeastern part of Mainland China during the 17th century.

3. 'Ping Opera' was the dominant theater in Beijing (previously known as Beiping) and was constructed as national opera by the KMT government before it moved to Taiwan.
4. The Council of Cultural Affairs was set up in 1981 and managed cultural and arts developments in Taiwan until 2012, when it was renamed the Ministry of Culture. Before 1981, there was no clear institutional structure to manage the cultural affairs in Taiwan.
5. 'National' music, painting, and theater are also called *Chinese music, Chinese painting*, and *Chinese opera*. As important forms, they have become symbolic of KMT China and have dominated cultural development for over 40 years.
6. In the 1960s and 1970s, Taiwan experienced fundamental change in two important respects: the population increased 1.6 times (from 1960 to 1977), and the Gross National Product (GNP) increased 12 times. As society became more affluent and more challenges arose from both domestic civil society and the international arena, the need to change the basic structure and operation of the KMT government became more apparent. In 1971, three major events of particular significance to Taiwan occurred, beginning Taiwan's challenge of the rule of the KMT government. In April, the problem of Diao-Yu Island led to a demonstration by college students and a certain degree of intellectual support for Communist China. In October, the KMT government announced its withdrawal from the United Nations because Communist China had been admitted to that organization as the representative of the whole of China. In September, the Taiwanese Presbyterate stated that 'Taiwan must become a new and independent country.'
7. In addition to the Council of Cultural Affairs (which was converted to the Ministry of Culture later), the Council of Indigenous Peoples (CIP) and the Hakka Affairs Council (HAC) were set up in 1996 and 2001 to support the cultures of the indigenous people and the Hakka. These three organizations are responsible for cultural and arts development in the central level. Meanwhile, most local governments set up a cultural unit or ethnic committee to deal with cultural affairs.
8. From http://www.apc.gov.tw/laws/The Law for Indigenous Education.htm (in Chinese).
9. Article 2 of the Law for Indigenous Education.
10. From http://www.apc.gov.tw/laws/The Plans to Promote Indigenous Culture for Six Years.htm (in Chinese).
11. Since the mid-1990s, migrant workers from East Asian countries such as the Philippines, Thailand, Indonesia, Vietnam and Malaysia have introduced new cultures into Taiwan. Today, the roughly 320,000 migrant workers (out of a total Taiwan population of around 23 million) put them on a similar footing, in terms of numbers, with Taiwan's indigenous peoples. How the government treats and integrates migrant workers into society should be viewed as a litmus test of national multicultural policies. In 1994, the Taiwan government ended limitations on 'foreign brides' entering Taiwan from Indonesia, Thailand, Vietnam and the Philippines. This new group, comprising mostly Taiwanese husbands and Southeast Asian wives, has attracted significant attention. In September 2002, with children of these marriages beginning primary school, the government was faced for the first time with the issue of how to educate these bi-cultural children.

12. I use Taipei as an index because the Taipei city council has consistently promoted the culture of migrant workers for the relatively long period of two years. Other cities and counties, while also holding activities for migrant workers, are not as well organized in their approach.
13. http://news.pts.org.tw/detail.php?NEENO=218705.
14. http://tasat.blogspot.tw/2013/02/2013.html.

References

Anderson, B. (1983) *Imagined Communities: Reflections on the Origin and Spread of Nationalism* (London: Verso).

Chiou, S.W. (1999) 'Local Internationalisation: The Philippines Brides in Japanese Villages', *Contemporary*, CXLI, 108–117 (in Chinese).

Cornwell, G.H and E.W. Stoddard (eds) (2001) *Global Multiculturalism: Comparative Perspectives on Ethnicity, Race and Nation* (Maryland: Rowman & Littlefield).

Hakka Affairs Council (2001) *The Plan to Promote the Hakka Culture within Six Years* (Taipei: Hakka Affairs Council) (in Chinese).

Hobsbawm, E.J. and T. Ranger (1995) *The Invention of Tradition* (Cambridge: Cambridge University Press).

Kuo, S.-H. (1989) *Dilemmas of Cultural Policy Formation in a Transitional Society: The Case of Taiwan, Republic of China* (Ann Arbor: University of Michigan).

Kymlicka, W. (1995) *Multicultural Citizenship: A Liberal Theory of Minority Right* (Oxford: Oxford University Press).

Liu, X.-J. (2002) 'Formosa Aboriginal Singing and Dance Troupe', *Grace and Beauty of the Century: Performing Arts in Taiwan* [audio CD] (Taipei: Council of Cultural Affari), 21–27 (in Chinese).

Parekh, B. (1991) 'British Citizenship and Cultural Difference', in G. Andrews (ed.), *Citizenship* (London: Lawrence and Wishart), 183–206.

Su, Zhao-Ying (1999), *The Development of Culture and Arts in the Counties of Taiwan – Conceptions and Practice* (Taipei: CCA).

Wang, L.-J. (2012) *The Development of Hakka Ethnicity and Cultural Policy in Taiwan* (Taipei: Best-Wise) (in Chinese).

Wu, H.-Y. (2008) *From Self-Searching to Strategic-Orientation: The Cloudgage Dance Theatre of Taiwan and the Social Change of Taiwan*. Unpublished PhD Dissertation. Taipei: National Taiwan University (in Chinese).

Xiao, A.-Q. (1991) *The Cultural and Moral Discourse of the KMT Regime*. Unpublished master's thesis. Taipei: National Taiwan University.

Xiao, A.-Q. (1999) 'The Development of Taiwanese Cultural Nationalism from the 1980s: The Analysis of Taiwanese Literature', *Taiwanese Sociological Review*, III, 1–51 (in Chinese).

Yang, D.-Y. (2003) *The Development of Performing Arts and Society in Contemporary Taiwan*. Unpublished master's thesis. Chung-Li: National Central University (in Chinese).

Zhou, H.-L. (1995). 'Chinese Opera, Nationalism and Cultural Policy', *Contemporary*, CVII, 56–59.

3
Online Games and Chinese National Identities

Anthony Y.H. Fung

The big question: market and the state

Cultural industries in the People Republic of China (PRC), from publications to music and the movie business, are often under strict control of the authorities. Political censorship plays a crucial role in reinforcing the state's hegemonic influence nationally. The sense is that, with its transformative power in defining cultural discourse and shaping national identity, media is always under the radar of the authoritarian state. And yet, new media businesses and online game industries, as emerging but highly profitable sectors, appear to be more difficult to control for two reasons. First, the state was not very involved in the growth of the two industries, and their rapid growth has made them challenging to manage in this later stage. Second, with China's ambition to extend its soft power overseas and boost its revenue from exports, the state needs to ensure political correctness and profitability at the same time. That said, censored cultural goods may still generate decent profits in the domestic market, which is controlled by the state, but will these products still appeal to overseas consumers and achieve commercial success?

The interplay between political forces and market forces puts cultural industries, the online games industries in particular, in a unique situation. On the one hand, Chinese online games industries have learnt from the West, adopted the Western form and structure, and operated under the foreign mode of management; cases of development of online games industries that rely on the West reflect the formation of global popular culture in China. On the other hand, the process of cultural globalization vis-à-vis forces of market localization has occurred under the umbrella of state control and monitoring. Such dynamics between politics and the market highlight a key question: is there an inherent exclusivity between globalizing forces with cultural hybridity and a local discourse of national identity?

Globalization has strengthened the interconnectedness among nation states, from economies to politics and culture. In the throes of the globalizing process – with emerging visions of a global village, border-crossing activities, capitalist ideologies embedded in free trade and global citizens with cosmopolitan outlook and worldview – one may wonder whether globalization will weaken the sense of national identity. Underlying this argument is the assumption that concepts such as 'the global' and 'the national' are contradictory. That is, when globalization prevails, the national influence would diminish. Globalization basically erases the differences among peoples of different nations, and hence blurs the distinction between 'us' as well as the 'others,' which is the basic foundation of cultural identification (Hall 1997). As the concept of hybrid identities is intertwined with 'the process of accelerated globalization,' 'differential and hybrid ethnic and national identifications' gain importance in an increasingly globalized world (Barker 1997, p. 191). Barker suggests that national identities are replaced by hybrid identities. In the era of globalization, audiences are exposed to a wide range of foreign cultures, and their sense of identity may not be confined to their own culture and nationality. In the context of China, where the media is censored and the state has strong control over cultural discourse, however, audiences only have limited access to foreign culture, and these cultural representations are often manipulated by the state. As such, foreign cultures have limited influence on the sense of being Chinese among audiences in China.

This chapter seeks to address the oldest issue of cultural policy through the newest cultural form – whether there is a fundamental exclusivity between a global market force and national political interests in the case online games. Given the rapid rise of the online games industry in recent years, Chinese authorities have realized that games as a global entertainment industry could also weaken the national identities of their own citizens. Thus, like other media and creative industries, the Chinese state is very vigilant about the influx of global games, and has chosen to exercise stringent control over its online games industries.

Identity, consumption and globalization

Identity is one of the focal points in contemporary social and cultural debates. The concept originates from psychology, first in Sigmund Freud's psychoanalytical theory and then Erik H. Erikson's concept of 'self identity.' The term is later widely cited and applied to research in different fields. Henri Tajfel (1982) developed 'social identity theory' in the 1980s and pointed out that a sense of otherness is at the core of the in-group and out-group mechanism. As the sense of otherness is one of the essential substances of identity, the notion of *identity* transforms 'all relations of identity into relations of difference' (Grossberg 2011, p. 92). People's senses of identity tend to be built around icons and symbols, which are emotional anchors of identification. This identification is not only an attitudinal or cognitive process; it clearly has an emotional aspect that binds individuals into a collectivity. Scheff (1994) points out that discussions of national and cultural identity – for instance, Anderson's concept of 'imagined community' (1983) – mostly focus on the cognitive, saying little about feelings and emotions, which are important components of national and cultural identity.

With the explosion of information in the globalized world, the process of cultural identification has changed. Using Baudrillard's (1994) concept of signifier and the signified, one can note that these are the two elements of cultural identification. For instance, a national flag represents a nation, and recognizing a national flag is a cultural identification to the nation represented. In a postmodern society, as Baudrillard observes, signifier, image, symbol and icon already precede the signified. As such, media, as the gatekeeper of all sorts of signifiers, plays a very crucial role in shaping people's perception of their identity.

Two major aspects of identity are discussed at length within academic literature in the West. First, the process of identification requires certain levels of imagination and internalization (Anderson 1983). As social actors seek meanings from identities, for themselves and by themselves, the process of identity construction involves part of individualization (Giddens 1991). Only if social actors internalize the cultural meanings and construct their sense of identity around these meanings, will their identities become real (Castells 1997). In other words, national identity is not just about external forces, but also a perception from within. The other aspect of identity is its constant variation in accordance with context and social structures at large. Such variation is not simply driven by the context but also by how the social actors imagine themselves and differentiate themselves from 'the others.' In other words, the broader context and structures not only constrain identity, but also offer an opportunity for identity to take shape (Giddens 1991). In the era of globalization especially, the interaction between different cultures constantly fixes and re-fixes identities based on the changing external environment.

As such, there is no longer a fixed status of identity. The new generation often searches for their identity through consumption, and the act
of consumption itself is a set of cultural practices that expresses an individual's sense of identity, which differentiates oneself from other social
groups. In a capitalist free market, there is a wide range of products –
some are from multinational corporations and some are produced by
domestic companies. Each product is a hybrid of different cultures. Take
World of Warcraft, a globally popular massively multiplayer online role-
playing game (MMORPG), for example: the game was developed by an
American company, Blizzard Entertainment, and the storyline is based
on the mythical imagination of Medieval European history. When it is
sold in the Chinese market, the language of the game is translated into
Chinese. The game illustrates the cultural hybrid of a cultural good in
the era of globalization. Thinking along the lines of a Gramscian textual
analysis, which is rooted in the Marxist notion of the base/superstruc-
ture relationship, questions worth pondering include: Do online games
in China serve as a national machine to strengthen the gamers' sense
of national identity? Or is it a battlefield between politically correct
ideology and the gamers' cultural resistance? Or are there any other
reasons, which are neither the state's control nor the gamers' acceptance, which make popular Chinese online games consistent to national
identity? Can the global versus local dilemma be resolved?

The cultural industries in China and government control

'Cultural industries,' sometimes known as 'creative industries,' has
become a buzz phrase in China. The terminology refers to industries
that create, produce, and distribute goods and services in the nature of
culture. Broadcasting, music, film, animation and online game industries are examples. The development of cultural industries is not only a
driving force in export and the boosting of GDP; it is also a tool of the
authoritarian state to strengthen its soft power overseas. It takes many
forms, but there are two dimensions worth highlighting. The first is the
dimension of global reliance. As the cultural industries in China are
relatively new, its initial development has to rely on global capital and
foreign help. The second dimension is ideological control. In view of
the strong influence of mass media, the Communist Party has long been
manipulative in the media landscape for propaganda and other political
purposes. In other words, the state has to ensure the ideological alignment between the content of media and the state's political agenda.

Cultural industries, like the media industry, could easily arouse sentiments, reshape ideology, and mobilize the public. The authoritarian state has to censor the content to protect its political interests. And yet, the stronger control the state has, the less freedom and creativity in content and product development the market has. That would affect whether the product is compelling and thus competitive, or not, in the market.

Online games are one of the fastest growing cultural industries in China. According to the statistics given by the Chinese government, the total annual revenue of Mainland China's online game industry in 2010 was US$5.7 billion, which included US$5.2 billion of the revenue from internet-based games (Ministry of Culture, 2010). The rising statistics provided by the state are in line with the industry forecast. Mirae Asset Global Investments Group predicts that the growth rate of the Chinese online games market will be 28%, and total revenue will be around US$7.4 billion in 2011 (People.com.cn, 2011). While it is anticipated that the growth rate of the global online games market will remain 14.8% for the upcoming 5 years, growth in China will stay around 20%. Investment bank Digi-Capital says that the revenue from China's online and mobile games industry is currently a third of the total revenues of the global online games industry (Sohu 2011). It is anticipated to increase to half of the total revenues by 2014.

Prior to 2004, the state's intervention in the online games industry was minimal, and the industry was only monitored by The Temporary Regulation for the Management of Computer Information Network International Connections, which was implemented in 1996. In 2004, the state issued new policies to control the online games industry, exemplified by the Notice on Forbidding the Broadcast of PC/Online Games Programs, which banned video games based on traditional media programs. Later, the Chinese authorities introduced The Regulation on Digital Publications in 2007, The Regulation on the Publishing of Digital Publications in 2008 and The Administration of Software Production in 2009. In August 2010, the state delegated such censorship to the provincial level (People's Congress Decision on the 5th Batch on the Cancellation of and Approval of Delegation on the Level of Management and Controlling Unit). Most of the controls were in the name of protecting minors such as the Online Game Parents Monitoring over Minors Project, Online Games Advising Project and Minors' Healthy Participation in Online Games Advisory. A few other projects were also implemented in 2010, including the Real Identity Registration Scheme and the National Green Online Project – which was software pre-loaded on any computer to filter 'undesirable' content. This initiative exposed the real motive of the state: to strengthen the control of the industries so as to prevent any dissident voices from infiltrating into this creative industry. And yet, the state's attempt to control the online games industry encountered strong resistance from the public and the international community. As the software was suspected to be linked with the state's political agenda of extending its Internet censorship, more than 80% of 'netizens' in China expressed their unwillingness to use the software. The US government also expressed concerns about the potential impact of the 'Green Dam' on freedom and trade.

Cultural specificity of Chinese online games

Although the Chinese authorities' direct control of online games industries received strong resistance from the market and the industries, Chinese online games have enjoyed visible success in the market. According to statistics, the number of Chinese online gamers has shot up exponentially since the early 2000s; it rose from 1.7 million in 2001 to 56 million in 2008 and 324 million in 2012 (CNNIC 2001; CNNIC 2009; CNNIC 2012). The domestic market size, revenue, and industry of online games in China also grew similarly rapidly. Up to 2010, MMORPG remained the most popular type of online game with 57.4% market share, compared with casual games (28.6%) and web games (14%). The game-world of the most popular MMORPG in China is often based on Chinese folklore, legends, wuxia[1] and historical stories, which is in line with the state's political interest. While many online games in the world sell across the globe and therefore attempt to discount their cultural origin, online games in China tend to be culturally specific. This cultural specificity not only contributes to the commercial success of these games, but also strengthens the gamers' sense of national identity. The cultural familiarity of the text attracts gamers, and the intensive and interactive online gaming process reinforces gamers' cognition of their national identity. Despite the fact that gamers strongly resist top-down nationalism, their engagement in online games with Chinese culture constitutes another form of cultural identification.

Journey to the West and *The Romance of the 3 Kingdoms* are two typical examples of domestic online games based on Chinese folklore and legends. Both stories are regarded as two of the four great classical novels, and most Chinese audiences are familiar with the text. The former is a fantasy novel set during the Tang Dynasty. The story tells of the journey of a Buddhist monk who sought to promote his religion in the West.

The text has been incorporated into numerous online games, such as *A Journey to the West* (in a series of 5), *Pocketpet Journey West*, and *The Q version of Journey to the West*. The latter story is based on a legend set in the historical time frame between the Han and Jin Dynasty, known as the Three Kingdoms Era. The story has been adapted in *Warriors of the 3 Kingdoms* (2011), *Chibi* (2007), *Yi San Guo* (2010), *QQ Three Kingdoms* (2012), *Map of the Three Kingdoms* (published annually from 2000 to 2013), and *Three Kingdoms Brawler* (2010), among others. Given the historical background, this type of folklore and legends contains strong connotation to ancient Chinese culture and Confucianism. Take *Romance of the 3 Kingdoms*, for example: the main reason for the popularity of the text is the famous characters, such as GUAN Yu, ZHUGE Liang and ZHANG Fei, who live their lives abiding to Confucian virtues. Guan represents *zhong* (loyalty), Zhuge is a symbol of *zhi* (wisdom), and Zhang is a sign of *yong* (courage). All of them work for the state *Shu* with faith and loyalty. When gamers participate in the online gaming related to the text, they will be assigned with a role, and they are supposed to think, behave and interact with other characters according to the storyline. With the intensive process of gaming, these virtues are likely to be internalized and reinforced among the gamers.

There is enough empirical evidence available to suggest a close relationship between long-term gaming and identity. Examining the social psychology of selected gamers and non-gamers, Waggoner (2009, p. 160) concluded with the argument that centered on the inseparability of real world identity, virtual identity, and the projected identity of gamers, suggesting the virtual or 'avatarial identity' acquired to a certain extent reflects and demarcates the real interests of gamers in their social lives. William et al. (2006) have documented various cases in which the construction of a fantasy world in video games is dialectically related to the construction of a gamer's self-identity and social reality. Among all cases discussed, Chee et al. (2006), based on Schultz's phenomenological approach for the ethnographic data, argued that the MMORPG game studied, *EverQuest*, is not 'just a game' (p. 171). They found that games in fact intimately connect players' online realities with their offline desires and passions and their sociability with other community members; above all, how players interact with each other in the game-world is perceived as genuine engagement in the real community.

To further illustrate the cultural specificity of the online games in China, *Genghis Khan* (2009) and *Heaven Sword and Dragon Sabre* (2010) are chosen as two case studies. Both games feature the same period in Chinese history, the Yuan Dynasty. The Yuan Dynasty refers to the rule of the Mongolian empire in China from 1279 to 1368, which was the first dynasty ruled by a foreign empire. Prior to the Yuan Dynasty, the Chinese empire had long been ruled by the Han Chinese ethnicity. It is worth noting that despite the same historical background, the two games have approached this part of history differently. *Genghis Khan* is a type of online game based on historical stories. Genghis Khan was the founder and emperor of the Mongol Empire, which governed China from 1260 to 1370. Genghis Khan is a historical persona who is widely considered to have been one of the most powerful and influential emperors in Chinese history. The territory of the Mongol Empire extended from East Asia to Central Asia.

A Beijing-based domestic online game company, Qilin Youxi, developed a series of online games based on this historical period. In this fantasy war-themed MMORPG, gamers can choose between four factions and twelve classes, including crusader, warrior, pyromancer, swordsmen, warlock, prophet, monk, shaman, guardian, rifleman, assassin and archer. The ultimate goal of any character is to conquer the world. The game became one of the most popular online games in China in 2009, exemplified by numerous awards, such as 'Favorite Online Game In Year 2009' in the Outstanding Game Award 2009 competition and 'Top Ten Most Popular National Online Game,' awarded by the China Game Industry Annual Conference 2009, among others. The games were even exported to Singapore, Malaysia and other foreign markets.

Strictly speaking, Genghis Khan was only an invader, and seeing him as a representative of an ancient emperor of China is rooted in a sense of Sinocentrism. Still, the game visualizes and fantasizes China's glorious past, with its capacity and ambition to invade and influence the West. Despite the cruelty from this foreign regime, the game text justifies the necessity of using force to rule, and draws links with the current ruling regime in China today. By participating in this online game, gamers celebrate the expanding national border during Khan's period. Thus, when it comes to border disputes nowadays, these gamers would be immediately sensitized to support whatever actions the Chinese take to defend their territory and border.

Guanggrong Shiming is another example. The game was developed by the Shanghai-based company Giant Interactive Group and was first launched in 2008. A new version of the game was released in 2013, which features the Diaoyu Islands; the image of the invader has been criticized for its allusion to Japanese soldiers (*Passion Times*, 2013).

Heaven Sword and Dragon Sabre (2010) is another type of online game, which is based on wuxia fiction. This literary genre has been widely adopted in online games, and JIN Yong's fictions remain the most popular ones. In 2011, there were more than 30 online games based on wuxia. *Heaven Sword and Dragon Sabre*, developed by The Perfect World, is an example. Like *Genghis Khan*, it is set during the Yuan Dynasty. As the late Yuan Dynasty was full of internal conflicts, the game is about the competition among three rebel powers and their conflict with the establishment. The historical perspective of *Heaven Sword and Dragon Sabre* is different from *Genghis Khan*. The Yuan Dynasty is portrayed as a foreign empire, and thus the common goal among the gamers is to revive the power of the Han Chinese.

Again, this fictional game is closely connected to current geopolitics: a time when China has border disputes with Japan, Vietnam, the Philippines, and so forth. In particular, recently Japan and China have had military confrontations over the Diaoyu Islands (Sekaku Island in Japanese). The Chinese state needed strong public sentiment to support its diplomatic action. In sum, despite the different ways in interpreting Chinese cultural identity, both games reveal that these commercial online games have become a space for cultural identification that coincidentally matches state agendas, seeking to make audiences feel proud of their rich Chinese culture, and thus strengthening their sense of national identity as well as respect for the establishment.

Online gaming and banal nationalism

Thus, despite the state's failure to directly create a cultural Chinese community or Chineseness across the globe through a top-down approach, the popularity of online games based on cultural history of China fulfills the state's agenda. Such cultural identification has emerged as a market force, which not only strengthens local gamers' cultural identification to their national identity but also connects overseas gamers and expands the dimension of the cultural aspects of national identity.

Chinese MMORPG are popular in the domestic market because they are attributed to a rising youth culture in China. Young people tend to consolidate their identity and reinforce their social role by appropriating cultural practices that are widely shared among their peers (Hebdige 1979), and it is then not difficult to imagine that gaming has become a popular phenomenon among the youth in China. Illustrating the idea of the activeness of the youth in political and social movements, Clark (2012) highlights that new media technology and the Internet has inevitably become a pivotal vehicle and platform for public participation and even intervention. With the increase in online games, online gaming would be readily embedded into the social life of young people. When playing online games, Chinese youngsters are likely to build up a 'virtual me' online, and they will more readily identify themselves with other youths in a virtual world (Cao and Downing 2008). In his study of Chinese youth, Clark (2012) also points out that Chinese audiences isolate themselves in gaming or 'plays' in front of their computers, but ironically, at the same time, they are pitching in with the global trend when they participate in video game playing.

Players in China belong to the 'Net generation, which has grown up with home computers, games, but most importantly, the Internet. Born in the unique historical period in which China governs tightly in politics but governs freely with the economy, this generation is keen to use digital media and is skillful in navigating information, technologies, and platforms. While the formal mass media is under tight control, the 'Net generation relies heavily on the Internet for information and news, and even feels empowered to challenge the ideological control of the state on online forums – something that the state-owned media channels would not allow. Everyday online activity now is simply a ritual for this generation. More importantly, this 'Net generation has grown up amidst enormous opportunities and uncertainties in a rising China, which is in line with Beck's concept of a 'risk society' (1992). Beck's concept refers to a society overwhelmed by the anxiety of people's perceived risks and consequences of modernization. On the one hand, China's economy has grown much faster than many economists predicted. According to *The Economist* (2012), if we measure China's GDP in nominal dollars, it is estimated that China will take over America and become the world's largest economy in 2027. On the other hand, *China Daily* reported that China's Gini coefficient was 0.61 in 2010, which was much higher than the global average of 0.44. In addition to the rising wealth gap, the issues of corruption, natural disasters and China's rising tension with its neighbor countries result in mixed sentiments, both pride and anxiety, particularly among the young generation. Online games serve as a virtual platform for them to release their stress and escape from pressing realities.

There are two kinds of nationalism, namely state-constructed nationalism (Zhao 2004) and banal nationalism (Billig 1995). The former refers to a kind of nationalism initiated by the state and implemented via a top-down approach. The Cultural Revolution, sometimes known as the Great Proletarian Cultural Revolution, from 1966 to 1976 is a good example. MAO Zedong, the Chairman of the Communist Party of China, was portrayed as a national hero, and his school of thought,

Maoism, was promoted and celebrated through a series of propaganda campaigns. Banal nationalism refers to a kind of nationalism that is reinforced through the practice of everyday life. As Billig puts it: '[the] metonymic image of banal nationalism is not a flag which is being consciously waved with fervent passion; it is the flag hanging unnoticed on the public building' (1995, p. 8). Edensor further elaborated that 'national identity is primarily constituted out of the proliferating signifiers of the nation and the everyday habits and routines which instil[l] a sense of being in national place' (2004, p. 101). The Beijing Olympics are another good example. Martinez (2010) analyzed the cultural texts from the Beijing Olympics and revealed that the Chinese media is value-laden, 'producing the Olympics through their own cultural imaginaries' (Fung 2011, p. 574).

Given the participatory and interactive nature of online games, the game-world is a platform for the construction of national identity. As MMORPG requires gamers to take a role in the game, gamers have to immerse themselves in virtual realities. Still, language and the communicative nature of MMORPG allow gamers to dissolve the boundaries between in-game realities and 'real world' realities (Williams et al. 2006). In the context of Chinese online games, gamers imagine themselves as part of the national history; no matter whether the history is modified or not, the way they perform the role and communicate with other gamers co-constructs the cultural definition of being Chinese.

Guo (2003) points out the difference between *political (state) nationalism* and *cultural nationalism*. Political nationalism refers to a kind of hegemonic nationalism that aims at top-down control and ideological homogenization of the authorities. Cultural nationalism takes the contexts into account, from international to ethnic and ideological, and includes people's will and beliefs. Regarding Chinese nationalism in particular, as Guo (2003) puts it: 'cultural nationalism imagines a Pan-Chinese cultural nation which includes all ethnic groups while rejecting the ethnocentric notion of China as a Han nation' (pp. 134–135), and this kind of cultural nationalism is in line with most popular Chinese online games with strong cultural specificity.

Hegemonic cultural capitalism

With a dual nature of politics and market, the development of online game industries in China, like other cultural industries, is in a dilemma. Unlike other free capitalist markets, Chinese online games not only need to generate profit through the demand-supply market mechanism, but also fulfill the state's political agenda, which seeks to reinforce the audiences' sense of national identity. In other words, the online game industries and the games are both serving and subservient to the state, and even in contemporary China, it is hard to imagine the state would allow popular content that is not concordant with its ideologies. There is inseparability of profits and political control, which results in a dilemma between politics and market. The state would like games to be a strong economic power, but the internal control seems to be hampering the competitive power of the Chinese games, in that game companies are unable to maximize their profits by producing crude entertainment that might not be aligned with state agendas. For individual companies, their revenues could be significantly reduced if their games were not allowed to be 'published' (meaning that they could not be distributed because these products did not pass the political standard of the authorities in the censorship process). For the state, their agenda is to protect locally produced online games with strong cultural specificity and promote them overseas as a way to couple political interest and economic viability.

In 2006, the state implemented the National Ethnic Original Production of Online Games Overseas Promotional Project – which was an explicit means to market Chinese culture overseas. In 2010, China's total export of games in 2010 reached US$230 million (Sina 2012). In 2011, 150 local games were exported overseas, reaching US$360 million in sales revenue. Approximately 90% of the Vietnamese game market and 68% of imported games in Malaysia were occupied by Chinese games. Meanwhile, Chinese game companies have been very proactive in going overseas. Perfect World is an example. Its self-developed games, *Perfect World International* (2006) and *My Own Swordsman* (2008) have been sold in 17 markets, from Latin America to North Asia and Southeast Asia. Its other works, *Zhu Xian* (2008) and *Red Cliff* (2008), have also been distributed in the North Asia and Southeast Asia markets respectively. In 2007, Perfect World acquired Japanese online game operator C & C Media with US$21 million and founded a Japan branch of the company.

Still, despite the proactive role the Chinese central government is trying to play, the growth of Chinese online games in overseas markets is more a market-driven phenomenon than a state initiative. Snail Game, a company headquartered in Suzhou, has already exported its *Voyage Century* to South Korea in 2004, before the National Ethnic Original Production of Online Game Overseas Promotional Project. What really contributes to the commercial success of Chinese online games overseas is their cultural specificity. If we take a closer look at the breakdowns of major overseas markets, Southeast Asia (51%) is ranked at the top, followed by Europe & North America (28%) and Japan & Korea (15%). Southeast Asian countries have considerably large Chinese communities. Take Malaysia for example, with its Chinese population of seven million. It is not surprising that Chinese online games appeal to these audiences. The cultural specificity of Chinese online games strengthens Chinese national identity not only within China but also across the region. This phenomenon, as I put it, is a kind of cultural regionalization, which extends China's soft power in the region.

All in all, the game-world is one of the sites in which the nationalistic logic of the state and the capitalist logic of the game companies are constantly competing. And yet, in the Chinese context, the strong cultural specificity of MMORPG resolves the conflicts between political force and market force. Online games, as fantasized reality and virtual community, can camouflage the real social problems. Amidst the rise of China's economy, the country faces numerous social problems. Corruption is one of the most pressing issues. According to the National Bureau of Statistics, 3,603 people were investigated for 'the misappropriation of public funds by the Chinese procurator's office' (NPR 2012) in 2010 and the media estimated that 'around $125 billion had been stashed overseas since the mid-1990s, by at least 16,000 officials' (NPR 2012). These games offer a way into dealing with these social issues.

Take the game genre of *wuxia* as an example: most of these games, including the case study discussed, *Heaven Sword and Dragon Sabre*, set the scene in a corrupted and chaotic society. Most 'martial heroes' featured in the game represents 'justice,' and each gamer is expected to win and to demonstrate the spirit of 'martial hero.' By winning the game, gamers' hope for justice is realized in the virtual world, and such satisfaction might reduce their sense of grievance about society, reinforcing a strong cultural identification under a very stable economy.

This is quite consistent with the theoretical argument that, in this digital world, the controlling stake of the state and capitalists continues to produce content – and games as well – that consumers can engage with for pleasure and escape from 'reality'; the digital culture and the fantasy constructed gradually supersede the 'real' (Preston 2001, p. 41). In the meantime, given the considerable size of Chinese overseas communities in Southeast Asia, the strong cultural specificity of Chinese online games also contributes to their commercial success in some overseas markets.

The combination of strong cultural identification and market forces leads to a form of 'hegemonic cultural capitalism,' which defines the unique nature of the online games industry in China. Revising Gramsci's notion of *cultural hegemony*, which refers to how the ruling class maintain their power and justify their legitimacy through controlling shared belief, the case study of online games industries in China puts the nation into a new perspective. While globalization theory suggests that the market-driven global force blurs the cultural boundaries among nations and thus weakens people's sense of national identity, Chinese online games, with their strong cultural specificity, reinforce the national discourse of Chinese identity and strengthen the state's hegemony through the logic of capitalism.

Acknowledgment

This work was fully supported by a grant from the Research Grant Council of Hong Kong Special Administrative Region. [Project no. 4001-SPPR-09]

Note

1. *Wuxia* which translates literally to 'martial hero' is a genre of literature where the stories are often based on a modified history with dramatic characters that demonstrate the Chinese ideal of hero. The popularity of the stories in this genre has seen it appear in various different arts forms ranging from opera, comics and now online games.

References

Anderson, B. (1983) *Imagined Communities: Reflections on the Origin and Spread of Nationalism* (London: Verso).

Barker, C. (1997). *Global Television: An Introduction*. Oxford: Blackwell.

Baudrillard, J. (1994) *Simulacra and Simulation* (Ann Arbor: University of Michigan Press).

Beck, U. (1992) *Risk Society: Towards a New Modernity* (New Delhi: Sage).

Billig, M. (1995) *Banal Nationalism* (Thousands Oaks, California: Sage).

Cao, Y., and Downing, J.D.H. (2008) The realities of virtual play: video games and their industry in China, *Media, Culture & Society*, 30(4), 515–529.

Castells, M. (1997) *The Power of Identity* (Malden, MA: Blackwell).

Chee, F., Vieta, M. and Smith, R. (2006) 'Online gaming and the interactional self: Identity interplay in situated practice', in J.P. Williams, S.Q. Hendricks and W.K. Winkler (eds), *Gaming as Culture: Essays on Reality, Identity, and Experience in Fantasy Games* (Jefferson, NC: McFarland Publishing), 154–174.

China Daily (2012) Income gap remains high, report shows, http://www.chinadaily.com.cn/cndy/2012–12/11/content_16004398.htm, date accessed July 26, 2013.

China Internet Network Information Center (2001) 7th Statistics Report on China's Internet Development, http://www.cnnic.net.cn/, data accessed March 18, 2011.

China Internet Network Information Center (2009) China's Online Gaming Market Report 2009, http://www.cnnic.net.cn/, data accessed March 18, 2011.

China Internet Network Information Center (2012) 29th Statistics Report on China's Internet Development, http://www.cnnic.net.cn/, data accessed March 18, 2011.

Clark, P. (2012) *Youth Culture in China: From Red Guards to Netizens* (New York: Cambridge University Press).

Ernkvist, M. and Strom, P. (2008) 'Enmeshed in Games with the Government: Governmental Policies and the Development of the Chinese Online Game Industry', *Games and Culture*, 3(1), 98–126.

Fung, A. (2011) Book Review on Documenting the Beijing Olympics, *Television & New Media*, 12(6), 573–574.

Giddens, A. (1991) *Modernity and Self-identity: Self and Society in the Late Modern Age* (Cambridge: Polity Press).

Graham, B.J. (1997) 'Ireland and Irishness: Place, Culture and Identity', in B. Graham (ed.), *In Search of Ireland: A Cultural Geography* (London: Routledge), 192–212.

Grossberg, L. (1996) "Identity and Cultural Studies: Is That All There Is?", in Stuart Hall and Paul du Gay (eds), *Questions of Cultural Identity* (London: Sage), 92.

Guo, Y. (2003) *Cultural Nationalism in Contemporary China* (Stanford: Stanford University Press).

Hall, S. (1997) (ed.) *Representation: Cultural Representations and Signifying Practices* (London: Sage).

Hebdige, D. (1979) *Subculture, the Meaning of Style* (London: Routledge).

Martinez, D.P. (ed.) (2010) *Documenting the Beijing Olympics* (London: Taylor & Francis).

Ministry of Culture (2010) 2010 Annual Report on China's Online Game Market (in Chinese), http://www.ccnt.gov.cn/, date accessed March 18, 2011.

NPR (2012) A Portrait Of Chinese Corruption, In Rosy Pink, http://www.npr.org/2012/06/29/155773618/a-portrait-of-chinese-corruption-in-rosy-pink, date accessed March 18, 2011.

Passion Times (2013) Online gaming to protect Diaoyu Islands, Chinese online games criticized as Militarism (in Chinese), http://www.passiontimes.hk/article/07–27–2013/4184, date accessed July 26, 2013.

People.com.cn (2011) Global online game market will reach 20 billion, US survey says (in Chinese), http://game.people.com.cn/GB/48644/48662/13574960.html, date accessed December 26, 2010.

Preston, P. (2001) *Reshaping Communications: Technology, Information, Social Change* (Thousand Oaks, CA: Sage).

Scheff, T. (1994) 'Emotions and identity: a theory of ethnic nationalism', in Craig Calhoun (ed.) *Social Theory and the Politics of Identity* (Oxford: Blackwell).

Sina (2012) Build an internationalized platform, http://www.pwie.com/en/news?newsId=9, date accessed September 23, 2013.

Sohu (2011) China's online and mobile game sales will account for half of global market in 2014 (in Chinese) http://news.sohu.com/20110226/n279541735.shtml, date accessed February 28, 2011.

Tajfel, H. (1982) 'Social Psychology of Intergroup Relations', *Annual Review of Psychology*, 33, 1–39.

The Economist (2012) China will overtake America within a decade. Want to bet? http://www.economist.com/blogs/freeexchange/2012/03/china-will-overtake-america-within-decade-want-bet, date accessed July 26, 2013.

Von Ruediger, J. (2005) *Globalized Culture and Consumption-Identities* (Baden-Baden: Bastard).

Waggoner, Z. (2009) *My Avatar, My Self: Identity in Video Role-Play Games* (Jefferson, NC: McFarland Publishing).

Williams, J.P., Hendricks, S.Q. and Winkler W.K. (2006) *Gaming as Culture: Essays on Reality, Identity, and Experience in Fantasy Games* (Jefferson, NC: McFarland Publishing).

Zaretsky, E. (1994) 'Identity theory, identity politics: Psychoanalysis, Marxism, post-structuralism', in Craig Calhoun (ed.), *Social Theory and the Politics of Identity* (Oxford: Blackwell).

Zhao, S. (2004) *A Nation-State by Construction: Dynamics of Modern Chinese Nationalism* (Stanford: Stanford University Press).

4

Nation Branding of Korea

Kiwon Hong

Globalization casts manifold issues over various fields in contemporary society. It is often perceived as a phenomenon that reinforces transnational interrelatedness and the exchange of economical, societal, technological, and cultural activities beyond national borders (Beck 2000). While the overall consensus would be that globalization constrains roles of nation states (Steger 1998), there exist different perspectives: there is the view that sees globalization as eventually leading nation states into being absorbed into the larger structure of a transnational state (Robinson 2001) to the argument that, in spite of globalizing forces, the existing patterns of institutions for governing nation state and its economy will still remain powerful (Giddens 2003). This chapter points out that nation states are devising strategies to deal with globalizing forces in various ways and discusses the rise of nation branding policy in South Korea within this context. The chapter views nation branding as part of the country's active strategies to manage and survive the forces of economic globalization. Through cultivating a distinct message and impression of the country and improving its prestige in the international arena, nation branding could function as a tool to strengthen the country's business competitiveness in the global market. Despite a strong economic agenda, Korea's nation branding has very strong cultural aspects to the degree that it should be seen as an extension of cultural policy.

In general, nation branding tends to select, simplify, and deploy certain aspects of a nation's identity via a bureaucratic process in order to enhance the country's marketability. Nevertheless, it is not shy about exploiting multiple layers of national identity in order to create distinctive and differentiated image of the nation. During this process, national cultural identity is created, recalled and displayed, leading to its imposition on and internalization by the public. In this sense, nation branding works as an 'implicit cultural policy' (Ahearn 2009), which has strong elements of 'cultural policy as display' (McGuigan 2004). The process of setting up and implementing a nation branding policy in Korea illustrates the precarious nature of such a project. This chapter argues that the policy, despite its reliance on 'branding' as a private sector practice, is a form of cultural policy that aims to reinforce national cultural identity internally and externally. The Korean case demonstrates the way the market-driven agenda of nation branding is reconciled and fused with a cultural agenda, and implemented under the heavy influences of the existing framework of cultural policy. In the following section, I will briefly introduce the theory of nation branding and discuss its definitional variations. Next, details of nation branding policy in Korea will be explained within the historical and institutional contexts of the country's cultural policy. The development of nation branding policy over time shows an evolutionary process from a commercial rationale to a cultural rationale. The concept of national cultural identity was latent throughout the process of the country's nation branding policy and has recently become more evident. In spite of the country's efforts to associate its image with commercial cultural industries that are increasingly successful overseas, it is its traditional culture that has come to occupy the central part of its nation branding project. Finally, I will highlight the institutional dynamics and organizational features that shape the project.

Cultural aspects in nation branding

Nation branding emerged from the idea that, in a globalized market, retaining a favorable image and reputation for a country is essential to improving its competitiveness. Branding would be required for countries not only to succeed in international trade but also to attract overseas economic resources, such as capital investment and human resources. It is often believed that a country should have a brand to achieve those objectives or otherwise be involved in branding itself. According to Anholt (2007), a brand pertains to a product, a service or an organization, considered in combination with its name, identity, and reputation. This concept would be difficult to apply directly to a country because the latter is not a fixed and unequivocal entity that carries out clearly defined functions. Branding, on the other hand, refers to the process of designing, planning, and communicating the name and identity in order to build or manage a reputation (Anholt 2007, p. 4). Via this activity, as many specialists of nation branding such as Kotler and Gertner (2002) would say, countries can gain a positive brand identity and thereby attain a competitive advantage in the global market place. Quite a few branding experts claim that even though there are essential differences between a company and a nation, the techniques of motivating, inspiring, and manipulating people whether they belong to a company or a nation would be similar (Olins 2002; Widler 2007, p. 145). Such arguments about nation branding presume that a nation is something that exists as a social reality. Different from the nation branders, a group of sociologists assert that the concept of a nation is a social construct. The socially constructed reality is an ongoing, dynamic process and thus is constantly reproduced by cultural, institutional, and media practices. In this vein, Kunovich (2009) defines a nation as a 'socially constructed sameness resulting from nationalism.' When constructing the sameness, various forces, for example economic, political, societal, and cultural, come into play. For Kunovich, national identity is a combination of civic factors and ethnic factors, which are the most important constituents of nationality and national identity. Meanwhile, Gellner (1987) recognized cultural commonality as a determinant for constructing national identity. He explains that people are of the same nation only if they share the same culture: that is, a system of ideas, signs, and ways of behaving and communicating. Anderson (2006) interprets national identity as a socio-cognitive construct both spatially and temporally inclusive, and both enabled and shaped by broader social forces. Following these theoretical assumptions on national identity, we could perceive nation branding as an exercise that targets the nation to reimagine and reconstruct its identity (Widler 2007, p. 145).

Recently scholars in marketing and branding studies have increasingly acknowledged cultural aspects of national identity. In his book *Competitive Identity: The Brand Management for Nations, Cities, and Regions*, Anholt (2007) describes why he would rather use the term 'competitive identity' instead of 'competitive brand.' He claims that branding strategy should be 'mining rather than forging: to dig out the history, the culture, the geography, the society of the place' (Anholt 2007, p. 75). He also puts emphasis on the *people* of the country. He predicts that the strategy of nation brand (competitive identity) will fail if it lacks fundamental truths about the place and its people. Holt (2004), again, recognizes the importance of cultural branding. He insists that 'cultural branding' outweighs general branding effects because it provides the consumers with long-lasting and intense feelings of cultural affiliation. Culture is seen as a tool to communicate and participate in the story and myth, a conduit through which a consumer can communicate. Cultural branding does not, Holt (2004) argues, smooth over contradicting aspects of culture but rather offers more interpretations with genuine stories about a society. In a way, a nation brand is established in a similar way to the way cultural identity is internalized in a society. According to Anholt (2007), brand identity expresses a core concept, which parallels the idea of national identity, and that brand image is a kind of perception that exists in the mind of the consumer. He explains that the population's own perception of the nation brand is a powerful driver of the external image. Thus, it is important for brand makers to focus on the nation's own people because they are in the long run the most influential brand channel (Widler 2007, p. 146). This has been demonstrated by research that countries with powerful reputations rated their own reputation highly (Anholt 2007, p. 56). Brand, as defined previously, should most of all be believed or endorsed by the nation's population itself. This is in line with branding advocates' arguments that nation branding has the function of building internal solidarity, pride, and a sense of patriotism in the domestic population. Some may describe it as domestic propaganda that sustains a new form of nationalism (Jansen 2008).

Nation branding in its essence has a relationship to the strategy and product of cultural diplomacy. Cultural diplomacy, which has its roots in the rise of public diplomacy, is a variation of foreign policy. It emerged from the post-Cold War environment, claiming that soft power would become important to accomplishing diplomatic goals (Nye 2004). It regards culture as an effective instrument for manipulation in achieving the national interest, which is a rather abstract and broad term to define. As nation branding and public diplomacy, including international public relations, become indistinguishable, it is easier to contract out the activity to internationally renowned private companies. This is why nation branding is criticized as a sort of 'privatized version of foreign policy' (Jansen 2008). As has been investigated, the cultural aspect of nation branding poses complex questions. There are questions about commercial initiatives that oddly coexist with nationalism, selection (out of diverse cultural forms and contents), the actual impact of nation branding policy, and the policy's location (it is an interface between different policy areas such as foreign policy, international relations, public relations, and cultural policy). Nation branding occupies a terrain where commercial motive and ideological intention collide, and this makes it difficult to see this activity simply as a marketing project. What policy areas the nation branding affiliates itself to will have a different impact, not only internationally but also domestically. The Korean case is an example that illustrates how these various features interact and gain characteristics of cultural policy.

Formation of nation branding as a public policy in Korea

Nation branding in Korea is a recent phenomenon. The country's repressive governments in the past utilized cultural resources for political and diplomatic purposes, but it was not exercised in a systematic way, as professional nation branding is conducted. The authoritarian government's cultural projects were implemented as a form of public relations exercise targeting both Korean society and overseas audiences, and were tightly controlled by government agencies. While the governments were concerned with promoting Korean culture abroad and raising the country's image, the main goals of their cultural projects were to propagate the government ideology and to induce Koreans' compliance with state policies. This is underpinned by the historical development of the government department in charge of this activity. From 1948 to 1961, a time of political turbulence in the development of the modern nation state in Korea, the Ministry of Public Information looked after matters of public opinion in collaboration with the Ministry of Culture and Education taking responsibility for cultural administration. This implies that there was a lot of intersection between the government's PR (propaganda, to be precise) and cultural policy. In 1961, the military regime gave birth to the Ministry of Culture and Public Information, officially merging these two functions. This system lasted for almost thirty years until public relations and cultural administration were separated into different ministries in 1990. The initial development of nation branding, which focused on the country's traditional culture and images, was partly overseen by the Ministry of Culture and Public Information's overseas offices, Korean Cultural Service Abroad.[1] The structure where public information policy and cultural policy were combined to carry out nation branding domestically and overseas meant that key agendas of domestic cultural policy also penetrated into the country' strategies for representing its image abroad. Throughout the period until the 1990s, military governments aligned Korea's national culture with the country's traditional culture. The governments found the justifications for such a conservative and past-oriented approach in the country's need to repair its cultural destruction, caused by colonialism and the Korean War, and reinstitute its spiritual culture, which was under serious threat from Westernization (Oh 1998; H.-K. Lee 2013).[2] During this period, mass produced popular culture was regarded generally as a Western import that had a negative and damaging effect on the national cultural identity of the country (H.-K. Lee 2013). The political and social messages that popular culture could convey were seen as a threat to the dictatorial regime. Under such a circumstance, it was the state bureaucracy that was in charge of defining Korean cultural identity based on selected traditional culture and arts and facilitating the identity to be internalized by the populace via various cultural projects funded and managed by the government.[3]

The severe financial crisis that called for the IMF bailout in 1997 impressed upon the government psyche the importance of strengthening the country's economic competitiveness for survival in a globalized market. It was an immediate task for the KIM Dae Jung administration (1998–2003) to sort out the financial crisis by actively accommodating neoliberalist public policies. Cultural policy was not an exception to this trend, and one of the supreme goals of cultural policy at that time was to quadruple exports in cultural industries. The economic crisis justified the rise of commercial aspirations in the cultural sector. The expansion of audience for Korean TV drama and the exponential growth of Korean pop culture in the Asian region were not only seen as a possible source of income for cultural industries, but also as a medium to enhance a positive image of Korea and its wider recognition abroad. Korean manufactured goods exposed through media content were a conduit of export. All these new changes explain why cultural industries came to occupy a significant place in the country's cultural policy agenda toward the end of the 1990s. The KIM Dae Jung administration replied to the new phenomena by setting up the country's first public committee for the purpose of enhancing national image.

For the country's nation branding, the spread of the Korean Wave seemed to play essential parts. However, it was an open secret that most of the revenue from cultural exports was generated by the games industry rather than the so-called Korean Wave industries such as TV drama and pop music (Cultural Industry Statistics 2009).[4] Nevertheless, these less lucrative industries were consistently held as important because their products were effective carriers of the country's cultural image and Korean way of life, and therefore would have a huge window effect on other industries and their exports. This explains that cultural industries have gradually acquired an important position in the country's public policy as they have successfully enhanced the international recognition of the country and have functioned as a facilitator for export. This is so regardless of how much public support is given to cultural industries in financial terms. The term 'Korean Wave' has now gained its own status as a well-recognizable and perhaps overused 'brand': there was nothing that could not be labeled as 'Korean Wave,' from cultural products to cosmetics and plastic surgery, as long as they were produced in, conducted in or exported from Korea (H-K. Lee 2013).

From a cultural perspective, however, the Korean Wave faces a dilemma as to how to position itself as neither imperialistic nor contemptibly commercial. While the ambivalent position of the government towards the Korean Wave continues, this double-edged sword of the Korean Wave has created the hybrid identity of Korean culture by fusing traditional cultural elements and commercial motivations. The Ministry of Culture, Sports and Tourism (MCST)'s *Han Style* project is an offspring of this combination. Facing a backlash against a view that Korean pop culture that was copying ideas from the Asian region, the government came up with branding content that essentially represented Korean culture, which would look less ambitious and therefore politically acceptable in neighboring countries. In 2006, a policy report was issued proposing six categories of Korean traditional culture that were not in the realm of commercialism, along with an economic estimation of their potential as an income generator. The list included the Korean alphabet, *Han-Geul*, Korean culinary arts, *Han-Sik*, Korean traditional clothing, *Han-Bok*, Korean traditional housing, *Han-Ok*, Korean traditional paper making, *Han-Ji*, and Korean traditional music, *Gug-Ak* (MCST 2006). Referring to the success of the 'Japanesque' style in the Western world in recent decades, the *Han Style* aspired to be a breakthrough in branding traditional Korean culture. However, it is noteworthy that the *Han Style* project was never pronounced as an explicit nation branding policy but has had an influence on other policies under the umbrella of nation branding.

Nation branding became heavily emphasized during LEE Myung Bak's administration (2008–2013) following intermittent involvement in the cultural sector. The government proclaimed itself a 'business friendly' administration, and its business orientation affected many areas of the country's public policy. President LEE himself was a former CEO of a company, part of one of Korea's biggest conglomerates, and firmly believed that the government's key responsibility was 'to provide business corporations with a favorable environment in which to do business' (December 28, 2008 in his speech at the Federation of Korean Industries as the president-elect). This had already been stated in his presidential pledge, 'World Class Country, Republic of Korea' (The Grand National Party 2008). The new government had a great interest in Korea being seen as a leader in the league of developed countries. The president believed that that the country did not have a distinct brand and proposed 'a country of a high class' as a brand that could correspond with the country's economic achievement. He emphasized that, by nation branding, the image of Korea as a 'respectable country' could be effectively spread internationally (Speech at the Liberation Day ceremony 2008). Soon after, the Presidential Council on Nation Branding (PCNB) was officially established as a pivot to formulate nation branding policy within the Office of the President. A Decree on the Enhancement of Nation Brand (2009) was enacted to consistently support nation branding policy.

The formation and evolution of nation branding practice during LEE's government provides a valid example of showing a multi-layered nature of nation branding, which is an mixture of nation marketing, public diplomacy, and cultural policy. The government wished to create a Korean brand that would have three main components: a respectable country that fulfills its international responsibilities, such as providing support for underdeveloped countries; a country that has world-leading corporations and therefore has formidable presence in the international market; and a country that is culturally competent, as shown by the success of the Korean Wave. These three were essential goals of nation branding underneath the officially pronounced vision of the Council: 'a country contributing to the world,' a 'country of respectable people,' a 'coexisting society,' and 'country of world class corporations.'

The Council's chairperson, EUH Yoon Dae, as a 'corporate friendly' economist, strongly represented pro-market and commercial agendas. In his interview with KIM Dong Yoon, the editor of *Bipyung Quarterly*, the chairperson emphasized that Korea, more precisely the country and people, should obtain a '"world class" reputation equivalent to that of private corporations' such as Samsung and Hyundai . He went on to say, 'nation branding is not about becoming a culturally significant country but "a respectable country".' By 'respectable' he meant a country that is willing to share the 'knowledge and know-how of economic achievement in a short period of time.' Consequently, the Council's nation branding promoted government-led Official Development Assistance (ODA) programs, adopted government practices inherited from the economic developmental period of the past. Referring to ODA practices as an 'expansion of (the) economic Korean Wave'[5] implies the government's intention to appeal to the people's national pride for both the country's economic achievement and cultural recognition.

As part of the nation branding project, the range of the Korean Wave was expanded with the repackaging of existing cultural activities, such as Korean language classes overseas and international cultural exchange activities. The Korean Wave was not only a brand for the internation-alization of Korean culture but had complicated, emotional meanings for Koreans. It was a symbol of Korean culture as a peripheral culture making its presence felt towards the core of world culture. For Koreans, it was a phenomenon where feelings of self-respect could be generated and the country's cultural identity could be projected.

As the leadership of the Council transferred from an economist to an historian and eventually to a journalist, the balance of emphasis in its perspective and actual programs moved more to the recognition of the cultural aspects of nation branding. Out of the Council's 55 individual programs led by participating ministries, 18 programs, amounting to one-third of the total, were implemented in the cultural policy field.[6] In addition to these, the programs that the Council directly executed were focused on recollecting Korea's traditional cultural identity. One example would be a project aiming at rediscovering the spiritual culture of 19th-century Korean literati, and the other would be a project concerned with registering traditional cultural heritages as UNESCO Heritage sites.

It is noteworthy that none of the cultural programs represented cultural industries' products that were already well known abroad. Still, the term 'Korean Wave' was used throughout official documents in a symbolic way when repackaging traditional cultural programs, referring to everything from registering UNESCO Heritage sites to providing over-seas libraries with Korean collections. Even when commissioning non-profit traditional performing arts, the term Korean Wave was adopted. Korean Wave was a 'pride factor' targeting a domestic population to internalize the brand of a successful and attractive Korean culture. Excluding cultural industries' projects in the country's nation branding programs and preventing the impression that these industries were supported by the government was necessary to avoid the accusation that the Korean Wave was a government-backed cultural imperialistic project. Still, nation branding in Korea could be seen as a progressive form of patriotism and a 2.0 version of nationalism, in that it utilized non-threatening fragments of culture, history, and geography (Aronczyk 2009). It is shown that traditional, spiritual, and non-profit culture would be a perfect fit to such a project.

Institutional and organizational dynamics in nation branding policy

Nation branding may be differently represented according to who is responsible for its formation and execution. This applies to the Korean case, where institutional settings and organizational characteristics affect the outcome of nation branding, as can be seen today. Korea's national branding policy has close ties to cultural policy because of its organizational adhesion to cultural bureaucracy and shared interest with cultural policy. Branding policy's association to national cultural identity seems to have decreased over time yet still remains strong. The swing of emphasis in nation branding throughout LEE's administration describes this feature well. At the very inception of nation branding, the Council adhered to branding theorists' market-driven suggestions.[7] The thirty-two members of the Council represented private sectors that had interests in raising Korea's image abroad, such as business corporations, IT firms, media professionals, and marketing companies.[8] From the private sector were CEOs of Cheil Advertising Company (whose CEO also served as chair for the Samsung Group Brand Management Council), Hyundai Card Corporation, SK Group, Korean Airlines, and Asiana Airlines.[9] Twelve ex-officio members from relevant ministries were co-opted (PCNB Whitepaper 2012).[10] While the government perceived nation branding from a public policy perspective, corporations linked their Corporate Social Responsibility (CSR) activities with nation branding programs, projecting into the branding process the firm's private motivations. Different participants had different aspects of Korean national and cultural images to reinforce, reflecting their sectoral interests. For example, airline companies would be pleased to a greater extent if the nation brand envisioned more place marketing elements, while IT companies would prefer an advanced image of technologies of Korea. Participating companies expressed their wishes to directly handle government programs, with which the officials raised concerns, based on the grounds of public interest (Interview with a former secretariat official, May 2013).

The role of MCST was influential, if not essential, in shaping the policy. Nation branding, for the past ten years, was never done through sub-contracting with private branding firms. Despite the presence and role of the Presidential Council, the secretariat of the Council that coordinated actual programs, along with the relevant ministries, was steered by MCST.[11] The ministry was responsible for the budget, overall coordination, and support. It also dispatched the largest number of personnel to the Council's administration. Although the Council appeared to be an independent body executing policy decisions, its budget consisted of a collection of related budgets from participating ministries.[12] The budget covered expenses for personnel, the administrative costs for running the Council, and project costs directly dispensable by the Council. The program budgets were reflected in each ministries' budget;

thus, nation branding programs were a mosaic of existing or newly devised ministerial programs if they had any relationship to the vision of the Council, rather than a coherent set of policies. Hence, not only a few signature programs steered by the secretariat, but also other smaller programs, would give color to what nation brand signified. Out of the twelve ministries that were involved in the Council's programs, MCST provided the largest number of programs and variety since it already had been working for cultural exchange and cultural diplomacy.

One interesting characteristic of the Council's policy was the exclusion of cultural industries from its programs. It is difficult to say if the growing interest in the Korean Wave abroad was a result of strategically planned or extensive governmental intervention. The government did fund organizations such as the Korea Foundation for International Cultural Industry Exchange (KOFICE) and several agencies, including Korea Creative Contents Agency (KOCCA) to promote cultural industries. However, in hard figures, the portion of the budget used solely to promote the Korean Wave abroad was not recognized as significant. Most of the cultural industries budget was for cultural technology development and human resource development accordingly (Korea Statistics on Cultural Industries 2009–2012).

Throughout the nation branding process, the Korean government was very careful about its relationship with cultural industries. As much as the role of government in the spread of Korean Wave was equivocal, the stance of governmental intervention in so-called Korean Wave industries was problematic. The Korean wave can be mobilized by the government to realize economic and political goals but being too overt and instituting deliberate policy endeavors to enlarge the wave could provoke a backlash (Jang and Paik 2012). In the same vein, it is asserted that 'the Korean government should not take a forefront role in the promotion of its Korean Wave... the state should not to take the main role on the stage of the entertainment business' (cited in Jang and Paik 2012). Cultural bureaucrats were aware that this was a field from which they needed to keep a balanced distance so as not to be accused of too much intervention in commercial cultural businesses. Under-representation of cultural industries as an instrument to boost nation branding is a tactful strategy of Korean cultural policy to achieve the sustainability of the Korean Wave against a backlash of potentially cultural imperialist and commercialist aspects. The policy's focus on traditional culture was also effective in terms of continuing and deepening cultural policy's efforts to define Korean cultural identity via culture and arts from the past.

Conclusion

Nation branding, in its various forms in reality, encompasses every activity that contribute to the creation of positive image of a country. It could be formulated as a pure marketing strategy from scratch, or could be practiced as a concerted action by relevant governmental bodies, as the Korean case illustrates. The specific socio-economic environment that a country faces affects the making of nation branding policy. The overwhelming influence of neoliberalism and commercialism throughout the world may not have an equal impact on every country. Nation branding in Korea is a case where those external forces fuse into the persistency of historical and institutional factors that have defined the country's cultural policy so far and form an implicit cultural policy. The historical context of where cultural policy was situated in Korea's public policy and what roles it plays has affected its current nation branding. The history of cultural policy as informing and shaping people's spiritual life has had an impact on defining the 'nation brand' as an abstract concept rather than a concrete and materializable idea. Culture, where it has been regarded as an essence to sustain the spiritual status of the country and its people, is a very broad notion that would absorb any strategic activities dealing with the nation's identity, image and brand. This still is the case in spite of the changes of government in Korea from military governments to liberal and more commercially minded ones over time.

In recent years, nation branding has become a key agenda for the government. While this emerging field of policy was crowded with many participants, both from the government and private sectors, who had their own agendas, the core of the policy was driven by cultural policy makers who connected nation branding to the cultural identity of the country and orchestrated the content of cultural identity with the least contestable themes and forms. Cultural policy makers administered the subtle position of both supporting cultural industries and being a nonpartisan advocate for the value of 'lofty culture,' mainly Korean traditional culture. Perhaps the strategy of tightrope walking between support for the commercially driven Korean Wave and support for non-commercial culture reflect cultural policy makers' autonomy from commercial and neoliberalizing forces. This type of bureaucratic stance may be considered positive in that it counterbalances market-driven approaches to nation branding. It would be difficult to assess the effect of nation branding policy as a 'marketing strategy' in the short term.

It is also difficult to evaluate the efficacy of Korea's nation branding either from the marketing or cultural side. Yet, the Korean case provides valid evidences for the nation branding to be represented as 'implicit cultural policy' in terms of its policy contents and way of implementation. Nation branding nurtured Korean society's self-respect and pride for its culture, binding the country and its people with certain cultural identities. Whatever the merits and utilities of nation branding will be in contemporary society, in order to achieve a marketing goal or a cultural policy goal, it should be firmly grounded on recognition by and participation of the constituents of society. It might be an imperative to bring nation branding to public discourse if it is to be a 'cultural policy proper' (McGuigan 2004).

Notes

1. 'Land of Morning Calm' which was first used in a book published in 1947 in London, was later adopted as the official term to brand Korea while hosting the 1988 Olympic Games (Doosan Dictionary 2010).
2. Most of the legislation concerning cultural heritage was introduced in this period. The most comprehensive law, Law on Protection of Cultural Heritage (1961), is an example.
3. There were cultural activists who argued that the military regime's idea of nation culture was based on selected cultural forms preferred by the ruling classes in the past (Song 1998).
4. TV dramas and pop music accounted for only 11% of the revenue for the whole cultural industries. When film is included, the figure only rises to 17%. The top three revenue makers, which accounted for more than half the overseas sales, came from the game industry, the character industry (OEM production and licensing), and the publication industry.
5. *The Second Basic Plan for Nation Branding* (2009–2011).
6. From the remaining two-thirds of programs, media related programs were the second largest, followed by private company joint campaigns, and public diplomacy programs (*PCNB White Paper* 2012).
7. It has been pointed out by a group of branding theorists that nation branding practices should adopt a more participatory perspective.
8. The Council has had three Chairs. The first was an economist and a strong advocate of deregulation and privatization. The second was an historian who also firmly shared political values with the president's office.
9. Out of the 32 members, 13 were from the economics, industry, and finance (40%). Academics from journalism and public relations were the next largest group, nine people, and a further nine people were from the arts and culture (12%).
10. The Ministries of Culture, Sports, and Tourism; Foreign Affairs and Trade; Strategy and Finance; Knowledge and Economy; Public Administration and Security; Education, Science, and Technology; Justice; Land, Transport, and Maritime Affairs; the Prime Minister's Office; Korea Communications

Commission; the Mayor of Seoul; and the Director from the Office of the President.

11. The secretariat consisted of the Office of Planning and Coordination, the Office of Corporations and IT, the Office of International Cooperation, and the Office of Culture and Citizenship. Private companies also dispatched their own personnel to work at the secretariat, which was rare in a public organization. About ten private corporations sent their delegates.

12. The Council was one of the top-rated, with the largest budget of 18 advisory councils under the Office of the President (with the yearly budget of about 87 billion Korean Won (US$82 million), Source from MCST Audit Report for the National Assembly) and the sixth largest of 499 government-affiliated councils in total. Figures taken from the Public Forum of People's Solidarity for Participatory Democracy, Public Administration Monitoring Center's *Evaluation of Lee Myung Bak Administration* (2012).

References

Ahearne, J. (2009) 'Cultural Policy Explicit and Implicit: A Distinction and Some Uses', *International Journal of Cultural Policy*, 15(2), 141–153.

Anderson, B.R.O. (2006) *Imagined Communities* (New York, London: Verso).

Anholt, S. (2003) *Brand New Justice* (Boston: Butterworth-Heinemann).

Anholt, S. (2007) *Competitive Identity* (New York: Palgrave Macmillan).

Anholt, S. (2008) 'Nation Branding in As, *Place Branding and Public Diplomacy*, 4(4), 265–269.

Aronczyk, M. (2009) 'How To Do Things with Brands: Uses of National Identity', *Canadian Journal of Communication*, 34(2), 291–296.

Beck, U. (2000) *What Is Globalization?* (Cambridge: Polity Press).

Burbach, R., Jeffries, F. AND Robinson, W.I. (2001) *Globalization and Postmodern Politics* (London: Sterling: London).

Cerulo, K.A. (1997) 'Identity Construction: New Issues, New Directions', *Annual Review of Sociology*, 23, 385–409.

Chung, J.-E. (2012) *From developmental to Neo-developmental Cultural Industries Policy: The Korean Experience of the 'Creative Turn'*, Ph.D. dissertation, University of Glasgow, Glasgow.

Dinnie, K. (2008) *Nation Branding* (Oxford, MA: Burlington).

Dinnie, K. and Lio, A. (2010) 'Enhancing China's Image in Japan: Developing the Nation Brand through Public Diplomacy', *Place Branding and Public Diplomacy*, 6(3), 198–206.

Dinnie, K. (2007) 'Competitive Identity: The New Brand Management for Nations, Cities and Regions', *Journal of Brand Management*, 14(6), 474–475.

Fetscherin, M. and Marmier, P. (2010) 'Switzerland's Nation Branding Initiative to Foster Science and Technology, Higher Education and Innovation: A Case Study', *Place Branding and Public Diplomacy*, 6(1), 58–67.

Gellner, E. (1987) *Culture, Identity, and Politics* (New York: Cambridge University Press).

Giddens, A. (2003) *Runaway World* (New York: Routledge).

Giddens, A., Duneier, M. and Appelbaum, R.P. (2007) *Introduction to Sociology*. (New York: W. W. Norton & Co).

Hofstede, G.H. (2001) *Culture's Consequences* (Thousand Oaks, California: Sage Publications).

Holt, D.B. (2004) *How Brands become Icons* (Harvard Business School Press: Boston, Mass).

Jang, G. and Paik, W.K. (2012) 'Korean Wave as Tool for Korea's New Cultural Diplomacy', *Advances in Applied Sociology*, 2(3), 196–202.

Kim, D.Y. (2009) 'National Image, National Status, and Cultural Foundation', *Bipyung (Criticism) Quarterly*, 22, 86–111.

Korea Ministry of Culture, Sports, and Tourism, (2006) *Research on the Globalizing Strategy of Han Style* (Seoul: KCTI).

Korea Ministry of Culture, Sports, and Tourism, (2008) *Master Plan of Presidential Council on Nation Branding 2008–2012* (Seoul: MCST).

Korea Ministry of Culture, Sports, and Tourism, (2009) *The Second Basic Plan for Presidential Council on Nation Branding 2009–2011* (Seoul: MCST).

Korea Ministry of Culture, Sports, and Tourism, (2009) *Cultural Industry Statistics* (Seoul: MCST).

Korea Ministry of Culture, Sports, and Tourism, (2010) *Content Industries White Paper* (Seoul: MCST).

Korea Ministry of Culture, Sports, and Tourism, (2012) *Presidential Council on Nation Branding White Paper* (Seoul: MCST).

Kotler, P. and Gertner, D. (2002) Country as Brand, Product, and Beyond: A Place Marketing and Brand Management Perspective, *Journal of Brand Management*, 9(4–5), 249–261.

Kunovich, R.M. (2009) 'The Sources and Consequences of National Identification', *American Sociological Review*, 74(4), 573–593.

Lee, H.-K. (2013) 'Cultural Policy and Korean Wave: From National Culture to Transnational Consumerism', in Y. Kim (ed.), *The Korean Wave: Korean Media Go Global* (London: Routledge).

Lee, G. (2009) 'A Soft Power Approach to Korean Wave', *The Review of Korean Studies*, 12(2), 123–137.

Lee, S., Toth, E.L. and Shin, H. (2008) 'Cognitive Categorization and Routes of National Reputation Formation: US Opinion Leaders' Views On South Korea', *Place Branding and Public Diplomacy*, 4(4), 272–286.

McGuigan, J. (2004) *Rethinking Cultural Policy* (Maidenhead: Open University).

Nye, J.S., Jr. (2004) 'Soft Power and American Foreign Policy', *Political Science Quarterly*, 119(2), 255–270.

Oh, M.S. (1998) 'A Study On Cultural Diversification and Korean Cultural Identity: Cultural Policy during 1960s-70s and Its Nationalistic Discourse', *Comparative Cultural Studies*, 4, 121–152.

Olins, W. (2002) 'Branding the Nation – The Historical Context', *Journal of Brand Management*, 9(4/5), 241–248.

Ooi, C. (2008) 'Reimagining Singapore as a Creative Nation: The Politics of Place Branding', *Place Branding and Public Diplomacy*, 4(4), 287–302.

Robinson, W.I. (2001) 'Social Theory and Globalization: The Rise of a Transnational State', *Theory and Society*, 30(2), 157–200.

Skinner, H. and Kubacki, K. (2007) 'Unravelling the Complex Relationship between Nationhood, National and Cultural Identity, and Place Branding', *Place Branding and Public Diplomacy*, 3(4), 305–316.

Song, D.H. (1998) 'The Quest of Alternative Art Styles for the "National" and the "People's Class" Cultural Movements in 1980s', *Comparative Cultural Studies*, 4.

Steger (1998) 'The Quest for Evolutionary Socialism', *The English Historical Review*, 113(454), 1359.

Tomlinson, J. (1999) *Globalization and Culture* (Chicago: University of Chicago Press).

Widler, J. (2007) 'Nation Branding: With Pride against Prejudice', *Place Branding and Public Diplomacy*, 3(2), 144–150.

Part II

Negotiations between Culture and the State

5

Culture and the State: From a Korean Perspective

Hye-Kyung Lee

This chapter is intended to theorize the relationship between culture and the state in the Republic of Korea (hereafter Korea) by looking into the historical development of, and the recent controversies around, its arts policy. There are two reasons for the chapter's focus on arts policy: firstly, preserving and developing the arts has traditionally been the main concern of Korean cultural policy; and secondly, the country's arts sector, which hardly survives without state funding and lacks society-wide support, has developed a very tight relationship with the state. The inquiry starts with an observation of the rise of political intervention in the cultural sector in Korea under the conservative government of LEE Myung Bak (2008–2013). One noticeable example is that, when the government was inaugurated in 2008, the Ministry of Culture, Sports and Tourism (MCST) forced the heads of 15 public cultural institutions to resign, and dismissed some who refused to do so, in order to replace them with those deemed ideologically close to the government. It was argued by the opposition Democratic Party that such a political move was part of the government's scheme to rebalance the power structure of the cultural sector: that is, to give power back to cultural practitioners and organizations with conservative traits, who were regarded as having been ignored by the previous two liberal governments (1998–2003 and 2003–2008). Many critics have interpreted this phenomenon as a reversal of the cultural sector's autonomization achieved during the last ten or so years, and the revival of the authoritarian cultural policy of the past. Such an understanding apparently entails an assumption that Korean cultural policy would progress again once a new, more democratic and culturally oriented government is elected in the future. Meanwhile, this chapter is more interested in asking why the country's cultural policy is so vulnerable to party politics and political pressure, why the government continues to occupy a strong position vis-à-vis the cultural sector, and why the sector has failed to raise a coherent voice against governmental interference. In spite of the democratization and neoliberalization of Korean society in the past two decades, fundamental characteristics of its cultural policy have changed little – why?

As a first step in considering the above questions, this chapter will critically review the culture-state relationship defined by the available cultural and arts policy literature, from a Korean perspective, and will then propose taking an historical and institutional approach. Then the chapter will narrow down its scope to the country's arts policy and examine three factors that have molded the basic shape and operation of the policy – the form of the state, social legitimation of the arts, and, finally, the organization of the arts sector. First, the chapter will find that the developmental state in Korea has been noticeably effective in creating formal institutions for arts policy but has been limited in fostering arts-centered rationalities and in bringing the arts to the everyday cultural life of the Korean public. Second, it will demonstrate that the social legitimation of the arts in Korea is reliant on a foundation where there seldom exists popular support for the arts and middle-class-based arts patronage has yet to fully emerge. The next point will be that the historically rooted ideological and organizational division in the arts sector has hindered it from forming a broad sectoral consensus and strengthening its position against the government. Democratization since the mid-1990s has opened up new opportunities to empower artists and arts professionals to take a more active part in arts policy making. However, the shortage of social legitimation and the deeply institutionalized division within makes the arts community turn to the state for legitimacy, power and resource. This implies that Korean arts policy – and cultural policy in general – is likely to be driven by the government of the day, rather than by a broad social consensus or the cultural sector's own agenda, and thus it will be left susceptible to the whims of politicians.

Culture, the state and cultural policy

Cultural policy objectives, content, structure and implementation are shaped by the relationship between culture and the state in a given society. The existing research, written primarily by Western academics, proposes a number of different, even conflicting, perspectives of this relationship. For example, there are writings envisioning the state as a safeguard for culture and cultural diversity against market failure

(Heilbrun and Gray 1993) and neoliberalist pressure (Voon 2006) while some scholars suspect that the state, as an entity organized and managed primarily by political decisions and public administration, is prone to instrumentalize and colonize culture with political logics and rationalities (McGuigan 2004; Vestheim 1994). The existing literature's view of culture is not unified either. Culture is often seen as a realm differentiated from politics (McGuigan 2004) while it is also regarded as part of the liberal state's governing mechanism, via which people are given freedom and assistance so that they can direct and regulate their own conduct (T. Bennett 1998; Foucault 1991).

While calling for more focused debates on the relationship between culture and the state, this chapter attends to the following aspects of cultural policy. Firstly, state cultural policy, such as public subsidy, heavily involves value judgments and the state's selection of legitimate culture (O. Bennett 1997). Secondly, the development of culture as a relatively autonomous field (Bourdieu 1993) is a product of an historical process (DiMaggio 1986; H.-K. Lee 2008), which may be more pertinent to Western liberal democracies. Thirdly, there exists a huge variance between cultural policies in different countries (Toepler and Zimmer 2002).

Considering that generalizing and abstracting the culture-state relationship is difficult, as it is a product of the historical, political and social trajectory of a given society, we can get some inspiration from comparative viewpoints. Instead of fitting into one of the existing conceptual models or regimes identified by comparative cultural policy literature (e.g., Hillman-Chartrand and McCaughey 1989), we can understand cultural policy as a project of a 'unique combination of events,' socio-political factors ('their form of government...their economic and social development...religion') and traditions of cultural patrimony (Cummings and Katz 1987, p. 5). Similarly, we can view it 'as being shaped, mediated, and channeled by the history, tradition, and institutional arrangements of any given country' (Toepler and Zimmer 2002, p. 32; Zimmer and Toepler 1996). Here, history encompasses not only the tradition of cultural patrimony but also the country's historical trajectory that broadly determines the political and socioeconomic life of the public. Institution refers to both formal and informal rules for social interaction, from laws and organizations to norms and consensus (Powell and DiMaggio 1991; Scott 2001). From this point of view, cultural policy can be defined as a historically rooted and institutionalized relationship between culture and the state, which demonstrates continuity and path dependency.

This chapter argues that the culture-state relationship in Korea is heavily conditioned by the form of the state, social legitimation of culture, and the organization of the cultural sector itself. As the state form affects not only the political but also the social and economic arrangement of a country, it is crucial to discuss the form, orientation and capacity of the state in Korea. From the available research based on Western experiences, we can note that culture found social legitimacy in elite groups' (and other social groups') consensus on its value, and this legitimacy justified state cultural funding, albeit to a varying degree (Cummings and Katz 1987; DiMaggio 1986; H.-K. Lee, 2008). The legitimacy also served as a crucial prerequisite for culture's autonomization from other social forces such as politics and commerce. Meanwhile, culture's shortage of such legitimacy could result in a culture-state dynamic that fundamentally differs from those found in Western European and North American societies. Korea is such a case. Finally, we need to pay attention to the organization of the cultural sector itself as it may determine the sector's competence to formulate a sectoral agenda and to negotiate with governmental actors. The following sections will show that the above three factors have been historically interwoven and have influenced the contours of the country's policy for the arts over time.

Arts and the state in Korea

Arts policy under the developmental state

In order to understand contemporary Korea since the Second World War, one needs to consider two determining factors. The first one is that the country suffered seriously from internal ideological conflicts (the division between the South as a US protectorate and the North as that of the Soviet Union after the country's independence in 1945, the establishment of two nation states in 1948, and the Korean War from 1950 to 1953) and their legacy has been strongly felt in varied areas of social life. Simply speaking, Korean society has not yet overcome the 'red complex' and many Koreans – particularly those on the conservative spectrum and the elderly – are susceptible to the dichotomist view that frames political opinions and activities challenging the conservative regime as 'leftist' and even 'pro-North Korea'. Another factor is the 'developmental state' as the dominant form of the state in Korea since the 1960s. Developmental state refers to the form of the state where state institutions function as the prime engine of economic advancement by proactively regulating, guiding and coordinating market forces (Öniş 1991; Weiss 1998; White and Wade

1998). In addition to Japan and Germany, 'Asian tigers,' including Korea are seen as typical developmental states, although all of them are currently under the pressures of neoliberalization. The Korean developmental state started with PARK Chung Hee, who took power via a military coup d'état, pledging to end poverty and modernize the country through industrialization. Holding a tight grip on market forces, the government successfully fostered export-driven economic growth, which led to 'the miracle of Han River.' The Korean development state had elements of corporatism, but they differed from those found in Western – for example Nordic – welfare states. In Korea, labor was excluded in the state-capital corporation, and there was a huge imbalance between the state and private organizations, even big business conglomerates, in their power and capacity (Eckert 1990–1991; Kwon 1999; Öniş 1991). Consecutive military governments used the country's remarkable economic performance to compensate for its democracy deficit. Under ideological campaigns of anti-communism and national security, political opposition and bottom-up civil movements were suppressed. As White and Wade (1988) note, it was the government who created a pseudo-civil sector by setting up non-governmental groups, when necessary, in order to control them. In spite of their size and nation-wide membership, these pseudo civil groups' role was limited to assisting the government and its policies (H.-S. Kim 2012; Kwon 1999). In many areas, including culture and the arts, there was a very close coupling between the political and the social. The end of the 1980s saw a spark of political activism, and this was followed by the maturation of the country's democracy and the surge of civil society throughout the 1990s and afterward. However, Korean society and its cultural policy are still greatly affected by the country's complex historical and political path.

The institutionalization of cultural and arts policy in Korea in the 1960s and 1970s was embedded in the political circumstances at the time, where the military government tried to control and use them to govern the populace. With the enactment of the Public Performance Law (1961), Motion Picture Law (1966) and Recorded Music Law (1967), the formation of the Ministry of Culture and Public Information in 1968, the enactment of Culture and Arts Promotion Law (1972), the creation of the Korea Culture and Arts Foundation in 1973 and the introduction of the 5-Year Cultural Developmental Plan in 1974, the government clearly aimed to regulate cultural and artistic outputs and utilize them to achieve governmental goals of the 'revitalization of the nation,' the 'renaissance of national culture,' and the formation of ideological and moral consensus among the populace (Han 2010; H.-S. Kim 2012; W. Kim 2012; Oh 1998).

This process necessitated the suppression of 'unhealthy' – immoral, decadent, anti-government, anti-war and leftist – contents of the arts and popular culture that challenged the regime and its ideologies. Cultural and arts policy in Korea was viewed in the same way as state-driven economic planning. Over time, state cultural policy goals changed to incorporate the agenda of cultural welfare, public accessibility, the internationalization of Korean culture, deregulation and decentralization. However, the role of the state as a primary planner, funder, implementer, regulator and service provider was taken for granted. The rapid expansion of formal institutions such as relevant laws, arts subsidy, arts venues, national arts organizations and infrastructure was carried out without society-wide discussion around the value of the arts. Hence, it was not surprising to see these institutions scarcely having any substantial impact on the public's cultural life and attitudes towards the arts. The omnipresence of the state in every stage of policy making became a habit of Korean arts policy, and this has not been really challenged until today. Arts policy making and management have been undertaken by generalist bureaucrats who do not necessarily possess arts-specific knowledge and skills. While arts are treated as an object of state planning and bureaucratic consideration, their particularities are less likely to be recognized.

Problems with social legitimization of the arts

Unlike Western European and North American countries, it is hard to say that the development of arts policy in Korea was rooted in society-wide or middle-class support for the arts. The relatively weak social legitimacy of the arts is a consequence of the historical and social conditions of Korean society. One factor is the low esteem in which artists and other types of cultural producers have traditionally held. For instance, most performing artists used to be classified as one of the lowest classes, and many masters suffered from a lack of social respect until recently (Jin 2007; J.-Y. Lee 2005; National Institute of Korean History 2007; Uoo 2009). Throughout the colonial period, Korean arts forms rooted in collective and folk traditions were on the one hand, suppressed by the colonial government who saw them as potential triggers for political uprisings and on the other, despised by Westernized intellectuals as backward-looking, demoralizing and escapist, far from securing the status of 'fine arts' (Yoo 1998). The country's independence (1945), the creation of a new nation state (1948), and its economic growth since the 1960s hardly guaranteed artists' social legitimation. A series of cultural policies such as the Cultural Property Protection Law (1962), national folklore contests and prizes, and the creation of national traditional arts organizations helped them become acknowledged as part of the 'national culture' and an 'intangible cultural property.' However, this process was driven by the government without wider public or middle-class support (H.-S. Kim 2012; J.-Y. Lee 2005). In spite of newly gained recognition and government support, they quickly became a minority pursuit amid the Westernization of Korean society.

The Westernization accompanied Koreans' uncritical adoption of the Western distinction between high and popular cultures. European fine arts were easily accepted as 'high culture' and became mainstream in both arts education and arts-making practice. For decades after the Korean War, university-level arts education grew, producing a large number of qualified artists in various disciplines of Western arts. For example, as of 1997, 25,000 students applied to universities to study music, which primarily meant Western classical music, and 93.1% of full-time music professorships at universities and colleges were held by experts in Western classical music (Hwang 2009, p. 59). However, Western art forms have hardly secured a firm place in Korean people's cultural life. There are no solid longitudinal studies, but available survey results show that only a small minority of the population enjoy the arts, either Western or traditional Korean. As of 1995, the number of visits by Korean adults to musical concerts, dance performances, and art exhibitions was 0.51, 0.07 and 0.51 per head per year, while the number of visits to the cinema was 6.6 (MCS 1995). A more recent survey indicates that the average number of visits to art venues has been between 0.01 and 0.2 except visits to the cinema (3.3 to 4 visits per year) (MCST and KCTI 2010). The Korean people's overall indifference to the arts may explain why the National Theater of Korea (formed in 1950) has suffered from a lack of audience and social support throughout its entire life, with some periodic exceptions (Yoo 1998). For the same reason, individual Western music performers, including the most prestigious, hardly make a living based on performances alone and rely heavily on other salaries, especially those from working at educational institutions (Hwang 2009, p. 61). The fact that being associated with higher education institutions is almost the only way to secure social respect and a stable income explains the noticeable concentration of cultural power and authority in the hands of arts professors at universities. Combined with the sector's weak capacity for self-control, however, this has resulted in some problematic consequences: the arts sector has been subject to 'recurring' scandals about the plagiarism of degree dissertations, nepotism, the abuse of power and corruption involving the university entrance exam (*National Arts* 2003).

To take an example, almost every year Koreans hear news reports on some arts professors' wrong and corrupt dealings with their department's recruitment of students. Even arts departments at high-ranking universities and the most prestigious arts colleges are not free from such scandals. From a functionalist view, arts experts are seen typically as professionals who produce and distribute unique knowledge useful for the entire society and whose work is best monitored and evaluated by professionals themselves. Similarly, existing cultural sociological investigations (e.g., Bourdieu 1993) maintain that the field of artistic production takes peer-evaluation as the dominant mode of social control of artists' expertise. However, the arts sector in Korea has shown notable shortcomings in this area despite the existence of varied formal institutions, such as associations and professional qualifications. The failure of self-control is likely to portray the arts as a sector that needs more transparency and public scrutiny.

It is important to note that the country has not (yet) seen the development of middle-class cultural patronage. In Korea, 'middle class' is a socioeconomic concept that is mainly concerned with wealth, income, education and job. Deprived of the cultural legacies of the old literati classes that were disrupted and disappeared amid a series of historical events and Westernization, the formation of a middle-class in contemporary Korea was a product of the condensed economic growth since the 1960s, flexible social mobility, and meritocratic education. This process did not necessitate the acquisition of cultural capitals. The Korean middle classes' lack of, or indifference to, cultural capitals can be compared with their abundance of political capitals, exemplified by their active involvement in the democratization process since the late 1980s and their everyday interest in politics. The post-1997 period has witnessed a rapid neoliberalization of Korean society, which noticeably widened social inequality and job insecurity, reduced social mobility, and polarized middle classes (between declining and upward moving ones). The upper and surviving middle classes' consciousness of class distinction via culture has gradually been rising (D.-Y. Lee 2010). Perhaps this might explain classical music and ballet's recent success in audience development (MCST and KAMS 2010). Nevertheless, it can still be widely observed that the upper and middle classes are concerned more with material (e.g., buying luxury goods) and educational (e.g., sending children to schools in the US, UK or Canada) than with cultural distinction (Kang 2008). It is within this context that private support for the arts is hugely underdeveloped in Korea, except arts support programs run by big business conglomerates. For the Korean upper and middle classes, the affairs of the arts – for example, funding them or securing their autonomy from politics and the market – has seldom been an issue that matters to their class or status consciousness. It is unsurprising that these classes were nonchalant towards the LEE Myung Bak government's overt political pressure on the arts world and conservative politicians' attempt to mobilize artists for party political purposes.

Internal divisions historical, ideological and organizational

The arts sector in Korea is densely organized. Yechong (or the Federation of Arts and Cultural Organizations in Korea) and Minyechong (or the Korean People's Artists Federation) are the two largest national federations, which respectively cover approximately 1,300,000 and 100,000 artists. Each federation consists of a number of art form associations and has branches at provincial and municipal levels. Typically, Yechong is regarded as conservative while Minyechong progressive. Although there are numerous artists who are not members, the federations are key participants in the country's arts policy, and the government regards them as representing the country's arts community. Yet, it should be noted that the sector's tight organization does not guarantee that it, as a civil sector, has substantial powers of negotiation vis-à-vis the government. On the contrary, its heavy dependency on and close relationship with the government has been a key characteristic of Korean arts policy. This coincides with the sector's internal division and tension, which prevent it from representing artists' common interests to the government. This division is a product of the country's historical and political trajectory, and similar divisions are also found in other social and professional areas. The story goes back to the colonial period, when the sector saw tension between socialist and nationalist sections, and the tension continued and deepened after independence as the Korean peninsula was put under heavy ideological influence by the USA and the USSR. The ideological conflict within the divided Korea and the subsequent Korean War forced many artists to choose either South or North, and most socialist artists chose the latter. Under the authoritarian military regime, the arts were tightly regulated by the state, which did not allow politically plural voices (H.-S. Kim 2012; W. Kim 2012; Oh 1998). It was within such a political environment that Yechong was born in 1962, under the endorsement and financial support of the military government in order 'to gather artists who had been scattered according to their view of the state and political ideologies' and represent their interests (Yechong 1979, p. 13). As the only leading organization in the sector, it worked closely with the government, which wanted backing from the arts community. It was routinely mobilized to hold politically charged events, for example arts festivals to celebrate the birth of the Third Republic, friendly volleyball matches involving army, government officials and members of the public, and lectures on national security, the 'new village movement', 'October Yushin' (the political reform led by President PARK Chung Hee) and the assassination of the First Lady (Yechong 1979, pp. 13–24). Its co-option by the military regime is aptly demonstrated by its announcement of a statement in favor of General CHUN Do Hwan, who became a successor to the assassinated President PARK after a coup d'état and a massacre in Gwangju in 1980 (Shin 1989, p. 178). In return, the federation could get easy access to state funding and even political power. For example, its chairperson was normally expected to be invited into politics by the ruling party. Toward the end of the 1980s, artists who were critical of the regime began to organize themselves: Minyechong was set up in 1988 and actively took part in political and labor movements in the 1980s and 1990s. The political democratization and the emergence of civil society in the 1990s led to the growth of Minyechong and other organizations that approached the arts from social and civil movement perspectives. This brought unprece-dented pluralism to the organization of the sector and arts policy discus-sion, challenging the legitimacy of the existing institutions. Ironically, however, the pluralist environment made the internal division and tension within the arts sector more strongly felt.

Old and new dynamics in arts policy

The political democratization and economic neoliberalization in the 1990s induced substantial changes to Korean society. One of them was the surge of belief in small government and deregulation, which facili-tated the emergence of the civil society as a public policy partner. The arts sector witnessed the government's growing willingness to engage more arts practitioners and experts in policy making. Reflecting on the shortcomings of state-dominated arts policy, both the two liberal govern-ments (1998–2003, 2003–2008) and the sector felt the need to develop 'expert-led' policy making, which would be buffered from political inter-vention and party politics. This created a new space where progressive groups of artists and cultural activists, who had challenged the existing arrangement of arts policy, were invited to take part in policy discussion. However, the diversification of the government's policy partners was regarded by conservatives as favoritism by the liberal governments and a threat to the existing funding and power structure in the sector. In particular, conservative artists and commentators were not happy about the fact that key positions in public cultural institutions were taken by those who had been active in bringing social and political issues to the arts or had been close to Minyechong, the federation of progressive artists. They opposed the appointments by issuing formal statements and commenting in the media, sparking fierce debates. In particular, Yechong was extremely critical of the changes in arts policy under the liberal governments and saw it as a 'fundamental restructuring of the arts community' or even the deployment of a 'cultural red army' (*Shindonga* 2003). Such a response caused unprecedented tension within the sector and gave birth to a new kind of 'politicization' of arts policy, which takes for granted an alliance between a given government and artist groups with the same political position.

This was also the case with film policy. The Korean Film Council and Arts Council Korea, the most visible legacies of the liberal governments' attempt to institute expert-led cultural policy making, were at the heart of controversies throughout the period (see H.-K. Lee 2012 for more details). The Korean Film Council was set up in 1999 as an arm's length agency but, from the very beginning, it seriously suffered from ceaseless disputes on how power and financial resources should be distributed between different – namely conservative and progressive – sections in the industry (Han 2010; *National Arts* 2003). The creation of Arts Council Korea in 2005 and its close relationship with Minyechong triggered similar debates, deepening the existing mistrust between the progressive and conservative camps of artists. The liberal governments tried to embrace both federations (e.g., by giving the same amount of annual funding to them and engaging both of them in policy making), yet conservative groups who believed that they better represented the sector in terms of membership size and thus deserved more funding and attention saw it as unfair treatment (*Shindonga* 2003).

This situation was even dubbed as a 'culture war' by some right-wing commentators and news media that explicitly favored the conservative section and incited Korean society's red complex by accusing the progressive federation of being 'leftist,' 'socialist,' 'pro-North Korea' and 'anti-American' (e.g., S.-H. Kim 2008; S.-W. Kim 2009) and compared progressive artists' taking key positions as 'the invasion of the North Korean army' (*Shindonga* 2006). The concern of conservatives who waged the culture war was more with (re-)securing financial resource, appointments and prestige within the sector (e.g., *Shindonga* 2003 and 2006) than with initiating genuine political and ideological debates on cultural policy ideals, visions, goals and measures. Their use of the term 'leftist' was extremely arbitrary, as it frequently referred to those who challenged their vested interests embedded in the existing institutions in Korean cultural and arts policy. Artists and experts in the progressive camp acknowledged that they were engaged in a battle to shift the power structure within the sector, but their aim went beyond the distribution of funding and key appointments. They wished to tackle the weaknesses of the existing system – for instance, nepotism, corruption related to university entrance exams, and the abuse of power by arts professors – and tried to present a new vision of arts policy by adopting a broad and more socially oriented perspective of culture and promoting diversity and decentralization (*National Arts* 2003). However, their battle was only half successful, as it spurred a huge backlash throughout the period of liberal governments and especially when a conservative government was formed in 2008. The newly elected government of LEE Myung Bak (2008–2013) tried to shift the power balance in the cultural sector primarily by filling key positions in public cultural institutions with those who were close to the government. Such an action was interpreted as fulfilling the wants of conservative artists who 'supported LEE Myung Bak in order to compensate for the lost 10 years' (*Sisa Journal* 2008) and mobilizing support from the conservative camp. The unlawful dismissal of the then chairmen of the Arts Council Korea in 2008 occurred as part of this process, but conservative artists and commentators saw this as an inevitable and righteous measure to restore balance in the sector (H.-K. Lee 2012). This explains why the arts sector failed to raise a unified voice against governmental intervention with Arts Council Korea and also to call for an arm's length relationship with the government. The arts sector's internal tension was visible at regional and local levels, too, where Yechong and Minyechong constitute two of the four pillars of local cultural policy making, together with local authorities and local cultural centers.

The crucial issue here is that the politicization of arts policy deters the sector from developing a sense of common interests and a shared understanding of the arts-government relationship. The British system of the arm's length principle was much admired over decades as an ideal model for Korean arts policy; however, conservative artists and politicians simply put it aside when they thought that it could benefit progressive groups and activists. As the arts sector could not self-coordinate different interests within itself, the government was called back to perform the job, despite the prevailing rhetoric of small government and artist-led policy making. While being busy with debating on power and resource distribution within, the sector was rather powerless about the surge in the market-centered view of culture. The government began to pay attention to cultural industries from the mid-1990s and rapidly expanded its budget on and policy measures for these industries throughout the 2000s. This came with the reconceptualization of cultural industries as 'content industries.' Gradually, the arts, traditional culture, craft and heritage became newly defined as content for cultural commodities. However, both conservative and progressive groups of artists and activists failed to come up with an alternative framework that could convincingly call for social and public values of the arts and persuasively critique the overt commercial turn in Korean cultural policy.

Agenda for future research

This chapter defines the arts sector's vulnerability to political pressure and the asymmetrical power relation between the arts and the state as a key characteristic of Korean arts policy. It has attempted to make sense of the phenomenon by looking into the arts' engagement with the political and the social as well as the sector's internal conditions. In particular, it has focused on the authoritarian developmental state in the past and its legacies on arts policy and broader cultural policy, the weak social legitimacy of the arts, and finally, the arts sector's internal division, which has become firmly institutionalized over decades. The historical and institutional approach taken by the chapter could be useful, to a certain degree, for examining state cultural policy in other East Asian countries which share with Korea the strong presence of the state in cultural affairs, the rapid process of Westernization, the lack of popular support and middle-class patronage for the arts, and/or ideological divisions within the cultural sector itself.

This chapter's findings raise a few agendas for studying Korean cultural and arts policy. The first agenda is concerned with the state's capacity and roles. Having witnessed a noticeably strong capability of the state in planning and implementing arts policy, financing the arts and providing infrastructure, one can raise the question of whether the state can develop the ability to critically reflect on its own capacity. Asking such a question is useful because past and present experience clearly demonstrates the centrality of the state in arts policy and the unfeasibility of an immediate reduction of state power over arts provision,

administration and funding, in spite of the gradual trends of decentralization and marketization. The lack of the arts sector's financial as well as
symbolic resources – social legitimacy, middle-class support and sectoral
consensus – means that it would take time for the sector to take more
decisive roles in policy making and for the arts to be genuinely internalized in Korean people's cultural life. In this context, it is meaningful to
ask if and how the government – especially the central government –
can reflect on its own conduct in its relation to the arts and raise self-
awareness of the danger in the abuse of its capacity and the mobilization
of artists for political purposes. Such a reflexive ability is much needed,
given the current circumstance that the government is supposed to play
crucial roles as a balancing actor and a coordinator of different interests
within the arts sector.

The second research agenda is the link between the autonomy of
the arts from the state and the former's social legitimacy. Considering
the current economic and social context of Korean society (that is, the
increasing inequality, income polarization and reduced social mobility),
the future is likely to see middle-class identity and lifestyle being more
tied with cultural consumption. This might mean that fostering and
expanding middle-class audiences would be an effective strategy for the
arts sector to secure both financial and symbolic resources. However,
the shortage of class-based arts patronage and authority over the arts
also implies that Korean arts policy could be open to more democratic
understanding of arts and their roles in society. Here, it seems useful
to note that the Korean public tends to prioritize the issues of cultural
infrastructure, cultural welfare, public accessibility and cultural education over arts funding (World Research 2010, p. 18). More democratic
interpretation of the arts, the expansion of arts education, the provision
of easily accessible cultural facilities and securing popular support could
be an alternative to middle-class patronage for the arts. If this is desir-
able, what are the roles played by the state and the arts sector to foster
broad social consensus on values of the arts and leading the advancement of more socially grounded arts policy?

The final agenda is the arts sector's internal conditions. The chapter
finds that the institutionalized conflict within the sector is likely to
politicize arts policy making by projecting it as a battle for power and
resource, not as a process of democratic discussion and negotiation.
Similarly, the arts sector's self-control mechanism is difficult to develop
as such efforts could be seen as power struggle between different sections
in the sector. Without reflexive self-control and autonomy from political forces, the arts sector hardly functions as a civil sector. How can

the historically rooted division within the arts sector, which has been exacerbated and politically mobilized in the past, be dissolved? Again, the government playing a balancing act would be one way to deal with it. A fundamental solution, however, should come from the arts sector itself: for example, its own reflexive exercises to look back at the arts-state relationship throughout recent history and try to establish a shared understanding, beyond the existing internal division, of how the relationship can be constructively reformulated. Such effort might include the sector's strengthened self-consciousness as a civil force and linkage with the wider civil society.

Acknowledgments

This research has benefited from the Korea Foundation's Field Research Fellowship Grant that allowed the author to conduct fieldwork in Seoul from December 2012 to February 2013.

References

Bennett, O. (1997) 'Cultural Policy, Cultural Pessimism and Postmodernity', *European Journal of Cultural Policy*, 4(1), 67–84.

Bennett, T. (1998) *Culture: A Reformer's Science* (London: Sage).

Bourdieu, P. (1993) *The Field of Cultural Production* (Cambridge: Polity).

Cummings, M.C. and Katz, R.S. (1989) 'Relations between Government and the Arts in Western Europe and North America', in M.C. Cummings and J.M.D. Schuster (eds), *Who's to Pay for the Arts: The International Search for Models of Arts Support* (New York: American Council for the Arts), 5–13.

DiMaggio, P.J. (1986) 'Cultural Entrepreneurship in Nineteenth-Century Boston', in P.J. DiMaggio (ed.), *Nonprofit Enterprise in the Arts* (Oxford: Open University Press), 41–61.

Eckert, C.J. (1990–1991) 'The South Korean Bourgeoisie: A Class in Search of Hegemony', *Journal of Korean Studies*, 7, 115–148.

Foucault, M. (1991) 'Governmentality', in G. Burchell, C. Gordon and P. Miller (eds), *The Foucault Effect: Studies in Governmentality* (London: Harvester Wheatsheaf), 87–104.

Han, S.-J. (2010) 'A Study on the Role of Ideology in the Film Supporting Policy: The Case of the Korean Film Council', *Korea Journal of Public Administration*, 48(2), 309–337.

Heilbrun, J. and Gray, C.M. (1993) *The Economics of Arts and Culture* (Cambridge: Cambridge University Press).

Hillman-Chartrand, H. and McCaughey, C. (1989) 'The Arm's Length Principle and the Arts: An International Perspective – Past, Present and Future', in M.C. Cummings and J.M.D. Schuster (eds), *Who's to Pay for the Arts: The International Search for Models of Arts Support* (New York: American Council for the Arts), 43–73.

Hwang, O. (2009) 'No "Korean Wave" Here: Western Classical Music and the Changing Value System in South Korea', *Southeast Review of Asian Studies*, 31, 56–68.

Jin, O.-S. (2007) *Norummachi* (Seoul: Tree of Thought).

Kang, J.-M. (2008) 'Middle Classes Imprisoned', *Hankyoreh 21*, (699).

Kim, H.-S. (2012) *Cultural Policy and Cultural Control of Park Jung Hee Administration in the 1970s* (Seoul: Sunin Publishing).

Kim, S.-H. (2008) *Cultural and Arts Policy of the New Government* (Seoul: Jipmoondang).

Kim, S.-W. (2009) *An Analysis of Minyechong: Anti-American Warriors in the Cultural Sector* (Seoul: CFE).

Kim, W. (2012) 'Competition in Claiming for the Ownership of "the Korean"', *Society and History*, 93, 185–235.

Kwon, H.-J. (1999) *The Welfare State in Korea: The Politics of Legitimation* (Basingstoke: Macmillan).

Lee, D.-Y. (2010) *The Age of Cultural Capital: The Logic of Formation of Cultural Capitals in Korea* (Seoul: Culture Science).

Lee, J.-Y. (2005) *Korean Intangible Cultural Property Policy: Its History and Future* (Seoul: Kwan-dong Publishing).

Lee, H.-K. (2008) 'Uses of Civilising Claims: Three Moments in the British Theatre History', *Poetics*, 36(4), 287–300.

Lee, H.-K. (2012) 'Progress without Consensus: "Instituting Arts Council in South Korea"', *International Journal of Cultural Policy*, 18(3), 323–339.

McGuigan, J. (2004) *Rethinking Cultural Policy* (Maidenhead: Open University Press).

MCS [Ministry of Culture and Sports] (1995) *Survey on Public Opinions* (Seoul: MCS).

MCST and KAMS [Korea Arts Management Service] (2010) *Survey of Classical Music and Ballet Audiences* (Seoul: MSCT and KAMS).

MCST and KCTI [Korea Culture & Tourism Institute] (2010) *Survey Report on Cultural Enjoyment* (Seoul: MCST and KCTI).

National Arts (2003) 'How to Make Sense of "Cultural Power"', *National Arts*, April, 33–47.

National Institute of Korean History (2007) *The Lives and Trajectories of Artists of Humble Classes* (Seoul: Dusan Donga).

Oh, M.-S. (1998) 'Cultural Policy and National Culture Discourse in the 1960s and 1970s', *Comparative Cultural Studies*, 4, 121–152.

Öniş, Z. (1991) 'The Logic of the Developmental State (Review)', *Comparative Politics*, 24(1), 109–126.

Powell, W.W. and DiMaggio, P.J. (eds) (1991) *The New Institutionalism in Organizational Analysis* (Chicago: University of Chicago Press).

Scott, W.R. (2001) *Institutions and Organizations* (2nd edition) (London: Sage).

Shin, K.-L. (1989). 'The Meaning of the Birth of Minyechong', *Arts and Criticism*, 15, 173–183.

Shindonga (2003) '"Move Forward Minyechong!; Move Backward Yechong!"', *Shindonga*, 46(11), 258–268.

Shindonga (2006) 'This is Worse than South Korea Conquered by North Korean Army', *Shindonga*, 49(12), 230–242.

Sisa Journal (2008) 'The Lost 10 Years and Recovering of Cultural Power: Who Will be Appointed as Cultural Minister?', *Sisa Journal*, 925, 81.

Toepler, S. and Zimmer, A. (2002) 'Subsidizing the Arts: Government and the Arts in Western Europe and the United States', in D. Crane, N. Kawashima and K. Kawasaki (eds), *Global Culture: Media, Arts, Policy and Globalization* (London: Routledge), 29–48.

Vestheim, G. (1994) 'Instrumental Cultural Policy in Scandinavian Countries: A Critical Historical Perspective', *European Journal of Cultural Policy*, 1(1), 57–71.

Voon, T. (2006) 'The UNESCO and WTO: A Clash of Cultures?', *International and Comparative of Law Quarterly*, 55(3), 635–652.

Weiss, L. (1998) *The Myth of the Powerless State: Governing the Economy in a Global Era* (Cambridge: Polity).

White, G. and Wade, R. (1988) 'Developmental States and Markets in East Asia', in G. White (ed.), *Developmental States in East Asia* (Basingstoke: Macmillan), 1–29.

Yechong (1979) *Yechong White Paper* (Seoul: Yechong).

Yoo, M. (1998) *The History of the Korean Modern Theatre* (Seoul: Taehaksa).

Uoo, I. (2009) 'Patronage of Performing Arts in Chosun Period', in N. Park, J. Ryu, J. Song, I. Uoo, G. Cho and H. Park (eds), *The History of Arts Patronage in Korea* (Seoul: Mimesis), 175–233.

Zimmer, A. and Toepler, S. (1996). 'Cultural Politics and the Welfare State: The Case of Sweden, Germany, and the United States', *Journal of Arts Management, Law and Society*, 26(3), 167–193.

World Research (2010) *Survey on Cultural Vision and Policy* (Seoul: MCST).

6
Negotiation and Adaptation: Singapore Theater as Civil Society

Lorraine Lim

The relationship between the arts sector and the Singaporean government can best be characterized as an uneasy one. For a newly independent nation, the promotion of arts was seen as a luxury; issues such as sustained economic growth and social stability were deemed more important. It was only in 1990, more than two decades after independence, that the Singapore government published its first recognizable official cultural policy document. This is not to say that there were little or no arts events happening in Singapore before the 1990s. Rather, the arts sector flourished from the 1980s up to the early 1990s because the 'pragmatic, philistine modernity promoted by the government' was indifferent to arts, as the arts sector then 'was not considered important enough to warrant attention' (Wee 2003, p. 86). This resulted in an arts sector that operated under relatively few restrictions. During this time, arts production in Singapore, particularly in theatre, offered a space to address issues that were 'in distinction from established ways of thinking and operating in Singapore' (Krishnan 1997, p. 17).

It was during the 1990s that the Singapore government realized that the arts could play a key role in driving economic growth; the arts could transform Singapore's image as a financial sector to a global arts city and also help strengthen the citizenry's national identity. In an effort, perhaps, to make up for lost time, the government would release five cultural policy documents within the next 10 years[1]. These documents would outline in specific detail how the arts sector, along with the wider creative industries, could help Singapore achieve all these goals. For a nation where the government and the state are often considered one and the same, the eventual inclusion of the arts into the government's economic policies was not surprising. While arts practitioners would welcome interest from the government, this attention was also

104

a double-edged sword where their work was now, at the same time, coming under increasing scrutiny.

For the government, the arts were to be supported for two rationales. The first was for arts products that would showcase Singapore to the world, and the second was for artists to create arts products that were 'dedicated…to the support and edification of institutions and prevailing political structures' (Chong 2010, p. 139). While there were artists who were content to work within these goals, there were also arts practitioners who were not willing to create art within these parameters and continued to explore 'issues of memory, ethnicity, and other identity issues' (Wee 2003, p. 85).[2] The art created by the latter group problematized issues of national identity and examined the consequences of social policies. These works did not fulfill either of the two government rationales. As a result, tensions between what type of arts the government wanted to support and what type of arts Singaporean artists wanted to present were exemplified throughout the 1990s and 2000s with productions that tested the limits and boundaries of what was considered acceptable.

This was particularly evident in the theater scene. All arts performances, except for certain performance types,[3] require an arts entertainment license, which can only be obtained when the synopsis of the performance was submitted beforehand to the National Arts Council (NAC), it was not unheard of for performances to be denied an arts entertainment license or for other performances to be subjected to censorship before being issued with a license. Artists now, whether they liked it or not, had to learn how to negotiate with the state on what could or could not be performed or presented in public.

The way in which artists and arts groups engaged with the government about what could be presented publicly has thus resulted into what is currently an uneasy relationship. What must be understood is that 'all exercises in government planning and policy-making' since independence had to fulfill one 'defining criterion of pragmatism,' which was 'the question of whether the policy will stimulate or retard economic growth' (Lee 2010, p. 4). However, this issue when applied to the arts would prove problematic because the raison d'etre of art itself 'whether visual, performance or of other modalities, privileges itself as the arena in which complexities of social life are examined, issues raised and the boundaries of conventions tested and transcended' (Chua 2005, p. 69). What would therefore come under contest from the 1990s would be the role and function of the arts in Singapore society. The incorporation of the arts into an economic rubric has, as Singaporean sociologist CHUA

Beng Huat points out, 'not proven to be easily digestible' (2005 p. 69). This disconnect between what the arts sector seeks to achieve and what the government would like the arts sector to create is an important point, as it highlights how for some, if not all, artists and arts organizations, economics is not as important as the necessity to highlight social issues that are pertinent to Singaporeans.

I would like to examine this point further in this chapter. By drawing parallels between the arts in Singapore and the concept of 'civil society,' I would argue that the arts sector in Singapore contains many of the traits that a civil society possesses. This is not to state that the arts in Singapore is a 'civil society' per se, but rather that it works as one through the way it fulfills the functions of a civil society. The position the arts sector plays in Singapore can only be understood within a Singaporean context due to the way the country has developed, with its high levels of state intervention and competing desires of the functions of the arts in Singapore. For purposes of clarity, the term 'Civil Society' will be capitalized with reference to society as a whole, while 'civil society' will be used to denote a civil society as an organization or a group.

I will use examples from theater in Singapore in particular to demonstrate my points, as theater is one of the best-known art forms in Singapore in terms of its history and development. By highlighting how government intervention and restrictions limit the scope of engagement of civil societies in Singapore, I will provide examples on how the arts sector is able to circumvent some of these restrictions because of the way in which ideas are presented within a fixed frame of a performance or an exhibition and highlight how the arts are able to fulfill this role even when work is not allowed to be presented publicly. While I would argue that their influence is limited in effecting change, being able to bring issues into the public consciousness is a key success in a society where the media is strictly controlled by the government.

Understanding civil society within a Singaporean context

Discussions on civil societies in Singapore have focused mainly on two aspects. The first examines the dominant role played by the ruling government represented by the People's Action Party (PAP) who has governed Singapore since independence in 1965 and the way in which spaces for civil society engagement are managed. The literature here highlights measures undertaken by the Singapore government to enable or limit actions to allow citizens a greater say in national policy-making.

The second aspect focuses on how civil organizations function in Singapore today within these limitations and how effective these civil societies have been in facilitating social and political change. Here the debate examines how civil societies within Singapore are better understood as 'civic societies,' whereby the 'civic' responsibilities of citizens are promoted as opposed to those of the 'rights' of citizenship espoused in the conventional and political understanding of the concept of 'civil society' (Lee 2005, pp. 137–138). In short, by placing the emphasis on 'civic,' civil societies in Singapore are thus meant to promote ways in which citizens ought to behave themselves within society rather than to champion for civil rights such as freedom of speech, for example, thus depoliticizing the work that these societies engage with.

It has been argued that Singaporeans are generally content with the limited rights enjoyed as citizens, as long as the government continues to produce economic growth in society (see Chua 1995). However, by the 1980s, Singaporean citizenry had changed markedly. Increased educational and economic opportunities had created a 'large class of well-educated and successful Singaporeans' who were beginning to seek 'greater democratization, including greater participation for themselves in the polity' (Vasil 2000, p. 240). The government's response to these demands for a greater public input into national policy-making is best described as a preference for 'co-option' rather than democratization: the government would prefer civil society activists 'exercise their independent, critical minds but from a position inside rather than outside the government,' and where their overall strategy is for 'more public consultation without abdicating the responsibility to govern' (Lee 2008, p. 642; Chua 1995, p. 206). This is reflected in legislation that states that civil voluntary associations are 'barred by the [*Societies*] *Act* from making political statements beyond the interests of their respectively defined constituencies' (Chua 1995, p. 205).

What this effectively creates for Civil Society in Singapore is a clear demarcation of the roles of civil societies and how they should not be seen to impinge on the role of the state. At the same time, the government firmly believes that the 'collective wellbeing is safe guarded by good government by honorable leaders' whereby what is good for the state is good for society (Chua 1995, p. 185). So while civil societies must tread the line between state and society, the government does not need to distinguish between these lines and is therefore able to justify 'state intervention in all spheres of life, rationalized as pre-emptive interventions' to protect society and should be viewed 'as measures of good government rather than abuses of individuals' rights' (Chua 1995,

p. 187). A key obstacle to the development of a Civil Society in Singapore is hampered by the continued assumption from the government that an average Singapore's citizen's preference is 'incoherent' and that 'public opinion is a poor guide for formulating policy' (Ho 2000, p. 440). The oft-cited quotation from Singapore's first Prime Minister LEE Kuan Yew about the inability of 'the chap who can't pass primary six'[4] to understand the 'consequences of his choice' on issues such as 'language, culture and religion' is an attitude that pervades the Singapore government till this day (Han et al. 1997, p. 134).

What must also be acknowledged is the opaque way in which the government polices the line between state and society, often described with the term 'OB markers,' taken from golf terminology to signify when a golf ball has gone 'out-of-bounds.' The well-known rebuke from the government from an editorial written by local author Catherine Lim is a case in point.[5] Other methods of policing include using defamation laws to deal with individuals that the government has perceived to have interfered with local domestic policies. All these measures have created an atmosphere whereby the citizenry would rather practice self-censorship then leave themselves open to attacks from the government.[6]

However, the government is aware of the need to provide channels for Singaporeans to have some say into the creation of policy, and a solution has been to create official feedback channels where citizens can provide responses to government policies. Designating Hong Lim Park as a Speaker's Corner was another measure to foster this idea of the availability of a space for people to air their views. However, all persons who wish to speak at Speaker's Corner are required to register in advance, stating on an online form what their talk would be about, how long and when it would take place, and provide their contact details. It is clear that while the government values, or seeks to value the opinions of Singapore citizenry, the last thing they want to foster is the development of a perceived Western style of civil society whereby citizens are able to pursue 'individual desires and interests' with a total disregard for the 'heterogeneity' of society (Kenny and Germain 2005, p. 6; Schiffauer 2004, p. 92). The way in which the Singapore government tries to maintain this balance is perhaps best exemplified in the Arts and Culture Strategic Review (ACSR), initiated in 2010.

The whole process was managed by a steering committee made up of members from government bodies such as the then-Ministry of Information, Communication and the Arts, the Ministry of Education, and private companies in Singapore. Local arts practitioners would highlight that there was not a single artist on the steering committee (Chia 2010a).

The ACSR was conducted as a review of past and present cultural strategies with an aim to develop new strategies that were better able to address current changes within the global economic environment and the demographic of Singapore society and the impact of new media. The final report highlights that it was ACSR's intent to 'provide the public with a greater stake in shaping (Singapore's) cultural environment, engender a greater sense of public ownership of Singapore's arts and culture' (2012 p. 13). This was achieved in the following ways: focus group discussions, in-depth interviews, a month-long online public consultation, a quantitative survey, and five public forums (ACSR 2012, pp. 13–14). These public consultations were, however, not an opportunity for Singaporeans to offer suggestions about what they wanted from the arts sector. Instead, they were organized for Singaporeans to respond to the 'preliminary recommendations' of the committee (ACSR 2012, p. 13). The public was therefore asked to offer their opinions within preconceived, set parameters.

It is interesting to note the ACSR's response to any 'differing views on ACSR's preliminary recommendations' was to state that these opinions had 'helped ACSR to sharpen its recommendations' (2012 p. 14). What is clear from the ACSR is a demonstration of how the government seeks to manage and include the opinions of its citizens in determining future government policy. Asking its citizenry to provide feedback within set boundaries highlights the civic responsibilities of a citizen in offering their view on policies, yet does not allow them to pursue their own ideas or interests.

It is not possible to define what a 'true' civil society is (see Edwards 2009); however, it is perhaps possible to understand the government's perception of what a 'true' civil society is through working out the mechanisms it uses to determine how civil societies should function within a Singaporean context. For the government, a 'true' civil society would be one where citizens are able to suggest or raise concerns about domestic policy so as to effect change, and one where there are no boundaries between the role of the state and Civil Society.

Theater as a civil society

How then do the arts in Singapore manage, with the work that it presents, to highlight issues that are not within government-determined boundaries but also to create an impression that it is possible to question government policy that might be perceived as out-of-bounds?

I would contend that the arts sector in Singapore is able to function as a quasi-civil society in the following three ways: first, the arts highlight social issues that the government does not want to discuss publicly by creating or adapting works that touch upon politically sensitive issues. Second, the arts sector challenges the gray area of what can be discussed in public. Finally, I would argue that both these methods have created a 'space' where the citizenry is now aware that there is a possibility to at least discuss these issues in public without fear of repercussion, even if they are not able to directly effect change.

Just as the Societies Act, originally enacted in 1966, determines the boundaries in which civil societies function in Singapore, NAC, the government body that funds the arts, also creates boundaries as to what issues artists and arts organizations can create through its funding guidelines While explicitly stating that 'artistic merit is a key factor in funding decisions,' the NAC also gives 'consideration to whether the work is potentially a negative influence to society' (2012 p. 10). It goes on to state that funding would be prioritized for work that does not

a) advocate or lobby for lifestyles seen as objectionable by the general public;
b) denigrate or debase a person, group or class of individuals on the basis of race or religion or serve to create conflict or misunderstanding in our multi-cultural and multi-religious society;
c) undermine the authority or legitimacy of the government and public institutions, or threaten the nation's security or stability. (NAC 2012, p. 10)[7]

Two issues are highlighted with these guidelines. First, the terminology used is extremely vague. For example, how is it possible for any artist or arts organization to know who constitutes the 'general public'? Further to that, is it actually possible to determine what kind of material leads to 'conflict' or 'misunderstanding'? This is an issue that I will return to later in the chapter. Second, these guidelines also imply that the arts in Singapore should only support and reinforce the current status quo of society, by not questioning the role of the government and its policies. These guidelines are not the only rules that artists have to play within. There is still the issue of censorship. As all arts performances, except for certain performance types, require an arts entertainment license that can only be obtained via the Media Development Authority (MDA) by submitting the script for vetting, many performances have been denied licenses, which sometimes is not due to the content but also to the format. A performance by local theatre group Drama Box offers a way to understand how artists are constantly negotiating with these rules.

Creating and adapting work

In 2010, Drama Box's production, *shh...a date with the community*, a collection of three short plays on homosexuality, sex education, and religious radicalization was denied a performance license. It was not only the content that was deemed problematic but also the style of the performance. The plays were to be staged in the style of forum theatre, whereby the audience is asked to intervene during the performance itself to create a resolution to the issue being presented. Drama Box's original application was to stage the performance outdoors as a way to engage with the community, but the company was informed by the MDA that a performance license would be issued only if the performance was moved indoors, as the content of the plays were considered of a 'sensitive nature'; sexual acts, for example, between homosexuals are considered illegal (MDA in Tan 2010).

Also, by performing the plays in the style of forum theatre, MDA stated that any 'discussion (generated) is fluid and not within your control' (MDA in Tan 2010). Forum theatre has had a long, problematic history within the Singapore arts scene, but the main point of contention with forum theatre is the unscripted nature of it.[8] After all, how can the MDA determine if a performance should be awarded a performance license when no one, not even the performers, will know what is going to happen in the performance itself? In response, Drama Box offered to erect cloth banners around the performance area, with the 'mature content advisory' printed on them, so that any passersby would be aware of what was occurring. This suggestion was rejected, as the panels were not deemed to be large enough, and passersby would still be able to view the performance.

I will contend here that both the content and the style of performance come a little too close to comfort for the authorities in recreating the condition of a 'true' civil society, as it would have allowed audiences members to express their opinions freely, and their opinions could effect change within the performance itself. In short, forum theater is a performance style that cannot be predetermined by the government, and the aim of the performance style itself is meant to offer the audience a way to intervene directly.

The ruling from the MDA to move the performance indoors is thus an attempt to ensure that the opportunity for the public to respond to the issues presented would be limited. What makes the performance even more problematic is that working without a script and allowing audience intervention meant that it was not possible for there to be any form of control over the final 'outcome' of the performance where there was a possibility that the audience would have come to the conclusion that current domestic policy was flawed. There was a real fear, imagined or not, that this performance, if it had gone on as requested by Drama Box, could have fulfilled some of the roles of a civil society: that is, to question the current state of specific issues in Singapore and to offer concrete suggestions about what could be done to change the status quo.

It is possible here to argue how artists are able to address social issues such as these without being seen as intruding upon the state, as their work is presented within a performance, a fixed frame that contains fictitious characters. This is an advantage that artists have within Singaporean society that civil societies are unable to tap into. By also offering suggestions to what is a fictitious performance, there is no fear of repercussion, as the situation that is being commented on is not real. Yet it must be acknowledged that being able to present these topics in public takes away the notion that certain issues are taboo.

In the end, Drama Box did not go ahead with their original performance and instead re-applied for another license with a performance addressing the issue of divorce and its impact on families, once again performed in the style of forum theatre. This application was awarded a license and took place outdoors. Arguably, the denial of the original performance license signified that the state was still able to restrict and circumvent the role of artists in a way similar to civil societies in Singapore. However, what also has to be considered is press coverage of this issue, coupled with the discussion generated about these performances – not only of its content and performance style – only sought to raise the profile of the issues being discussed within the plays, which would not have happened had the license not been denied.

The notion that there is no such thing as bad publicity is one that the local arts scene has used to their advantage in recent years. One must bear in mind that the media is tightly controlled in Singapore. In 2013, Singapore was 149th out of 179 countries according to the World Press Freedom Index – ranking just above Iraq. The local arts scene has used the media to their advantage through their responses to funding decisions.

Challenging the gray area

In 2009, local theatre group W!ld Rice would be made an example of when they deviated too far from fulfilling the funding conditions as set out by the NAC: its government funding was reduced.[9] The subsequent justification for this cut and response from W!ld Rice was played out in the local press. NAC would state that the deduction was due to the group consistently producing work that was 'incompatible with the core values promoted by the Government and society or disparage the Government' (Chia 2010c). Ivan Heng, artistic director of the group, would counter this accusation by pointing out that 'despite repeated requests for clarification from the National Arts Council, it has not defined Singapore's core values, nor has it told us how the plays have eroded them' (Tan 2011).

ONG Keng Sen, another theatre practitioner, highlighted the lack of transparency about how funding decisions were made, stating that it was positive step that the NAC was now 'forced into some kind of articulation' so artists would be able to work out what the funding body was looking for, rather than simply second guessing what was acceptable or unacceptable material (Chia 2010b). This exchange was significant because it highlights two issues. The first is the vague terminology, which was pointed out earlier in this chapter, about what kind of work can be considered a negative influence on society. The second issue is the way funding decisions are made at NAC. There have been calls by the arts community for more transparency about how funding decisions are made, and this incident served to highlight the suspicion by many artists that the NAC was not so much acting as an arts funder as they were a moral vanguard. The fact that the funding cut was largely symbolic, representing just under a 0.5% reduction in W!ld Rice's budget, further seems to indicate that this was a way of reminding W!ld Rice that it still had to work within the boundaries set out by the government.

What is important about this incident is the call from arts practitioners for the authorities to be clear on what the boundaries are. The issue of transparency has always blighted the arts. The current system is unclear about what issues are permissible, and this has created tension between the arts community and the authorities. It is obvious that a large gray area is beneficial to the authorities, as it allows them to impose restrictions when they see fit; however, it must also be acknowledged that in a society, when the opportunities to express oneself are heavily circumscribed, having an exchange of what constitutes the gray area conducted over the local press creates a much needed space for discussion.

Creating a new 'space' for discussion

In their article, 'Renaissance City Singapore: A study of arts spaces,' Chang and Lee state that the production of art 'betrays insights into the psychological/mental spaces of the artist as well as the creative space allowed him/ her by society' (2003 p. 129). This point highlights how art can act as a catalyst for the debate of issues that the citizenry might consider out-of-bounds. As an arts entertainment license is required for any performance to be staged, by default any production that goes forward in Singapore has tacitly been approved by the government. This would signify consent from the state that participants would not be getting into any trouble for discussing these issues in the perform-ance. I would argue that when this occurs, an idea that started within the mental space of a single artist or group can now be disseminated through the audience via its performance. This in turn creates a mental space within the people who have seen the show, highlighting that it is possible to discuss these ideas in public without fear of repercussion.

The campaign for equal rights for homosexuals in Singapore is one such example. In 2003, then Prime Minister GOH Chok Tong would state in an interview with *Time* magazine that the Singapore civil service would employ gay people as long as they declared their sexual orientation on the application forms. However, this did not mean the government condoned homosexuality. In 2005, a gay (LGBT) plotline from the American television drama *Desperate Housewives* was censored when it was broadcast on national television. However, in parallel at this time, various theatre productions were dealing with LGBT themes. Adaptations of plays written by European writers, such as *Bent*, as well as plays by local writers such as Alfian Sa'at and Eleanor Wong, which deal with the LGBT experience within a Singaporean context, were staged. The link between the theater and LGBT community would be made explicit in 2007 during the debate about whether the law that criminal-ized homosexual acts should be repealed. W!ld Rice would organize a forum in conjunction with the play *Happy Endings: Asian Boys Vol. 3*, an LGBT play that it was staging at this same time.

While the law was not repealed, what could not be underestimated was how the issue of LGBT rights was brought into the national consciousness through the staging of these productions. Since then, there have been further collaborations between artists and the LGBT community in Singapore, culminating in the annual Pink Dot SG Event, where members of the public are invited to show solidarity with the LGBT community by wearing pink and congregating in Hong Lim Park. Participation in the 2012 event was estimated at 15,000 people (Mahtani 2012). This example demonstrates once again that artists are able to highlight contentious issues to a wider audience and show that it is possible to discuss these issues publicly without fear.

In recent years, the arts community – through staging their own productions that address issues of politics or national conscription, or through the use of their venues to highlight issues of government policy on migrant labor and the mandatory death penalty for drug-trafficking – have managed to provide a platform and create both a physical and mental space for the discussion of various issues that have an impact on domestic policy.

What next?

What the government has to acknowledge is that the changing demographic of Singaporeans, which includes an expanding middle class and the increasing use of social media, will make it difficult to circumscribe areas where policy can or cannot be discussed. Furthermore, Singaporeans are becoming more political due to their increased 'education, media exposure and political awareness', traits which have 'vastly increased since independence' (Ho 2000, p. 449). With continued intervention as to how Singaporeans can express their opinions, it would be hard to see how a rational, responsible Civil Society can develop in Singapore. Although current and past examples of civil societies and their ability to generate informed debate on policy in Singapore have been positive so far, there has not been a corresponding change in attitude from the government about citizenry participation in politics.

The use of online and social media has seen a huge increase in recent years due to its ubiquity. Where intervention in domestic policy is limited, as the media is state-controlled, online platforms such as blogs, YouTube and Facebook provide avenues for Singaporeans to debate policy issues and offer alternative perspectives. However, MDA now requires all websites that 'report an average of at least one article per week on Singapore's news and current affairs over a period of two months' and 'are visited by at least 50,000 unique IP addresses from Singapore each month over a period of two months' to obtain a license (MDA 2013). In addition, online news websites are also required to put up a bond worth S$50,000 (£25,000 or US$40,000 equivalent). While MDA states that these new regulations are meant to bring online media under the same regulations as traditional media platforms such as newspapers, initial reactions to this ruling have accused the MDA of trying to censor websites in an attempt to control what is being said about government policies on the Internet.

Due to this outlook, the nature of civil societies in Singapore would most likely remain in a nascent state, where it would be able to bring issues to the forefront but be unable to generate genuine change. This is an area in which the arts sector can play a part. Local artists and intellectuals have attempted to create debate and generate change by conducting their own public forums and creating an Arts Manifesto (2012) to address issues of the governance and practice of the arts in Singapore. While the Arts Manifesto focused on issues concerning the arts, it is also possible to see how issues of censorship and freedom of expression have bigger implications. Artists have also managed to gain representation within Parliament by coming together and supporting arts practitioners in becoming Nominated Members of Parliament.[10]

This chapter set out to explore how it was possible to view the arts sector as a group that demonstrates many of the traits of a civil society – creating opportunities where politically contentious issues can be debated and suggestions can be offered while also allowing citizens the space to discuss these topics without fear. While the ability to change policy is limited due to the denial of arts entertainment licenses or through censorship, being able to address these specific subject matters across the media still provides a platform to profile these issues to a wider audience. In the near future, it is likely that the relationship between the arts sector and the government will continue to be an uneasy and yet vital one for society in Singapore. By constantly negotiating with the state on the possibilities of change, the arts sector is fulfilling an important function in a city-state where the opportunities for a citizen to have his or her say are limited.

Notes

1. These documents are the Renaissance City Report (2000), the Creative Industries Development Strategy (2002), Renaissance City Report 2.0 (2003) and Renaissance City Report III in two parts (2008).
2. The arts and cultural sector would thus see the flourishing and co-existence of two different types of arts groups. In theatre, for example, groups such as the Singapore Repertory Theatre (SRT) would mostly present local versions of productions from Broadway in New York and the West End in London. At the same time, other theatre groups such as The Necessary Stage would focus on presenting work written by local writers. The existence of these groups serves to show that there is a diversity of audiences in Singapore as they compete for different types of audiences.
3. Exempted performances include 'getai,' 'lion' or 'dragon' dances or traditional cultural performances or those meant for children … performances of purely instrumental music (classical or otherwise), performances of classical music of ethnic origin, choral music, jazz music, performances of traditional dramas or folk dramas, for example, Bangsawan, conventional Shakespearean plays; performances of traditional puppetry or folk puppetry; performances of traditional or folk dance, performances of traditional opera from the East and the West; performances of ballroom or community dance including cha cha, foxtrot, rumba, salsa etc.; displays or exhibitions of art objects, paintings

in various mediums and commemorative items such as coins, stamps etc. (Censorship Review Committee 2010, p. 83).

4. Primary Six is the equivalent of Year 7 in the English School System or 7th Grade in the American School System.

5. In 1994, Catherine Lim would criticize aspects of the Singapore government through an editorial titled 'PAP and the People: A Great Affective Divide.' The government responded by stating that if she wished to air any political views, she should consider running for political office.

6. Foreign publications such as the Far Eastern Economic Review and the International Herald Tribune have been successfully sued for defamation and have had to pay fines for publishing articles that were critical of the Singapore government.

7. These funding guidelines were taken from the Seed Funding Grant Application but are also found in all its other grant applications.

8. The main issue with forum theatre is the nature of the performance itself, which is unscripted. In 1994, a performance artist was arrested after snipping off his pubic hair in protest to an anti-gay incident. Soon after, all funding of forum theatre was withdrawn, only to be reinstated in 2004.

9. W!ld Rice was formed in 2000 and quickly made its reputation through staging works by Singaporean writers as well as local adaptations of well-known works such as George Orwell's *Animal Farm*. The latter, could have been viewed as a comment on the current political situation in Singapore. It would continue to build on its reputation for dealing with social issues in Singapore through plays written by Singaporeans that addressed homosexuality (Eleanor Wong's *Trilogy* in 2003, Alfian Sa'at's *Asian Boys Trilogy* in 2004). In 2006, it would launch the highly successful Singapore Theatre Festival, which would champion local writing. The funding cut in 2009 could perhaps be viewed as rebuke for staging the play *The Campaign to Confer the Public Service Star on JBJ* in 2007 as well as for plays that were presented in the 2008 edition of the Singapore Theatre Festival that looked at Singapore's founding father, Sir Stamford Raffles, and also provided a discussion session that examined issues of religion and race, freedom of speech, and democracy. JBJ are the initials of J.B. Jeyeratnam, a prominent local opposition politician in Singapore.

10. The Singapore Parliament is made up of three different types of members. The first and largest group are the elected Members of Parliament (MPs). The second group, known as Non-Constituency Members of Parliament, are MPs who are not voted in at the General Elections. Up to nine of them can be appointed, and they belong to opposition political parties. The last group are Nominated Members of Parliament (NMPs) who are not affiliated with any political party and are meant to represent the views of the community. NMPs are appointed for 30 months by a Special Select Committee of Parliament.

References

Censorship Review Committee (2010) *Censorship Review Committee 2010 Report* (Singapore: CRC 2010 Secretariat).

Chia, A. (2010a) 'High-level Panel to Jazz Up Arts and Culture Scene', *Straits Times*, September 3.

Chia, A. (2010b) 'Funds Cut: Is it Censorship? Artists Say NAC's "Core Values" Criteria for Funding are Subjective', *Straits Times*, May 7.

Chia, A. (2010c) 'Cut and thrust of arts funding: Arts council should not use funding cuts to weed out critical Works', *Straits Times*, December 8.

Chang, T-C. and Lee, W-K. (2003) 'Renaissance City Singapore: A Study of Arts Spaces', *Area*, 35(2), 128–141.

Chong, T. (2010) 'The State and the New Society: The Role of the Arts in Singapore Nation-building', *Asian Studies Review*, 34, 131–149.

Chua, B-H. (1995) *Communitarian Ideology and Democracy in Singapore* (London and New York: Routledge).

Chua, B-H. (2005) 'Liberalization Without Democratization: Singapore in the Next Decade', in F. Loh and J. Öjendal (eds), *Southeast Asian Responses to Globalization Restructuring Governance and Deepening Democracy* (Denmark and Singapore: Nordic Institute of Asian Studies Press and Institute of Southeast Asian Studies).

Edwards, M. (2009) *Civil Society* (2nd edition) (Cambridge, UK and Malden, US: Polity Press).

Han, F-K., Fernandez, W. and Tan, S. (1997) *Lee Kuan Yew: The Man and His Ideas* (Singapore: Times Edition).

Hill, M. and Lian, K-F. (1995) *The Politics of Nation Building and Citizenship in Singapore* (London and New York: Routledge).

Ho, K-L. (2000) 'Citizen Participation and Policy Making in Singapore Conditions and Predicaments', *Asian Survey*, 40(3), 436–455.

Kenny, M. and Germain R.D. (2005) 'The Idea(l) of Global Civil Society Introduction', in M. Kenny and R.D. Germain (eds), *The Idea of Global Civil Society: Politics and Ethics in a Globalizing Era* (London and New York: Routledge).

Krishnan, S. (1997) 'Introduction', in S. Krishnan (ed.), *9 Lives 10 Years of Singapore Theatre 1987–1997* (Singapore: The Necessary Stage).

Lee, T. (2005) 'Gestural Politics: Civil Society in "New" Singapore', *Sojourn: Journal of Social Issues in Southeast Asia*, 20(2), 132–154.

Lee, E. (2008) *Singapore the Unexpected Nation* (Singapore: Institute of Southeast Asian Studies).

Lee, T. (2010) *The Media, Cultural Control and Government in Singapore* (London and New York: Routledge).

Mahtani, S. (2012) Pink Dot in Singapore Highlights Gay Rights Debate, http://blogs.wsj.com/searealtime/2012/07/02/pink-dot-in-singapore-highlights-changing-gay-rights-debate, date accessed May 30, 2013.

Media Development Authority (2013) Fact Sheet – Online News Sites to Be Placed On a More Consistent Licensing Framework as Traditional News Platforms, http://mda.gov.sg/NewsAndEvents/PressRelease/2013/Pages/28052013.aspx, date accessed May 30, 2013.

Ministry of Culture, Community and Youth (2012) *The Report of the Arts and Culture Strategic Review* (Singapore: Ministry of Culture, Community and Youth).

National Arts Council (2013) 'Seed Funding Grant Application Guidelines', http://nac.gov.sg/docs/grants/fy13-seed-grant-application-guidelines.pdf, date accessed May 30, 2013.

Tan, C. (2010) 'No Go for Arts Event; the Media Development Authority Wants Forum Theatre Piece to be Moved Indoors Due to Sensitive Nature of Topics', *Straits Times*, August 26.

Tan, C. (2011) 'Council to Give Arts Funding 25% Boost; 16 Groups to Get almost \$2 Million in Total', *Straits Times*, March 31.

Schiffauer, W. (2004) 'Cosmopolitans are Cosmopolitans: On the Relevance of Local Identification in Globalizing Society', in J. Friedman and S. Randeria (eds), *Worlds on the Move: Globalization, Migration and Cultural Security* (London and New York: I.B. Tauris).

Vasil, R. (2000) *Governing Singapore: A History of National Development and Democracy* (Australia: Allen and Unwin).

Wee, C.J. W-L. (2003) 'Creating High Culture in the Globalized "Culture Desert" of Singapore', *The Drama Review*, 47(4), 84–97.

7
ReOrienting Cultural Policy: Cultural Statecraft and Cultural Governance in Taiwan and China

Jerry C.Y. Liu

Culture, governance and cultural governance

Three key terms need to be defined in brevity – first of all, 'culture.' The multiplicity of meanings around the idea of culture and the inter-relationship of these meanings is well-recognized. However, the analysis here focuses mainly on the aspect of culture that is related to the deeply embedded values, beliefs, signifying system, or 'informing spirit' behind the perceivable activities of a society (Gong 1995, p. 41; Yu 1992, pp. 20–21), rather than taking culture in an all-encompassing and neutral sense, as the 'complex whole' of a society (Tylor 1958, p. 1), or 'a whole way of life' (Williams 1982, pp. xvi, 295) in the material world and everyday mundane. As to be illustrated in the memorials of Ming statecraft, this is particularly so in Chinese intellectual tradition. Culture can be seen as *'a particular way of life, which expresses certain meanings and values'* (Turner 1996, p. 52, the author's emphasis) and makes one group of people distinct from others. This, when applied to the pragmatics of policies, stands for the intrinsic values and meanings underlying a cultural institution, or a particular way of management and decision-making of culture in a state.

The practical and institutional sides of culture lead to another key concept of the study, 'governance.' In public administration, Rhodes (1996) specifies six uses of governance, including the minimal state, corporate governance, new public management, good governance, socio-cybernetic systems, and self-organizing networks. Rhodes asserts that governance throws new light on changes in government, including the hollowing out of the state, new public management, and intergovernmental management. These are a challenge to governability because they become autonomous and resist central guidance. Taking on the issue of culture and governance, Valentine (2002, p. 53) suggests governance is the governmentality of postmodern culture, of culture without authority. Governance has emerged as the replacement of a top-down structure of rule by a differentiated polity of networks without a single direction-determining center.

Along this line, Dillon and Valentine (2002) emphasize that governance abandons the concern with overarching cultural representations and is devoted to the invention of diverse practices situated within and drawing upon the cultural heterogeneity and dynamics that constitute its condition of operation. For Bennett (1998, p. 110), the novelty of governance is that it continues the aim of governmentality to make populations self-regulating. Recent studies on culture and governance indicate that self-governing, decentralization, or diverse forms of collaboration, participation and networking among governments and other agents are key features of governance.

In the face of a global 'cultural turn,' the concept of 'cultural governance' becomes powerful because it elegantly brings together the idea of culture, which embraces notions of aesthetic, artistic, historical values and beliefs, and the symbolic exchange of meaning of a society on the one hand; and the concept of governance, which connotes new designs of power, resource allocation, government, organizational control, senses of decentralization, networking, partnership, communication, self-reflection and self-regulation on the other hand (Liu 2011). Stuart Hall (1997, p. 238) even pleads to 'place culture at the center' of governance and to 'rule by culture.' Focusing on culture as the 'signifying system' has resulted in this chapter developing its framework of cultural governance in the following three interrelated and interpenetrated analytical levels:[1]

a) Cultural governance as 'regulating the public through culture': This means, first, the management, administration or regulation of public cultural affairs such as the governing/administering of arts, heritage and cultural industries via regulation and support (cultural policy in a narrower sense). Besides, it is also taken to include the state's civilizing process of public manners and behaviors through cultural institutions, media and public forums (cultural governance from the top-down).

b) Cultural governance as 'the self-regulation and self-reflection of both the governed and governors': Cultural governance opens up the possibilities of the self-governing of the conduct/ethics/morality of both policymakers themselves (cultural governance from inside-out) and of citizens (by preventing the governors from misconduct and by allowing the governed to develop a multiple-centered and collaborative form of network governance). Such a rise of self-awareness and autonomy of citizens (cultural governance from the bottom-up) gains ground to be differentiated from the Gramscian notion of 'cultural hegemony.'

c) Cultural governance as 'governing by culture': This denotes that the government does not only take culture as the rhetoric or means, but also as the ends of governance. Cultural governance in this context stands not only for art-cultural administration, but also how cultural values and ideas in the symbolic communication process can be placed at the center of all political and economic policy debates (cultural governance in a much wider sense). By adhering to the embedded cultural values of a society, the state cultural institutions are situated in a specific cultural milieu; hence, they reveal a particular way of management and governance (cultural governance from outside in).

Based on the above-defined levels of cultural governance (hereafter referred to as 'Cultural Governance (a), (b), or (c)'), I ask, is it is possible to envision a localized discourse of cultural governance in Taiwan and China? If so, what is its content? How would it differ from Western discourses? And what pragmatic implications would it carry? By looking into the historic works of Chinese cultural statecraft (*jingshi* or *jingji* in the *Collected Essays on Royal Ming Statecraft* of the late 14th to 17th century),[2] the chapter explores the possibilities of applying Oriental cultural logics to cultural policy in Taiwan, and to a lesser extent, China today, as well as its limitations.

Discourses of cultural governance in the Occident

In modern Western intellectual tradition, three particular discourses lead in the discussion of cultural governance and cultural policy, namely, the state, market and communication (McGuigan 2004). This chapter deals mainly with the state. The Western state-culture arguments, particularly the realist state, often resort to the power, interest and institution discourses. These can be traced from Machiavelli's *The Prince*, A. Gramsci's (1971) cultural hegemony, L. Althusser's (1971) ideological state apparatus, to that of M. Foucault (1991) and T. Bennett's (1998, 2007) culture and governmentality. Foucault and Bennett take special notice of the cultural elements in government and probe into the governing rationality, mentality and technology of the state. For them, modern European cultural institutions (such as museums, libraries and galleries) are new governmental instruments, which serve to construct and defend the public space as rational and scientific. The specializing and classifying institutions that perform as parts of the well-managed and calculated state regime, seek to regulate and civilize the morals, manners and conducts of the population (CG (a)) (Bennett 1995, p. 22). Along with the process of modernization, an instrumental mode of government that emphasizes goal-achievement evaluation, self-interest, managerial efficiency, and check and balance of powers starts to play an upper hand in modern European regimes of cultural governance.

I do not mean that there is no humanistic tradition in the West. And I do note that European scholars (especially the postmodernists) are devising a far more humanistic and decentered approach in cultural policy and governance. Yet, as Parsons observed, the rationalistic thought and scientific spirit in Europe, which began in the 12th century and culminated in the 17th and 18th centuries' Enlightenment, 'liberated' human thinking from the confinement of religious and cultural traditions. This way of thinking has since then permeated European society. A calculative and empirical logic, which justified the 'dehumanizing tendency' by praising human rationality in pursuing profitable goals with practical means, thus was often labelled as 'instrumental.' Under this very process, the concept of 'rationality' becomes more and more 'identified with interest – concern with a thing or person only in so far as it or he may be usable as a means or should be taken account of as an intrinsically relevant condition' (Parsons 1937, p. 660). This much-reduced narrative of Occidental governmentality, however, still carries some truth in it today. It is a matter of degree or propensity. The Confucian way of cultural governance *before* the West is a very different one.

Confucian *jingshi* learning: Chinese cultural statecraft *before* the West

Analyzing the scholarship of cultural policy and governance studies in Taiwan and China, one finds that very few actually bother to look into the historiography of Chinese cultural governance before 1895 (Japanese occupation of Taiwan). Many use the convenient textbook history to give Taiwanese cultural governance a conformed periodization of the political-economic centered historic account (that is, the international competition period, Ming Zheng's Rule Period, Qing Chinese *feudal* period (1640s–1894), Japanese colonial period (1895–1945) and KMT authoritarian period). The political-economic centered interpretation often gives the earlier Taiwanese/Chinese cultural policy a feudalist outlook, which then follows a dis-embedded Western theorization of an authoritarian state and ideological control. Since it neglects the potent connectivity and transformation of the traditional Chinese cultural rationality in China and Taiwan, it fails to provide the present of Taiwanese cultural governance a proper discourse. It also fails to explain the recurring morally and ethically oriented cultural logics for cultural policy in Taiwan and China. We need a *ReOrientation* of the history of cultural governance.

Taking the earlier definitions and benchmarks of cultural governance, one finds the function of Ming Chinese cultural statecraft innovative or even postmodern. Firstly, culture in the form of embedded ideals and values was (is) placed very much at the center of traditional Chinese statecraft (CG (c)). The Ming Chinese *jingshi* learning or the concept of *jingshi zhiyong*, which is often translated as Chinese 'statecraft,' literally means to manage the world or the age through classic learning so as to elaborate its pragmatic efficacy. Such terms express the Confucian commitment to apply practical solutions for the improvement of the world, while carrying 'simultaneously a moral orientation, a repertoire of practical activity, and a category of knowledge' (Brook 2000). Ming Chinese *jingshi* learning provides a cultural-historically specific context for the ReOrient thesis, through which one may explore the interpenetrating relations between culture, government, and political economy.

Secondly, traditional discourses of government in China manifest a peculiar characteristic of self-restraint (conduct of conduct for the governed as well as the governors, that is, CG (b)), which could hardly be found in Europe after Machiavelli. Such a self-restraining feature was reflected in the Chinese state's idealistic governing principle that Confucius termed *weizheng yide* ('to rule by virtue or benevolence'). By this Confucius meant that instead of using political interests and criminal punishments as the standards of governance, the rulers or politicians should 'guide people with virtue, and rule them with rites or courtesies' (*The Analects* 1954, section 2).

In Liu (2008), during the Ming Dynasty (1367–1572), among 899 compiled official correspondences to the throne,[3] nearly 30% of them addressed issues specifically about the tradition of virtuous rule. Most of the letters were reminders for the emperor to obey the sacred teachings, rituals, or ancestral instructions, and to reject unnecessary luxuries, pleasures, and tributes from abroad (see Table 7.1). The second largest category regards the judiciary, honor and impeachment of bureaucrats, which accounts for another 21.8 % of the communications. Since the contents of the letters were circulating mainly on issues of promoting the integral conducts and suppressing the disloyal or indecent behaviors or corruptions of the bureaucrats, memoranda under this heading can be taken as the reciprocal moral and ethical restraints among the civil officials (this represents both CG (a), a top-down model of civilizing process, and CG (b), self-regulating governors).

Beyond these two headings, there are letters concerning institutions, technology and procedures of government. Not only are the ratios of the 'non-ruling-virtue-centered' memorials low, even in communications

Table 7.1 Classification of letters from Chinese civil officers to the emperor at Ming times (c. 1367–1572)

Number classifications		Number of letters		Percentage	
1. Virtuous Rule	1.1 Sacred Teachings, Rites and Ancestral Instruction	265	224	29.5%	24.9%
	1.2 Declining Luxuries, Pleasures and Tributes		41		4.6%
2. Judiciary, Honoring the Decent and Impeaching Misconduct		192		21.4%	
3. Civil Service and Current Affairs		104		11.5%	
4. Finance, Taxation and Labor Recruitment		76		8.5%	
5. Infrastructure, Welfare and Social Orders		64		7.1%	
6. Military and Security		133		14.8%	
7. Feudal Awards and Palace Affairs		65		7.2%	
Total		899		100%	

Source: Sun Xun ed. Huang Ming Shu Chao (Transcripts of the Royal Ming Memoranda). d. 1584. Collected in Xu-Xiu Si-Ku Quan-Shu (Compilation of the Sequel to Complete Collection of the Four Treasuries). Vol. 463–464. Shanghai, Shanghai Gu-Ji Publisher, 1995 Reprints; Jia San-Jin ed., Huang Ming Liang Chao Shu Chao (Transcripts on the Royal Ming Memoranda in Jia-Jing and Long-Qing Reigns) (1522–1572), Zhang Han ed., Huang Ming Shu Yi Ji Lue (Selective Compilations of the Royal Ming Memoranda), d. 1551. (Liu 2008).

regarding finance, taxation, and security issues, an overpowering moral cultural argument still overshadows the context. The focus of official letters reflects very much the benevolent ruling principle of the Ming. The figures stand for the authentic view of how the Ming civil officers or literati (here the editors of essays) visualize the 'conduct of conduct,' or the mentality of governors. And despite oppositions, the idealistic ruling principles were put into practice in the finance, taxation, and foreign trade policies of the Ming state rather than merely presented as a bureaucratic rhetoric.[4] Cultural ideals and values were placed at the center of political and economic policy debates and agendas (CG (c)).

The statistical breakdown of traditional Chinese *jingshi* works illustrates clearly the ReOrient thesis of cultural governance. Chinese *jingshi* practices or governmentality were probably never so good at maximizing the state's profit and wealth and power, the precision of number, and the efficiency, efficacy, procedure, and technologies of governments compared to the modern Western state apparatuses, institutions, policy-making and implementation after the 17th and 18th century. However, it should be noted that such thoughts and conducts of self-reflexivity, self-constraining and self-regulation are emphasized from inside by the governors themselves (CG (b)), which in the contemporary context resembles the postmodern reform of 'cultural governance' in Valentine (2002) and Dillon's and Valentine's (2002) sense afore.

ReOrienting contemporary cultural policy

Cultural administration and policy in Taiwan (1950s–2010s): a brief sketch

Due to earlier Japanese occupation (1895–1945) and the direct military threat from the People's Republic of China (PRC) from the Nationalist government's retreat to Taiwan in 1949 to the 1960s, the main efforts of state cultural policy had been focused on getting rid of Japanese colonial culture and the re-establishment of the traditional Confucian order. Based on General CHIANG Kai-Shek's *Two Papers on Education and Entertainment* in supplement to Dr. SUN Yat-San*'s Principle of People's Livelihood* in 1953, cultural policy in Taiwan adhered to a very strong flavor of Confucian moral-ethical didacticism (Yang 2000, p. 53; Chiang 1985, pp. 307–402).

In contrast to the PRC's devastating Cultural Revolution during the 1960s, the government of Taiwan carried out the so-called 'Chinese Cultural Renaissance Movements,' which aimed to conserve traditional Chinese cultural roots in Taiwan, and serve as a counter- ideological and cultural war to MAO Zedong's Communist regime. Official brochures like the *Models for Citizen Etiquette, Essential Information for the Citizen's Daily Life,* and *Acts for Promoting Thrift in Ceremonies of Folk Religion* were devised to promote Confucian teachings such as the pursuit of a simple, plain and frugal life. Even dramas that were performed outside a temple were asked to follow the principles of loyalty, filial piety, moral integrity and righteousness. Under the dual cultural and political considerations, the Committee for Promoting Chinese Cultural Reconstruction Movement was established in 1967. The philosophy behind such moral-ethical didacticism was an extension of traditional Chinese thought for unified and balanced material and spiritual relations in human lives. Culture evolving along this Ming and Qing Confucian *jingshi* legacy means a continuous civilizing process and social cultivation under the guidance of moral and ethical values (CG (a)) (Liu 2006; Gong 1995, p. 41; Yu 1992, pp. 20–21).

The 1970s–1980s was a period of deregulation. Since 1977, the Executive Yuan of Taiwan announced another five-year plan to consolidate cultural construction, with the emphasis on education and recreation. The Council of Cultural Affairs (CCA) was founded on 11 November 1981 as the highest central cultural administrative body to coordinate and *guide* (still) the various ministries and councils to promote national culture. With Western influences, the CCA started to address concrete measures in preserving local cultural heritages, promoting culture, artistic activities, and folk arts. The series of deregulating measures in culture peaked on 15 July 1987, when Taiwan lifted martial law.

The cultural outset of Taiwan changed drastically in the 1990s, due to the abolishment of martial law, along with restrictions on establishing political parties and mass media. Since the lifting of these restrictions, the newspaper industry thrived. Corresponding growth can be observed in the number of radio stations, which grew from 31 in 1971 to 174 in 2003. In 2003, there were 51 cable radios and TV systems in Taiwan with more than 100 channels, whose programes ranged from music, sports, children's education, cartoon, news, drama, movie, religion, stock market, and discovery channels to glove puppet shows and local variety shows (CCA 2004). The modern, postmodern and multicultural currents were rampant throughout the island during the 1990s and 2000s. The indigenous ethnic and 'New Taiwanese' consciousness, together with the emerging demands of cultural facilities from the population, pushed the government to re-evaluate its cultural policy fundamentally. Thus, one starts to see the emergence of a bottom-up civilian and medium self-autonomy and self-regulation in Taiwan (CG (b)). In

May 2000, the pro-independent Democratic Progressive Party's new government re-designated Taiwan's cultural policy to foster a 'renaissance of Taiwanese culture' (Liu 2006).

The 2000 and 2004 Cultural White Paper (CCA 2000, 2004) still stresses attaining guiding principles and objectives such as 'rectifying the fast-food culture mentality' and 'unifying cultural administrative authority.' Pursuing a modern outlook on cultural policy, the CCA also called for the public to participate actively in cultural activities to cultivate cultural creativity and competitiveness. It encouraged corporate sponsorship, investment or patronage of arts groups and activities, and highlights the integration of culture, education and technology. Moreover, extending art to the countryside and equipping young children and people in the grassroots with competencies in art appreciation, the CCA (2001) stepped up promotion of popular art in schools at every level (a top-down, then bottom-up, policy approach). The deregulated creative industries sought to unleash their inner dynamism through all possible forms, including newspapers, cinemas, cable TVs, leisure farms, hotels, plaza hotels, resorts and resort hotels, clubs, theme parks and shopping malls (Zhang and Lin 2000, p. 4). The diverse cultural practices of people now came hand-in-hand with the profit-making creative industries. They put the state's didactic interventions of culture under direct challenge. The two levels of cultural governance (that is, cultural governance as civilizing process and as self-regulating process) therefore collaborate at certain junctures, and at times contradict each other, in Taiwan.

2012 was a significant year for cultural governance in Taiwan. The establishment of a new Ministry of Culture (MOC) marked a new era for Taiwanese cultural policy. On 20 May 2012, the MOC replaced the former CCA and became the highest administrative body. As stipulated in Article 2 of the Organization Act of Ministry of Culture, the competences of the Ministry included the drafting, planning and promotion of cultural policy and cultural regulations; and the founding, supervision, managing, supporting, rewarding, and promotion of cultural facilities, institutions, heritages, museums, community regeneration, arts, and life aesthetics. The MOC was also expanded to incorporate new competences in the areas of radio, TV, film, popular music, publication, creative industries, and training of cultural talents. The new Minister, LUNG Ying-Tai, announced her four new policy objectives as the reification of cultural rights for citizens, development of an creative environment for aestheticism, conservation and assurance of cultural values (history, democracy, openness, freedom, and diversity all lead to the assurance of Taiwan's cultural value), and the promotion of competitiveness for creative industries. Policy measures of soilization (the grass root approach), internationalization, and cloudization (digitalization) would converge and contribute to Taiwan's soft power.

In 2013, the MOC restarted the legislation process of the Culture Basic Law to instigate a comprehensive restructuring of the regime of cultural governance (Liu 2013). The expansion of the MOC and a newly conceived Culture Basic Law suggest the extension of a conventional cultural policy from a narrower sense to a much wider context of cultural governance in Taiwan today.

Culture and civil service system in Taiwan

Since the 3rd century, the Chinese government had recruited civil officers from intellectuals in the plebeian stratum through public examination. By the end of AD 1000, some 400,000 candidates sat exams each year, with hundreds of aspirants chasing an official post (O'Brien et al. 1999, p. 86). In 2011, there were 343,323 civil servants in Taiwan, within a population of 23 million. And in 2012, 105,487 examinees vied for 5,927 positions in state civil examinations, with an average recruiting rate of 5.62%. As the NDTV (2013) reports, around 40% of university students in Taiwan are willing to undertake civil examinations so as to be able to work for the government, while the ratio in China is even higher at 76.5%, compared to only 3% in the US (and 5.3% in France).

Confucian canons have been the main texts of exams after the Song-Ming periods (Jin and Liu 1994, p. 97), and the underlying ethos and values have long become the repertoires and blueprints of civil servants' cultural engineering in China. The figures above indicate that there exists a much wider and deeper connection between the state cultural governors and the self-regulating intellectuals in Taiwan and China, in both their value and knowledge base. As the civil exam system carries on in Taiwan and China today, Confucian teachings still serve as the bedrock of cultural governance for all civil officers.

The Examination Yuan (2012) is the highest civil examination authority in Taiwan. With the Ministry of Examination, they set the examining subjects, traits of specialized knowledge, and core competencies, and institute professional ethics for all civil servants. Emphasis on fostering a self-regulating governor or cultural bureaucrat through Confucian ideals still forms the overtone of contemporary civil exams (CG (b)). Chinese Language, for instance, is a compulsory exam subject for all civil posts. The 2009 composition topic requested the examinees to elucidate the role of modern public civil servants (it counts for 60%). The instructions read,

> Civil officers in the past had to commit all their efforts and minds to serve the people. They shouldn't abuse their position and power, manipulate the rule and make things difficult, and they must not be corrupt. The Song Emperor Taizhong quoted the writing of the Lord Meng Su of the Later Shu Kingdom, and wrote down the *Maxim for Civil Officials* in person. It was promulgated to the country and was inscribed on big stones to alert all civil officers in the state ... This is the so-called 'Stone Inscribed Commandment.' Please set your own title and elaborate the meaning of the quote. (Ministry of Examination 2009)

In 2012, examinees were asked to elaborate upon the theme of 'How a modern civil servant should act to measure the sense of humanness, practical reason and regulations, while adhering to the refining principle of integrity and self-cultivation with a benevolent heart so that he/she can provide satisfactory service for the public.' Again, this alone contained a weightage of 60% of the Chinese Language subject.

It is not difficult at all to define the 'conduct of conduct' of civil servants in Taiwan. Cultural bureaucrats are recruited via a rigorous exam based on Confucian values. They are expected to embrace core values such as integrity, loyalty to the Constitution and State, the heart of benevolence, and frugality, declining lavishness, and behaving virtuously. 'Modern' and 'instrumental' capabilities such as efficiency, professional expertise, management skills, creativity, and an innovative spirit in administration are further developed around the core ethos. They are considered as key 'pragmatic' competences of the civil officers today.

State intervention in media and public cultural forums

Cultural governance, as the symbolic communication of moral-ethical values and meanings, can be best observed in governmental intervention in media and public cultural forums. A typical example is China's recent announcement of an Order on the Restriction of Entertainment. In 2011, the State Administration of Radio, Film and Television (SARFT 2011) in China released an official Opinion about Strengthening the Management of Programs in Satellite Television Variety Channels (hereafter the Opinion). The Opinion requests the 34 satellite television variety channels to (a) increase the percentages (no less than two hours per day) of news and economic, cultural, educational, documentary and children programs; (b) create a new TV program category called the Reconstruction of Thoughts and Morality to promote Chinese traditional virtues and the core value system of socialism; (c) adhere to the priority of social benefits, and to insist on the organic integration of social and economic benefits so as to establish a scientifically objective and just general evaluation system on TV programs (based not only on audience ratings, but also on the impact of audience guidance, influence, program dissemination, and professionalism); (d) to designate experts in all administration apparatuses to monitor and inspect the problem of vulgar tendencies after 1 January 2012. Any programs that contain problematic portrayals of political, value and stylish orientations will be issued warnings, criticized, and ordered to revise their programmes, and will have their broadcasting time adjusted, or may even be banned, depending on the extent and degree to which they have breached the principles. The Opinion explains that many television channels have invited Hong Kong and Taiwanese stars to attend variety show programs, at which critical problems of vulgar and immoral social behaviors have occurred. It argues that these have seriously influenced the audience's spiritual life, their pursuit of the spiritual and aesthetic worlds, and the practices of social moralities and norms (SARFT 2012; *Beijing Daily* 2011).

On 9 April 2012, the Deputy Director of SARFT stated that after 100 days of the implementation of The Opinion, the screen media was much cleaner, better, and healthier. First, the prime time TV programs became far more various. The number of entertainment-oriented programs dropped from 126 to 38. Second, more than 20 new news programs that provided guidance to the public forum, and broadcasting hours were increased by one-third compared to the same period the previous year. Third, 36 new TV programs were created to strengthen the principles of moral reconstruction. The 34 satellite television channels adhere to the Confucian ethos that literature or 'culture is a vehicle to carry out the function of Tao' (*People's Daily* 2012). There is clearly an influence of official moral idealism and didacticism present here.

Many would argue that China's overtly top-down media policy has no scope for cultural governance, as cultural governance is supposed to be done 'indirectly' by giving freedom and autonomy to people and allowing them to self-govern their conduct. LIU Sun-Heng (2012) asserts that media and entertaining programs are solely reflecting the social reality, therefore the government should not simply beautify the reality by promoting healthy and harmonious images on the screen. In my opinion, what is manifested is another explicit contradiction in cultural governance that is between a civilizing process (CG (a)) where the state tries to directly address problems that it see seriously affecting the public's spiritual life, and the citizenry's pursuit of self-governance and cultural autonomy (CG (b)), where so-called vulgar values and behavior are considered part of individual choice and freedom, even if they are morally degrading. Obviously, here, a 'civilizing' state has triumphed over its citizens in China.

Turning to Taiwan, 2012 was also a significant year for its cultural public sphere. The scandal around 'Dreamers' (an expensive stage performance) highlighted alleged corruption and misallocation of state art subsidies during the celebration of the ROC's 100th anniversary and resulted in a controversy about state cultural governance. Despite a later decision of non-prosecution, the former chair of CCA stepped down due to the 'Dreamers' event. Following this event, a group of cultural activists and art curators in Taiwan established the Preparatory Office for the Foundation for the Renewal of Culture. The Foundation called for autonomy and diversity of art and culture in Taiwan, and subsequently organized a public petition to seek support for its nine major requests to 'improve' cultural policy. Here the cultural activists and curators have pointed out the limitations of traditional Confucian cultural governance. Even cultural bureaucrats, who are selected via the exam system based on the Confucian ideal, cannot withstand the challenges of commercial allures in Taiwan.

Nonetheless, due to the pressure of public forums and intense media coverage, for the first time in Taiwanese history, candidates for the office of the President, including the incumbent President MA Yingju, had to participate in an open debate focusing solely on the issues of cultural policy in Taiwan. 12 questions (ranging from the allocation of state cultural budget to cultural rights) were directed to the candidates during the debate by 12 renowned artists and cultural workers in Taiwan. The three-hour cultural policy debate was broadcast to the general public live on air and online by the Taiwan Public Television Service in 2012. Following that, the new Minister of Culture even felt obliged to convene nine consecutive National Forums on Cultural Affairs between 28 June and 16 August in 2012.

An explicit contradiction occurred again between the two different levels of cultural governance in Taiwan. Yet, unlike the case in China, the top-down state civilizing model (CG (a)) seems to give way to the ideals of self-restraining governors and the citizen's self-regulating cultural public sphere or media forum (CG(b)).

It is true that the pervasive Oriental moral-ethical value orientations give a much wider space for the state to intervene in media and public cultural forums, yet the 'articulation of politics, public and person, as a contested terrain through affective – aesthetic and emotional – modes of communication' (McGuigan 2010, p. 15) also encourages the general public in Taiwan to engage more rigorously in mass media policy reforms and the cultural public sphere above. Borrowing Michel de Certeau's words (1984, pp. xi–v), citizens in Taiwan seem to be subverting the state imposed Confucian moral-ethical order not by rejecting it, or devising a new order, but by accepting it and re-appropriating it. Instead of revolting against the state's cultural strategy, people in Taiwan are making use of the Confucian order by taking it for granted in their everyday lives, and applying this embedded value system in turn to constrain their governors and impel them to 'self-regulate.' Decision makers are asked to conform to such self-imposed ruling principles in order to gain their political legitimacy. Culture, in the way of tactics, is influencing the practice of policymakers by containing them in a self-imposed cultural or moral milieu, within which public policies are set into culture and values debates (again CG (c)) (Liu 2008).

Conclusion: a paradigm shift of cultural governance?

People in the West today probably find it difficult to accept notions of 'instruction,' or 'rectification' of culture. Even though culture in an artistic, musical, and idealistic form still retains its function of elevating the people's mindset, no policymaker in the West today would use terms such as 'moral purification' as a principle of cultural policy.[5] The emphasis on the meaning and spirit of the cultural system, or the 'deep structure or subconscious of culture' (Sun 1992, pp. 6–7), however, has been a persistent feature in the Northeast Asian states' cultural legacy and cultural policies (Liu 2009, p. 200). We recognize that the notion of 'self-regulation' may, in a way, connote the public's (or the governed's) 'self-acting imperative' or 'self-management' to conform to the norms and forms of behaviors that are promoted by governments (Bennett 1995, p. 23). The Confucian pro-humanistic rationality, however, does reveal a peculiar trait of self-restraint and self-reflexivity of the governors, too, which is rarely found in modern Western discourses. ReOrienting, therefore, can be seen as both the cultural governance from inside-out and a particular cultural governance in the Confucian way.

The investigation of Chinese *jingshi* statecraft shows the possibility of ReOrienting in cultural governance. The long-standing civil servant exam in China and Taiwan is a clear manifestation of such aspirations and ideals. However, as is revealed by the examples of Chinese media policy and Taiwan's 'Dreamers' event, there are still gaps between cultural governance as logic/ideal and cultural governance as reality. The self-restraining civil service system does not always prevent the governor from misallocating cultural resources and stop the alleged abuse of the governor's personal relations. At the same time, overemphasis on a pro-humanistic cultural logic comes at the cost of the precision of quantitative figures, and the efficiency and efficacy of the state's governing technologies. In addition, a government of virtue or goodwill does not, in reality, prevent it from instigating strong censorship and suppression of civilians' freedom of expression. All these point to the limitations of traditional Oriental cultural statecraft.

One way to fill the gaps is the 'reflexivity' found in the activities of Taiwanese cultural activists and curators, and their calls for a self-autonomous cultural public sphere, within which the state cultural policy can be monitored, reviewed, and reoriented from the bottom-up. Such reflection (involving civil actors) could be seen as a modern revision, reinterpretation and reapplication of Confucian logics in contemporary cultural governance. Cultural governance therefore stands for both the self-regulation of the governors and the rise of self-awareness of the governed in Taiwan. Apart from reflexivity, citizens in Taiwan today subvert the superimposed Confucian moral-ethical order, not by protesting against it, but by re-appropriating it. The moral-ethical values are taken as a commonsensical order in people's everyday lives, and all policymakers are in turn circumscribed by such a self-imposed order to govern themselves.

To make sense of modern cultural governance in Taiwan and China, what is needed is a 'cultural turn' or even 'paradigm shift' of governance. Such a cultural turn indicates a shift of the underlying governing rationale from that of Machiavellian interest, instrumental calculation, wealth and power, and government technology, to that of symbolic exchanges and culture debates – value, aesthetics, moral-ethical ideals, and humanistic traits (Liu 2011). By ReOrienting, I therefore mean to 'reflect,' 'reinterpret,' and 're-appropriate' the Confucian or East Asian cultural values and reflexively examine their roles in shaping both the discourse and practice of cultural policy. Western discourses cannot simply be transplanted into Taiwan and China today. For the East, one has to start thinking of cultural governance by bridging the Western cultural modernities with embedded Oriental values such as humanness, unity, benevolence, virtuous rule, moral integrity, loyalty and sentiments of aestheticism.

Going back to my initial analytical framework, cultural governance thus suggests not only the administration or regulation of the public art affairs (CG (a)). It means also to self-regulate through culture, to rule by culture, and to place culture at the center of all policy-making processes (CG (c)). The ReOrienting of cultural governance therefore signifies a re-articulation of value and meaning with modern bureaucratic calculation and efficiency in cultural administration. In a way, the East and the West become their mutual remedies in cultural governance.

Notes

1. The author appreciates the pertinent comments from the editors, who helped to clarify the three analytical levels of cultural governance.
2. I have examined the documents of the Ming Dynasty (1368–1644) for two main reasons. First, it is only in the late period of the Ming that European missionaries and delegates arrived in China and initiated systematic contact with the Chinese empire. Analyses of the Ming statecraft literature would reveal a pre-European influenced governmentality in China. Secondly, the late Ming Dynasty is also the critical period when Chinese intellectuals started compiling sequential civil officers' memorials to the emperor to test the pragmatic efficacy of Confucian classics.
3. As cited in Table 7.1, the 899 letters were selectively compiled in the *Transcripts of the Royal Ming Memoranda* (d. 1584), *Transcripts on the Royal Ming Memoranda in Jia-Jing and Long-Qing Reigns* (d. 1522–1572) and *Selective Compilations of the Royal Ming Memoranda* (d. 1551) by Ming scholars and officers. The percentages presented here are derived from a calculation of the compiled letters rather than of their absolute numbers. Since the ratios of letters under similar subheadings generally conform to one another across most compiled versions, it is reasonable to projects that such proportions stand for an authentic view of how the Ming civil officers or literati visualize the weight or balance among various state affairs, to which they thought the rulers and bureaucrats should dedicate their efforts accordingly. Carrying the study to the Qing regime, Liu (2010) categorizes another 12,157 pieces of writing across the 10 selected editions of *Collected Essays Imperial Qing Statecraft* (*Huangchao Jingshi Wenbian*) and its 22 sequels between 1776 and 1902, and finds a very similar cultural milieu of governmentality during the Qing China before 1895. From the late Ming period to the early Republic of China, more than 30 million words were published and republished in the format of collected essays of Qing statecraft. There is little doubt that the Ming and Qing collected essays on statecraft had formulated the persisting *jingshi* learning for modern Chinese intellectual tradition.
4. As Liu (2008) continues to argue, even the state bureaucracy realized that such cultural ideals might pragmatically contradict the fiscal and material interests of the state; the idealistic ruling principles had been put into practice in the

finance, taxation, and foreign trade policies of the Ming rather than stayed as governmental rhetoric. Due to the length limit here, we cannot examine the details of the Ming policy implementation.

5. It should be noted that similar things were spoken in 1950s France (Malraux) and 1970s Britain (Shaw), and I thank the reviewer for making the point. Yet, it is also clear that such European discourses did not carry in them a potent European 'legacy of statecraft' or 'regime of governmentality.' And we find neither strong European intellectual support, nor widespread popular reception, behind them today.

References

N.A. (1954) *The Analects*. Section 2 (Taipei: Qi-Ming Bookstore, Reprints).

Althusser, L. (1971) *Lenin and Philosophy and Other Essays* (London: New Left Books).

N.A. (2011) SARFT's Press Conference on the Opinion, *Beijing Daily*, http://zhengwu.beijing.gov.cn/zcjd/gjzcjd/ t1201387.htm, 27 October 2011, date accessed October 1, 2012.

Bennett, T. (1995) *The Birth of the Museum* (London and New York: Routledge).

Bennett, T. (1998) *Culture: A Reformer's Science* (London: Sage).

Bennett, T. (2007) *Critical Trajectories: Culture, Society and Intellectuals* (Oxford: Blackwell).

Brook, T. (2000) The Milieux of Scientific Activity in Ming China. Paper presented in the Conference on Regimes for the Generation of Useful and Reliable Knowledge in Europe and Asia 1368–1815, Windsor Great Park, April 14–16, 2000.

Council of Cultural Affairs. (2000) *Cultural White Paper* (Taipei: Council for Cultural Affair).

Council of Cultural Affairs. (2001) The Major Cultural Task for Council for Cultural Affairs (in Chinese), http://www.cca.gov.tw/, date accessed July 1, 2003.

Council of Cultural Affairs. (2004) *Cultural White Paper* (Taipei: Council for Cultural Affairs).

Chiang, K-S. (1985, First Published in 1953.) 'Two Supplementary theses of Education and Leisure to the Principle of People's Livelihood', in Sun Yat-San, *Three Principles of People* (in Chinese) (Taipei: Zhongyang Wenwe Publisher)

De Certeau, M. (1984) *The Practice of Everyday Life*. Steven Rendall (trans.) (Berkeley, Los Angeles and London: University of California Press).

Dillon, M. and Valentine, J. (2002) 'Introduction: Culture and Governance', *Cultural Values*, 6 (1& 2), 5–9.

Examination Yuan (2011) Introduction: Forward http://www.exam.gov.tw/cp.asp?xItem=1726&ctNode= 602&mp=5, date accessed October 12, 2012.

Foucault, M. (1991) 'Governmentality', in G. Burchill, C. Gordon and P. Miller (eds), *The Foucault Effect: Studies in Governmentality* (Chicago: University of Chicago Press).

Gong, P-C. (1995) *Thinking and Culture* (in Chinese) (Taipei: Yechiang Publisher).

Gramsci, A. (1971) *Selection from the Prison Notebooks*. Quentin Hoare and Geoffrey Nowell Smith (eds and trans.) (New York: International Publishers Co.).

Hall, S. (1997) 'The Centrality of Culture: Notes on the Cultural Revolutions of Our Time', in K. Thompson (ed.), *Media and Cultural Regulation* (London: Sage).

Jin, Guantao and Liu Qingfeng. (1994) *Prosperity and Crisis* (In Chinese) (Taipei: Fengyun Shidai).

Liu, J.C.Y. (2011) 'Discourses and Networks of Cultural Governance in Europe: A Critical Review' (in Chinese), *Intergrams*, 11(2), 1–15.

Liu, J.C.Y. (2013) 'Culture Basic Law: A Critical Reflection on Academia's Participation in the Legislative Process' (in Chinese), *Journal of the State and Society*, 13(3), 67–112.

Liu, J.C.Y. (2006) 'Leisure Governance in Transition: The Case of Taiwan', *Journal of Leisure Studies* 4(1), 73–91.

Liu, J.C.Y. (2008) 'Does Culture Matter? The Logics and Counter-logics of Culture in State Finance, Taxation and Tributary Trade Policies during the Ming Times c. 1300–1600', *The Icfai Journal of History and Culture*, 2(1), 24–60.

Liu, J.C.Y. (2009) 'Unity vis-à-vis Diversity: The Cultural Logics of Chinese and European Cultural Strategies through Macro-history', in Stephen Chan and Cerwyn Moore (eds), *Approaches to International Relations* (Volume 4) (London: Sage).

Liu, J.C.Y. (2010) The Logics of Soft Power: Culturing Chinese Statecraft in Modern World History (1826–1902). 2010 RCIA International Symposium on Culture and Political Economy: New Perspectives. Wenzao Ursuline College of Languages, Kaohsiung, Taiwan, September 17–19.

Liu, S-H. (2012) 'Comments on China: The Rigid Format of TV Program Caused by "The Order of Restriction on Entertainment" is not a Good Model' (in Chinese) *BBC*, http://www.bbc.co.uk/zhongwen/trad/comments_on_china/2011/10/111028_coc_china_tv_show.shtml, date accessed October 1, 2012.

McGuigan, J. (2004) *Rethinking Cultural Policy* (Berkshire: Open University Press).

McGuigan, J. (2010) *Cultural Analysis* (Los Angeles, London, New Delhi, Singapore, Washington DC: Sage).

Ministry of Examination. (2009) 'Online Database for Yearly Civil Examination Papers (In Chinese)', http://wwwc.moex.gov.tw/main/exam/wFrmExamQandASearch.aspx?menu_id=156, date accessed July 1, 2012.

New Tang Dynasty TV (2013) Figures in China: Chinese people gradually cannot afford themselves (in Chinese), July 5, 2013, http://www.ntdtv.com/xtr/b5/2013/07/05/a926155.html, date accessed October 7, 2013.

O'Brien, P.K., Jane Edmonds, Christian Humphries, Jannet King, Petra Kopp, Martha Leyton and Richard Widdows (eds) (1999) *Philip's Atlas of World History* (London: George Philip Limited).

Parsons, Talcott. (1937) *The Structure of Social Action* (New York and London: McGraw-Hill Book Company).

People's Daily (2012) One Hundred Days after the Implementation of the SARFT's Opinion about Strengthening the Management of Programs in Satellite Television Variety Channels, *People's Daily*, April 9, 2012, http://media.people.com.cn/GB/17599817.html, date accessed October 1, 2012.

Rhodes, R.A.W. (1996) 'The New Governance: Governing without Government', *Political Studies* XLIV, 652–667.

State Administration of Radio, Film and Television (2011), *The SARFT will Strengthen the Management of Programs in Satellite Television Variety Channels* (in Chinese), http://www.sarft.gov.cn/articles/2011/10/25/2011102517075580101 0.html, date accessed October 1, 2012.

Sun, L-C. (1992, First Published in 1990) *The Deep Structure of Chinese Culture* (in Chinese) (Hong Kong: Jixianshen).

Turner, G. (1996) *British Cultural Studies, An Introduction* (London and New York: Routledge, Second Edition.

Tylor, E.B. (1958) *Primitive Culture. Researches into the Development of Mythology, Philosophy, Religion, Art and Custom* (Gloucester, MA: Smith).

Valentine, J. (2002) 'Governance and Cultural Authority', *Cultural Values*, 6(1–2), 47–62.

Williams, R. (1982, First Published in 1958) *Cultural and Society* (London: The Hogarth Press).

Yang Z-K. (2000) *The Interaction and Adaptation of Tourism Policy, Administration and Laws* (in Chinese) (Taipei: Yangzhi Wenhua).

Yu Y-S. (1992) *Observing the Modern Meaning of Chinese Culture from Its Value System* (in Chinese) (Taipei: Shibao Wenhua).

Zhang G-X. and Ling Y-C. (2000) *Recreation Industry Management* (in Chinese) (Taipei: Yangchi Wenhua).

8

The Paradigm Shift in Local Cultural Policy in Japan

Mari Kobayashi

Past and current cultural policies in Japan

In this chapter, I would like to discuss recent changes in local cultural policy in Japan. These changes have taken place within the context of administrative structural reforms that have progressed in a rapid manner since 2000. I will analyze two particular reforms that have greatly affected the cultural sector in the country. The first would be the Basic Law for Promotion of Culture and Arts (BLPCA), and the second would be the 'Designated Manager System,' a new policy that was introduced to reform the management of public facilities under local government authority. My observations are based on field research that I have conducted with local government authorities, which is discussed in this chapter.[1] I will argue that these two reforms have caused a shift in the way in which local cultural policy in Japan is practiced, moving it from a top-down bureaucratic system to one that now actively seeks to include local residents in the decision-making process.

Before I begin my analysis, it would first be necessary to understand the overall context of local cultural policy in Japan. There has been a tacit understanding since the end of World War II that political parties should never use cultural matters for political purposes. This was due to how culture and the arts were used before and during World War II for political purposes to propagate governmental ideologies and to censor dissenting views. A government body to oversee arts and culture, the Agency for Cultural Affairs (ACA), was only created in 1968. The ACA was set within the Ministry of Education and its main tasks were determined by the remit of that ministry. Generally speaking, it was responsible for cultural promotion, the preservation of cultural heritage and properties, copyright protection for the arts, and the improvement and dissemination of Japanese language and religion.

During the 1980s, Japanese society paid greater attention to arts and culture. This was largely due to the economic boom during this time; the rise of corporate philanthropy and cultural patronage had a great impact on the promotion of arts and culture. It was during this time that local governments built many new multi-purpose theatres and concert halls, about 1800 throughout Japan. However, the bursting of the economic bubble in the 1990s would highlight two main issues surrounding the support of arts and culture in Japan.

The first was the lack of cultural funding for the production of cultural content such as performances and art exhibitions. This is why artists in Japan, in particular performance artists, called for an expansion of the cultural budget to the degree where it would become similar to that in European countries. This was because up to 1990, almost the entire public cultural budget was spent on the preservation of cultural properties and heritage and maintaining existing cultural infrastructure. Second, many of the cultural facilities built during the boom were underutilized, and the media would point out that many of these venues had been built without consideration on how they would be used and managed after construction. A lack of arts organizations or management personnel trained in cultural administration who were capable of running these venues was a part of this problem, but another related issue was that while many local govern-ments were willing to fund the construction costs, they were unlikely to fund ongoing operational expenses. In addition, while the economy remained sluggish, cultural budgets for local governments were being cut, and it was unlikely the situation would improve. Within this context, the creation of a law that addresses these issues would be needed.

In 2001, the National Assembly enacted BLPCA alongside other administrative structural reforms. What has to be pointed out here is that these central administrative reforms were undertaken during this time in the pursuit of cost reduction and efficiency in public admin-istration. The BLPCA law was passed unanimously. This law came to pass due to the efforts of a group of members within the assembly who had an interest in cultural policy. Known as *Ongaku Giin Renmei*, this group sought cross-party support to organize for the creation of a bill that would eventually lead to the enactment of BLPCA.[2]

Basic law for promotion of culture and arts: creating collaborations between local governments and residents

BLPCA consists of three parts: the General Provisions (Articles 1 to 6), Basic Policy (Article 7), and Basic Measures Concerning the Promotion of Culture and the Arts (Articles 8 to 35). The responsibilities of local governments are expressed in the fourth article as part of the section on General Provisions. In short, local governments would now be responsible for creating and executing policy for the promotion of culture and arts specific to their particular region. This responsibility is independent from central government and had to be considered with reference to each particular region. The central government would not be able to force local governments to provide or enact a policy on culture; therefore, the creation of cultural policy would be up to the discretion of local governments.

The importance of the 'local' and of 'diversity' can be seen in the eight fundamental principles of BLPCA, which are listed in Article 2 of the first part. It states that promotion of culture and arts had to take into consideration:

- Respect of the autonomy of entities that conduct cultural and artistic activities
- Respect for the creativity of entities that conduct cultural and artistic activities
- Building of an environment where Japan residents have access to the appreciation of, participation in, and creation of culture and the arts
- Development of culture and the arts in both Japan and worldwide
- Protection and development of diverse forms of culture and the arts
- Development of culture and the arts featuring regional characteristics
- Promotion of international exchange and cooperation related to culture and the arts
- Reflection of the opinions of a wide range of the Japanese population on measure to promote culture and the arts. (ACA 2012, p. 2)

Before the enactment of BLPCA, there were some local governments that had voluntarily enacted ordinances for the promotion of culture and the arts. The passing of this law, though, would encourage another 107 prefectures (towns and cities) to adopt the law. I would argue that this phenomenon is noteworthy in two aspects. First, it meant that local governments could continue to manage and maintain not only their own local cultural policy but also their cultural budgets. At the time of the passing of this law, the main task of many Cultural Affairs Divisions in local governments was managing their built cultural facilities. In other words, 'cultural promotion' of these divisions was essentially the management of local cultural venues. Thus, for many local governments, being able to create ordinances as a direct result of BLPCA would allow them to maintain their existing cultural budget. This was particularly important as there was a fear that this, being viewed as non-essential, was in danger of being reduced as administrative structural reforms were taking place, as mentioned earlier, with the goal of saving money. The second impact of this law was that local governments now had the opportunity to find new ways of constructing and implementing concrete cultural policy strategies with the active participation of their local residents so as to develop culture and the arts that had regional characteristics, one of the principles of Article 2 of this law. Local resident groups who had been active in promoting culture in their own community welcomed the potential for collaboration. These residents, who were usually aged between 30 and 50, while not usually keen on public administration, wanted to be able to participate directly in the decision-making process for local cultural policy. It was now possible for local governments to recognize these residents as partners.

This type of partnership can be seen in the recent development of cultural policy in the local government of Shizuoka Prefecture. In 2008, Shizuoka Prefecture would formulate a ten-year cultural promotion plan. This was a ten-year strategy, and a mid-term evaluation was conducted in 2012 so as to determine if the plan would be able to achieve its stated goal in 2018. The stages and strategies that were set out by the local government to achieve its goals in the cultural promotion plan can be summarized as follows.

- Stage One: Potential Power
  - There are rich cultural resources in Shizuoka Prefecture, but people do not recognize their value.
- Stage Two: Recognition
  - Residents recognize the existence and the value of regional cultural resources.
- Stage Three: Utilization
  - Through the utilization of cultural resources, residents and visitors will take notice of the region.
- Stage Four: Adding Value
  - Residents will take pride in their region and cultural resources, increasing efforts to add value to those resources.
- Stage five: Branding and Development of New Links
  - The region attracts people, is able to brand itself, and establishes links to new industries.
- Goal
  - Diverse and interesting culture develops in the region, and the region becomes an attractive place for both residents and visitors.

The steps under discussion during this evaluation were focused on Stage 2 'Recognition' and Stage 3 'Utilization' of this plan. During this evaluation stage, a key topic under discussion was 'who' would be utilizing these cultural resources. Was it the local government, or the citizens of the region? It was during this discussion that it was decided that the local residents and non-profit organizations would play the important role of executing the cultural promotion plan, while the local government would provide the necessary administrative systems and frameworks to organize the relevant strategies. This discussion clarified the role both the local government and the residents would play, defining the nature of their partnership on the plan.

Another example of close collaboration between local governments and residents can be seen with Koganei City's Cultural Promotion Plan. Three years after the enactment of BLPCA, Koganei City, located in Tokyo, decided that the city would establish the Ordinance of Arts and Cultural Promotion for its city. The administrative staff of the division of culture decided to construct this ordinance with the input of the citizens of the city. The goal of this ordinance was to use culture for urban development.

To create the ordinance and to achieve this plan, Koganei City signed an agreement with the University of Tokyo, and it at this point that a group of my research students and I become involved in this ordinance and the plan. In 2006, we became the secretariat for the ordinance, and our responsibility was to support the city through providing research and technical viewpoints. The committee for the ordinance for arts and culture consisted of nine people, three of whom were citizens from the general public, four were representatives for various organizations, and the remaining two were a writer and an associate professor at a university. Our tasks were to submit monthly agendas to the committee, create relevant discussion materials and collate feedback from the discussion from each meeting. Our preparation work for the committee consisted of researching and obtaining feedback from various citizens and organizations.

The purpose of this ordinance was to define the basic principles for the promotion of arts and culture in Koganei City, clarify the roles the city, residents and other organizations would play and enable residents to participate proactively in arts and cultural activities. In order to bring these goals into reality, we suggested that three elements were required in the structure of the ordinance. The first was that the plan under this ordinance had to run for ten years to give it enough time to achieve what it set out to do. The second was that an agency needed to be created specifically to promote the plan from this ordinance. Third, a system of evaluation was also needed.

From 2007 to 2008, the committee prepared to put together a basic plan for the promotion of arts and culture. It conducted some surveys about culture and the arts. One of them was to 2,800 of its residents who were selected through random sampling. The main purpose of these surveys were to determine how citizens could play an active role in promoting culture and the arts under this ordinance, working with public administration on equal and collaborative terms. This was a key issue as the committee recognized that the role of the citizen was just as important as, or even more important than, that of the administrative staff. This was because quick staff turnover might mean that public administrators would only be around for two or three years of the plan, and they might also not possess a deep understanding of local culture. This way of thinking was different from the standard way in which government policy is usually implemented. However, there was a recognition that cultural promotion plans have to be managed differently: culture in local areas is created by residents living in the particular area; therefore, it became clear during this process that citizens were required to play a key role in local cultural policy if the plan was to succeed. One of the challenges faced by the local government was how to encourage public administrative staff to work together with local residents. As these staff members were unfamiliar with how to engage with local residents, collaboration was often limited. A good solution would be that local residents take the initiatives and local government and public administrative staff create policy to complement and support these initiatives.

Since 2009, local residents, the committee, and the public administration have worked together to implement their cultural policy under this plan in Koganei City. In 2012, the committee would become an Arts Non-Profit Organization[3] (NPO), and rename itself *Artfull Action*. They would be financed by both Koganei City and Tokyo. They would also receive other subsidies to fund their activities. As an Arts NPO, its role was to 'create a rich civil society based on the principle of citizens' autonomy, through linking arts to the society and cooperating with NPOs in other areas' (Arts NPO Link 2013). The creation of *Artfull Action* was only possible because both the local government and residents wanted to work together to promote their local culture. This, in turn, occurred due to the enactment of the BLPCA.

These two examples show how the law has allowed local governments to seize the opportunity to work with their residents to fulfil key principles outlined in the BLPCA.

Designated Manager System: introducing new players

In a series of administrative reforms conducted in 2003, the central government revised the Local Government Act and introduced the 'Designated Manager System.' This system would have an impact on the way cultural facilities were managed by local governments. According to the committee of general affairs in the House of Representatives,[4] this revision was explained as follows: First, there was a recognition that the needs of residents have diversified; second, the private sector could be better placed to provide services to the public sector, and third, the 'knowledge of a private entrepreneur or company within the public sector could result in more effective and efficient management' (Hatanaka 2003). This adoption of the private sector into the public service domain could already be seen in the previous year when several municipalities drafted the proposal Structural Reform Special District Plan calling for public facilities to be managed by private companies. As a consequence, the Ministries of Public Management, Home Affairs, Post and Telecommunications would declare that it was possible to expand the range of management of public facilities to private entrepreneurs or companies.

It is here that we need to consider the role of local government and public facilities under their ownership. Local governments are responsible for providing services for residents that are not available through the private sector, often by constructing various types of public facilities such as welfare centers for the elderly, roads, parks and schools, etc. Cultural facilities were one of these public services that local governments felt that they had to provide for their local residents. However, what needed to be taken into consideration when it came to the construction of these facilities was that the mere existence of the facilities did not mean that the local government would also be able to provide the service it was built for. Local governments had not factored in the cost of the management and day-to-day expenses of these facilities before approving their construction. Without a clear goal and understanding of the purpose of these facilities, these venues were unsustainable in cost after their construction.

This problem was particularly obvious in relation to cultural facilities. Before the revision of the act in 2003, public facilities were either directly managed by the local government or the management of these venues were delegated to certain foundations that met specific requirements of the local government. These foundations are best understood as quasi-public corporations. With this new law, local governments could now designate any legal entity, hence the term 'designated manager,' to run their public facilities. The revision was undertaken during a trend of deregulation and privatization promoted by the government then in Japan. However, I would argue that this law revision does not equate to privatization; a distinction has to be made between allowing private companies to provide services at the lowest cost and the 'Designated Manager System,' where the designated manager executes the public service on behalf of the local government itself. This would mean that a private company or an NPO could be selected if they demonstrated that they could fulfil the public services required by the government. Procedures were put in place to ensure that cost was not the sole criterion for selection.

The local government would first have to decide if it could be the best provider of the public servicer in question. If the local government decided that perhaps a private company or NPO would be able to provide a better service, local ordinance would have to be revised to establish a framework in which the designated manager would be selected and also establish how long the contract for this service would be. This step has to be approved by local assembly before a selection process can be initiated. As the end of the selection process, local assembly would hold a debate on the suitability of the candidate. If the candidate is approved, the company or NPO would sign an agreement with the local assembly for a fixed term. The criteria for how a designated manager is chosen would depend on the needs that the local government sought. For many local governments seeking a manager for their cultural facilities, the key criteria seem to be based on first establishing a clear understanding of what the cultural facility's mission and purpose is. This is followed by an examination of how the local government sees the cultural facility working in tandem with local cultural policy. Finally, the local government also clearly defines what is expected of the successful designated manager and provides a budget at which it expects these services will be offered.

A special committee consisting of art experts, art managers, as well as policy makers in both public and cultural policy would be convened to select the candidate through a public presentation. It is clear that this process has been designed to ensure that the decision is not made based on the lowest cost. It ensures that local governments have considered the character of the facilities and also considered what content they would like these facilities to present. For many local governments, the location of the cultural facilities plays a large part in the decision-making process. For example, there are many professional arts companies in Tokyo, ranging from orchestras to drama, dance and opera companies, thus it might be that a suitable designated manager for a cultural facility in Tokyo would be a building management and maintenance company that would run the building efficiently allowing for as many companies as possible to rent and use the building. In cities where there are fewer arts organizations, a designated manager with different skill sets would be required.

It could be argued that the designated manager system is simply another form of privatization, and it is possible to see how this system has the potential to bring up issues that can occur when public facilities are managed by private companies. With the introduction of this system, existing foundations that had initially managed these cultural facilities could not compete with private companies and had to be dissolved at the loss of jobs. A fixed term contract also means that there is no incentive for the designated manager to invest in a cultural facility for the long-term. In addition, a fixed term contract also means that it is not possible to evaluate the long-term success or failure of a venue. A short-term contract might mean using quick fixes to cut costs, which might create long-term consequences through stage technology maintenance, for example, where the easiest way to cut costs would be to hire contract staff with little or no experience, which would eventually lead to a facility that would not be fit for the purpose at the end of the contract. Furthermore, there is no incentive to nurture or develop young artists, when hiring out venues to well-known artists or performers would be more lucrative for the designated manager. There are issues that do need to be considered within this system, but I would also like to highlight that this system also does have its positive aspects.

To begin with, it is now possible for local governments to seriously think about how cultural promotion in their region can be linked to the management of the cultural facilities. This requires them to formulate a cultural policy that takes into account their region and resources. This will enable local governments to develop a long-term cultural promotion ordinance that can continually be revised with each contract. Second, this system allows for a simplification of bureaucracy that had been created when these facilities used to be managed by quasi-government bodies such as foundations. Finally, local governments have to continually evaluate their mission and activities in relation to their cultural policy every time a contract is up for renewal. Local governments have managed the majority of these cultural facilities since they were built in the 1980s. While it is possible to argue that the main aim of the new system is to cut costs, this system also provided the impetus for many local governments to reconsider the way in which they had administered culture, leading to some serious re-thinking about their cultural policy in general. With the inclusion of citizens (due to the enactment of BLPCA), private companies and NPOs, the designated manager system arguably allows for a greater diversity of players within the local cultural field.

Tracing the paradigm shifts in local cultural policy

Collaborations between local governments and their residents were not born simply as a result of the enactment of BLPCA. There has been a history of local governments working with their residents since the 1970s. A key example would be the preservation of historic buildings; a law enacted in 1975 stated that historical districts were not only to be considered for their economic value but also for their cultural and historic significance. In order to preserve these districts, local governments had to develop collaborations with residents. However, this way of working gradually became less popular in the 1980s, when local governments began to think that the construction of new cultural venues would be the most effective way to promote local culture. The creation of these venues was undertaken without consultations with the local citizens. Their construction took place during a time in Japan when there was a growing recognition that culture and the arts were just as important as the material aspects of life. For many local governments, the best way to encourage this 'age of culture' would be through increasing cultural infrastructure.

Then, in the 1990s in Japan, there was greater citizen awareness in general that they could also affect the work done by both central and local governments. A key turning point was the 1996 Hanshin-Awaji Great Earthquake, where the activities of non-governmental groups and NPOs attracted the attention of the media with the work that they were doing with the affected. The severity of the earthquake meant that the resources and efforts of local authorities were insufficient, and a substantial part of this void was filled by various NPOs. One of the key areas NPOs were involved in was dealing with the psychological trauma and stress faced by the survivors.

Piccoro Theatre, known formally as *Amagasaki Seishounen Gekijo,* was a public theatre in Hyogo Prefecture with its own theatrical group. It visited temporary evacuation spaces and carried out cultural activities with children who were affected by the earthquake. This was a landmark occurrence at the time because conventional thinking in Japan then, when faced with natural disasters such as this, was to deem culture and the arts as irrelevant to other measures such as shelter and food. However, Piccoro Theatre's work allowed the affected children to express themselves and helped them overcome their trauma.

The experience of Hanshin-Awaji Great Earthquake was significant for two reasons: further recognition of the importance of arts and cultural activities, which had grown since the 1980s, and the idea that citizens working within non-governmental organizations could play a key role in cultural development in Japan. The corresponding increase in the number of Arts NPOs since the establishment of the Law for the Promotion of Non-Profit Organizations (see Endnote II) highlights the growing recognition that citizens can play a key role in the development of culture and the arts in regions.

In 2000, two reports released by the ACA and the Japan Foundation for Regional Art-Activities highlighted the problems with the management of cultural facilities in various regions in Japan and called for an overhaul of existing policy. The ACA's report, Investigation on the Activities of Public Cultural Facilities, recommended that for these venues to be sustainable, local governments would need to involve their residents in the management of these facilities and allow them to play a central role in the creation and presentation of arts and cultural activities in these venues. The report by the Japan Foundation of Regional Art-Activities

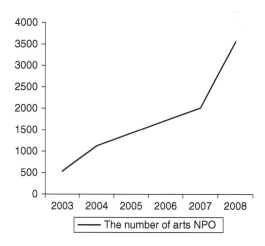

Figure 8.1   The Number of arts non-profit organizations
Source: Japan Foundation for Regional Art-Activities (2009).

called for local governments to recognize that organizational reform might be necessary for these venues to survive, and that local governments should be aware of the needs of the residents.

It was within such a context that BLPCA brought together the changes that had occurred in local cultural policy since the 1970s, recognizing the importance of cultural diversity in the regions, the role citizens could play in cultural development, and the productive ways local authorities could collaborate with citizens. The 'Designated Manager System' would exemplify these changes in relation to the management of cultural facilities in the region. In short, the enactment of BLPCA, together with the 'Designated Manager System,' demonstrates the shifts that have occurred in the way culture and the arts are viewed and supported in Japan from the 1970s to today.

Perhaps these shifts can be best understood in relation to the concepts of 'democratization of culture' and the 'cultural democracy.' Within this context, cultural democracy allows for people to take part in the decision-making process of cultural policy to promote the diversity of their views, whereas the latter is a bureaucratic top-down way to practice cultural policy. The concept of 'cultural democracy' was discussed in the 1960s in Europe (Matarasso and Landry 1999, pp. 13–14). It was a time when the methodologies of cultural administration were being questioned from the perspectives of various people with diverse cultural needs. For many European governments during this time, the democratization of culture, as practiced, meant building cultural facilities, fostering professional arts organizations, and popularizing the high arts and cultural knowledge. This form of cultural administration came under question in the 1970s, particularly in France and Germany, where there were calls for greater acceptance of the 'everyday expression of people' and for people to be involved in the 'fundamental debates about the nature and value of cultural identity and expression' (Matarasso and Landry 1999, pp. 13–14). I would argue that this change is now occurring in Japan through the two reforms that I have discussed within this chapter.

The changes in local cultural policy administration that have taken place since 2001 with the enactment of BLPCA have highlighted three trends that show how the management of culture in Japan today is now moving toward 'cultural democracy.' The first is that local governments now work with the active participation of citizens in developing local cultural policy. Through this participation, citizens are now able to understand the key purposes for developing cultural policy, and this allows them to lead and organize this policy with the local government through the instigation of particular strategies to address problems in local cultural provision. The aforementioned Koganei City, for example, has not only seen an increase in citizen participation in the decision-making process in regard to local cultural policy, they have also founded an Arts NPO. Through this NPO, they have managed to conduct various cultural projects that have been driven by the needs of the local residents. These include invitations to professional contemporary artists to work with elementary school children to produce artistic work, providing a gallery space for young artists in the city, and organizing lectures and seminars for local residents to discuss local cultural policy. The success of this citizen-driven NPO can be seen in it winning the contract to manage Koganei City's 55 year celebration event in 2014.

The second trend would be the way the 'Designated Manager System' has provided the impetus for many local governments to reconsider the way they administer culture, leading to some reflection on their cultural policies. This has led to Yokohama City, one of the biggest cities in Japan, developing a Policy Partnership System to manage its cultural institutions. It is now possible for both Art NPOs and private companies, and not just the local government, to provide cultural activities for the city, so citizens are able to choose from a wider selection of cultural activities.

Finally, with the increasing inclusion of citizens, private companies and NPOs in the way cultural policy is created and implemented, there is now a diversity of players within local cultural policy in Japan today. Through my research, I have found that there has been an increase in attendance of citizens aged 30–50 years of age in cultural activities. This was a demographic that had not been interested in arts and cultural activities, and this increase provides an indication that greater inclusion in the creation and implementation of cultural policy leads to the creation of new audiences.

In this chapter, I have shown how the way cultural policy in administered in Japan since 2001 has led to a change in the way cultural policy is developed and implemented at the local government level. These changes can best be understood in relation to the concept of 'cultural democracy,' where greater participation and cooperation between local governments, private companies and Arts NPOs in Japan has led to greater cultural diversity in various cities today. Essential to maintaining this paradigm shift is the continued collaboration between local governments, private companies and Arts NPO, where good working relationships between these partners would result in clearly defined cultural policies that are beneficial to their local communities.

Notes

1. The two case studies in this paper are drawn from Shizuoka Prefecture and Koganei City. I was a member of the Evaluation Committee for the Cultural Promotion Plan for Shizuoka Prefecture that took place in 2012. I was also a member of the committee, along with my graduate students, in providing research support for the development of Koganei City's Cultural Promotion Plan.
2. See M. Kobayashi (2004) *Bunka-Ken no Kakuritsu ni Mukete: Bunka Shinkouhou no Kokusai Hikaku to Nihon no Genjitsu* (*Toward Establishing Cultural Rights: Comparative Studies about Laws for Cultural Promotion and the Japanese Reality*) (Keiso-Shobo Publications) for a detailed study and analysis of the background and process of how the BLPCA was established.
3. The Law for the Promotion of Non-profit Organizations (NPO) was established in 1997 to describe work done by non-governmental and non-profit organizations. The first group to receive the designation of NPO was *Furano Engeki Koubou* (Furano Drama Workshop), an arts organization based in Hokkaido. It is generally accepted now that arts organizations that are also NPOs are referred to as Arts NPOs, to set them apart from other types of NPOs. As of August 2010, there are about 4,000 Arts NPO in Japan.
4. In Japan, the National Assembly consists of the House of Representatives and the House of Councillors.

References

Agency for Cultural Affairs (2012) Foundations for Cultural Administration, http://www.bunka.go.jp/english/pdf/h24_chapter_01.pdf, date accessed November 11, 2013.

Arts NPO Link (2003) Purpose and Objectives, http://arts-npo.org/artnpolink.html, date accessed November 13, 2013.

Hatanaka, S. (2003) Statement, Ministry of Public Management, Home Affairs, Post and Telecommunications, delivered May 27.

Japan Foundation for Regional Art-Activities (2009), Current State of Art NPOs, http://www.jafra.or.jp/j/library/letter/166/series.php, date accessed November 11, 2013.

Matarasso, F. and Landry, C. (1999) *Balancing act: Twenty-one strategic dilemmas in cultural policy* (Strasbourg: Council of Europe Publishing).

Part III

The Rise of Creative Industries Policy

9

The Reform of the Cultural System: Culture, Creativity and Innovation in China

Michael Keane and Elaine Jing Zhao

Dramatic changes have occurred in Chinese society over the past three decades. Many of these changes are attributable to the government's economic reforms presided over, firstly by MAO Zedong's successor DENG Xiaoping, and following DENG, JIANG Zemin, HU Jintao and XI Jinping. In this chapter, we focus on changes that have led to a revised understanding of culture. According to a Chinese Communist Party definition, informed by historical materialism, culture 'in a broad sense, refers to the sum total of all the material and spiritual wealth created by human beings in the course of the historical development of society; in a narrow sense, culture refers to ideology and related institutions and organizations' (*Cihai: Sea of Words*. Chinese Encyclopedia 1989, p. 1731). However, over the past three decades, the Chinese government has voluntarily relinquished control over many aspects of cultural production in exchange for the potential benefits of cohesion and increased productivity that social liberalization is seen to promote. Inevitably the market, rather than government propaganda, has become the arbiter of people's cultural tastes (Gerth 2010). It is important to bear in mind, however, that broadening of consumption practices does not necessarily constitute cultural pluralism. Indeed, the extent to which culture is commercializable remains contentious. In the view of conservatives, culture cannot be left to the forces of the market; yet the same conservatives assert that China's culture should be globally competitive.

Analysis of the cultural sphere needs to address the ways that cultural policy – in the form of laws, statutes, documents and regulations – organizes the relations between the production and dissemination of cultural forms. We commence with some understandings of cultural

155

policy in China before discussing the nature of the cultural system and its reform.

Given space constraints, our discussion is a broad outline of key events and shifts in the balance of cultural production – from public culture to commercial culture and more recently to amateur and user-generated content. We identify three periods of reform: 1978 to 1992, 1993 to 2002, and 2003 to 2013. Focusing on the last period, we look at the often-problematic transition from public cultural institution (*shiye*) to commercial industries (*chanye*). Since 2003, the 'reform of the cultural system' has given birth to other slogans and policy themes: namely soft power, innovation, and creativity. In this period, the 'twinning' of culture and creativity emerged, resulting in the term 'cultural and creative industries' (*wenhua chuangyi chanye*). In the final section, we turn to the most recent stage: the convergence of technological innovation and cultural creativity, and show how China is attempting to fast-track its culture and expand its soft power resources.

Cultural policy in China

There are two broad ways of understanding the objectives of cultural policy. First, cultural policy concerns the regulation of the 'marketplace of ideas and creative practice' (Craik 2007). From this perspective, government's role is to regulate production and consumption, often with the aim of developing national culture, promoting the macro environment for creative business, or, in some instances, helping to generate export potential. In most liberal democracies, the role of government is at a distance, enabling and making strategic policies. Second, cultural policy refers to policies that manage cultural resources and institutions, such as performing arts companies and public cultural assets. Governments often play an active, and sometimes interventionist, role in supporting cultural institutions (see Craik 2007).

In China, the implementation of cultural policy is caught up in strategies to promote the simultaneous development of public and private interests. In practical terms, this is the tension between public cultural institutions (*shiye*) and commercial enterprises (*chanye* or *qiye*). The cultural policy process is subject to tensions between competing interests; many seek to maintain what we might call a 'capital C' approach; that is, Chinese civilization is unique, and culture is for the most part invariable; alternatively, there are those prepared to allow Chinese culture space to evolve in response to competition. Adherents of the latter approach frequently promote the ideals of creativity, the autonomy of producers, and the imperatives of commercial (profit-making) industries (Keane 2013). A major difficulty, therefore, is ascertaining how deliberations take place across overlapping spheres of influence; a related difficulty is determining which of the many documents and pronouncements issued by government ministries and departments are significant.

Generally speaking, documents issued from leading government agencies in the lead up to the major planning periods – the National Five-Year Economic and Social Development Plans – serve as blueprints. The most authoritative documents are therefore issued by the Communist Party Central Committee. The wording is carefully constructed because central (*zhongyang*) documents have considerable 'guiding' authority, even more than speeches by leaders (Lawrence and Martin 2012). Policy documents embrace the rhetoric of socialism and acknowledge the enduring influence of elderly Party officials. As a consequence, much policy is deliberately vague and open to interpretation. Furthermore, many policies are difficult to enforce.

While policy is rigorously debated and formulated according to Marxist principles, its engagement by cultural producers is open to negotiation. The details of cultural policy and the actual adherence to statutes and regulations depend on the prevailing political climate, which tends to alternate from periods of relaxation *(fang)* to tightening *(shou)*. As several studies have shown, compliance depends on the willingness of regional cultural bodies to challenge policy (Keane 2001; Chin 2011).

Policy is incubated in formal think tanks such as the Chinese Academy of Social Science and tested in internal Chinese Communist Party (CCP) work groups, which are sometimes referred to as 'leading small groups.' Often these formal groups have connections to 'scholar-leaders' and 'leading scholars.' Scholar-leaders (*xuezhexing lingdao*) include industry leaders or officials who have a strong academic background. Scholar-leaders like Li Wuwei[1] may be members of the China's Peoples' Political Consultative Conference (CPPCC), a national and inclusive policy think tank,[2] or they may be leading entrepreneurs and consultants. Leading scholars (*qianyan xuezhe*) conduct leading-edge research.

Despite significant social changes over the past three decades, the language of cultural policy remains anchored to themes of nation-building and modernization. Cultural policy's bond with economic development policy, most evident during the past decade, constitutes a relatively new modality of governance. The shift from culture purely as propaganda work toward culture as 'pillar industry' (*zhizhu chanye*) in the most recent 12th Five-Year Economic and Social Development Plan has required a reconsideration of policy frameworks, bringing cultural production and distribution closer to the realm of industrial management with attendant requirements for actors to adhere to international legal regimes.

The cultural system

Understanding governance from a system perspective is endemic to Chinese thinking; not only does a systems model evoke a holistic notion of progress, but it allows government to pay a 'guiding role' in managing reform. The reform of the cultural system (*wenhua tizhi gaige*) embodies arguments about the relative weighting given to public and commercial forms of culture, as well as the modernization of China's technological innovation system (see below). It is important therefore to see the reform of the cultural system within the context of other systems undergoing reform: education, health, the economy, technology, manufacturing, and most importantly, politics.

The most important system theory in China is Marxism. Adapted to fit China's needs, Marxism advocated a systemic transformation that required a popular revolution to accomplish. However, by the end of the 1970s, the Sinicized variation of Marxist-Leninism adopted by MAO Zedong was in urgent need of revision. New system theories became popular. Intellectual debates in the mid-1980s picked up on the writings of futurists John Naisbitt and Alvin Toffler, who spoke of major social, economic and cultural changes wrought by technology.[3] Naisbitt went on to offer advice to China's policy makers (Naisbitt and Naisbitt 2010) while Toffler's ideas about post-industrial society led to him being acclaimed by the *People's Daily* as one of the most influential 'foreigners to shape China.'[4] The ideas of Daniel Bell were also influential (Bell 1989). Bell's 'post-industrial society' with its notion of stages of development offered an alternative to official Marxist-Leninism. The theory of the transition from a goods producing economy to a service economy had an echo of the utopianism of communism: the Chinese population would be delivered from their backwardness and the intellectual class would assume a leading role in the professional and technical classes.[5]

In the cultural field, systems reflect the tensions of historical progress. According to the authors of *The History of Chinese Culture (Zhongguo wenhua shi)*:

> The subsystems of material culture are the foundation of the systems view of culture...Only by way of rational organization can we safeguard the coordinated development of material and spiritual culture.

Spiritual culture (and its sub-systems) plays the guiding role; it protects and determines material culture, the construction of institutional culture and its orientation. (Hu and Zhang 1991, pp. 2–3)

A question that arises is: how is Chinese culture responding to changes in the overall economic, social and political system? Moreover, how is cultural policy in China impacted by international systems, given that China is now a member of international trade communities and is seeking to market its culture internationally? Is Chinese culture able to adapt? Accordingly, how can the cultural system be reformed?

Three periods of reform

From a global perspective, cultural activity can be broadly subdivided into three sectors: *publicly subsidized culture*, which includes opera, museums, performing troupes and galleries (although these often include commercial elements and corporate sponsorship); *commercial production* for which there is an audience and/or consumers willing to pay; and *amateur cultural activity*, which includes everything from community folk dancing to web-based creativity. In China the public sector has assumed priority. Until the 1980s, all artists and media workers were employed by the state as conduits for Communist Party propaganda. Broadcasting infrastructure in China also remains state-owned or at least managed by state-owned enterprises, while news media are firmly under government control.

It is in the sphere of amateur cultural activity where we see the greatest change. Prior to 1978, the domain of amateur cultural activity in China was subject to strict regulation (Wang 1995). Today amateur cultural activity merges with the marketplace: as we note below, reality TV shows present 'wanna be' celebrities, while the Internet accelerates a frenzy of bloggers, spoofers, and hackers.

According to HAN Yongjin (2005), the reform of the cultural system began in 1978 and has proceeded through three stages: (i) from 1978 to 1992: a period of cultural reconstruction took place in the wake of the Cultural Revolution with an emphasis of reform in performing arts (ii) from 1993–2002: major reforms occurred across all sectors; the emphasis in this period was on industrialization (*gongyehua*) and conglomeration (*jituanhua*); (iii) from 2003: the focus shifted to the deepening of the transformation from public cultural institution (*shiye*) to industry and enterprise (*chanye* and *qiye*) together with development of new financing and support models.

The first stage of cultural system reform began in 1978, two years after the end of the Cultural Revolution, a decade of excessive and sometimes chaotic government intervention in cultural practices. The Third Plenum of the Chinese Communist Party's 11th Central Committee set in train reforms, moving the nation from class struggle to economic reconstruction. In 1979, at the Fourth National Arts Workers Congress, DENG Xiaoping announced the end of political interference in cultural activities (Deng 1983), a reference to the previous era in which cultural pursuits were manipulated by MAO and his cultural ministers, including his wife JIANG Qing. This 'promise' to the arts communities, however, did not entail a retreat by the state. The less interventionist model of cultural jurisdiction that transpired was reflected in the so-called 'liberation of thought' (*sixiang jiefang*) and the endorsement of the principle of 'diversity' (*duoyanghua*), which was in turn encapsulated within the 'double hundred policy' (see Kraus 2004; Keane 2007). The double hundred campaign, 'letting a hundred flowers bloom and a hundred schools of thought contend,' was initiated by Chairman MAO in the late 1950s, and was supposedly designed to promote the flourishing of the arts and the progress of science. Whereas MAO encouraged different and competing ideologies to voice their opinions and was then able to flush out troublesome elements, DENG's use of the double hundred slogan entailed genuine liberalization of arts and cultural policy (see Kraus 2004).

Cultural production expanded and diversified. The so-called cultural fever (*wenhua re*) period of the mid-1980s saw a proliferation of new literary genres, popular musical styles, and television dramas. At the end of the decade, an anthology of writing by the popular Beijing author WANG Shuo's reportedly outsold the collected works of Chairman MAO (Barme 1992). February 1988 saw the first official endorsement of the term 'cultural market.'[6] Following DENG Xiaoping's 'southern tour' of Shenzhen and the new economic zones in 1992, China's cultural workers were instructed to go to the market; many publishing institutions lost financial support and were forced to seek out new business models, often outsourcing production to unlicensed studios (*gongzuoshi*) (Schell 1995; Keane 2007).

This marked the beginning of the second stage of reform. In the same year, the term 'cultural industry' was introduced, although its formulation into state policy would have to wait another nine years (see Pang 2012). During these years, commercial culture grew. The media market consolidated in the late 1990s as the government proclaimed that media institutions should follow the path to commercialization by becoming conglomerates (*jituan*), which were in effect an attempt to build local media champions (see Keane 2013). The second stage culminated in the late 1990s when the slogan 'cultural security' (*wenhua anquan*) was incubated in the lead up to China's entry into the WTO. China's determination to open to foreign investment meant reducing restrictions on cultural trade. The need to liberalize markets in strategic sectors, including advertising and cinema, led to zealous debates about state sovereignty.

An initial treatise on cultural security and globalization was authored by HU Huilin in February 2000 (Hu 2000). On August 12, 2003, HU Jintao raised the topic of 'Ensuring National Cultural Security' to the Politburo of the Central Committee of the CCP during the seventh central collective study meeting.[7] In the following Fourth and Sixth Plenary Session of the Sixteenth Central Committee, cultural security was included in a package of 'security measures': namely political security, economic security, information security and cultural security. Unsurprisingly, conservative academics rallied around the proposition that Chinese traditional culture would decline or die out if decadent external culture was allowed to be accessed so easily.

The proposed solution was that China should strengthen its 'soft power' (see Chu 2013; Keane 2013, 2010, 2010a, 2010b; Sun 2010; Barr 2011; Kurlanzick 2007). The notion of soft power is now mandatory in policy statements and news reports. In brief, soft power describes the capacity of a nation to exert influence aside from 'hard power' such as military and economic influence. According to Joseph Nye (1990) a nation's 'attractiveness' rests on three resources: culture, political values and foreign policies. In most instances, soft power is synonymous with a nation's 'cultural attractiveness,' but in the case of China, such attractiveness is yet to be manifest beyond its national borders.

Even before Joseph Nye, soft power had a prehistory in China. According to LI Mingjiang (2008, p. 292), the first Chinese article on soft power was written in 1993 by WANG Huning, now a member of the CCP Central Committee Secretariat. LI notes that 485 papers featuring the phrase 'soft power' in their titles were published between 1994 and 2007. By the time the CCP leadership passed from JIANG Zemin to HU Jintao, the political environment was open to a reassessment of China's domestic and international influence. Statistics collated by Chinese Academy of Social Sciences researchers showing increased consumption of overseas leisure and cultural products. In his keynote speech to the 17th National Congress of the Communist Party of China in 2007, President HU Jintao emphasized that China should stimulate cultural creativity as part of the nation's 'soft power':

We must keep to the orientation of advanced socialist culture, bring about a new upsurge in socialist cultural development, stimulate the cultural creativity of the whole nation, and enhance culture as part of the *soft power* of our country in order to better guarantee the people's basic cultural rights and interests, to enrich the cultural life in Chinese society and to inspire the spiritual outlook of the people to be more elevated and more progressive.

The transformation of the cultural market, its evolution toward the cultural and creative industries (*wenhua chuangyi chanye*) represents a shift from the propaganda state presided over by China's revolutionary leaders. The articulation of 'cultural creativity' as a discursive theme neatly accommodates conservative and progressive factions. The market, now represented as 'industry' (*chanye*), is viewed by reformers as a mechanism of progress and a positive force for change.

New directions

The third stage of reform embodies a broader transformation, bringing new media into deeper alignment with cultural policy. Under the reform of the cultural system in stages (i) and (ii) the tripartite categorization of institutions, markets and consumers organized cultural policy. The public broadcaster China Central TV (CCTV) is generally described as a public cultural institution (*shiye*) even though it draws a high degree of advertising revenue. Commercial entities like Huayi Brothers, a leading commercial film production company, or commercial art galleries like 798 in Beijing, are evidence of market transformations (i.e., *chanye*). Consumers (*xiaofeizhe*) are variously categorized as 'audiences' (*guanzhong*), 'users' (*yonghu*) or 'grassroots' (*caogen*).

Significantly, the impact of users and grassroots is changing the nature of cultural activity in China. The relationship between institutions, market and consumers is therefore shifting as millions of internet users generate low budget content, create online spoofs (*egao*) (Meng 2011), contribute to fan subtitles (Hu 2006), and circulate fictional stories (Zhao 2011).

Inherent in this change is a shift between formal and informal economies. As mentioned above the Chinese policy system is outwardly formal and highly structured but internally connected to numerous think tanks and epistemic communities. Similarly, cultural activity is represented in complex formations; much cultural output is formal: that is, it is officially ratified, censored and distributed according to geographical jurisdictions. Other output is informal: it confounds attempts by the state to restrict its territory: for instance, web-based forms of parody and user-generated content. While the value of the informal economy is impossible to estimate, there is little doubt that online communities are contributing to China's cultural identity.

These new challenges have also presented themselves as opportunities, echoing the Chinese word for crisis *weiji*, a composite of *wei* (impending danger) and *ji* (opportunity). Whereas the challenges are mostly evident in the emergence of grassroots, opportunities for reform have emerged as a result of the need to strengthen industries (*chanye*). For some policy reformers, strengthening industries (*chanye*) is a way of disciplining the 'informal cultural economy.'[8]

The cultural system once more came to national attention in July 2003 following a national work conference in Beijing. A central government policy document, *The Opinions on Trial Work in the Reform of the Cultural System*[9] proposed a further series of measures to separate public institutions (*shiye*) from industries (*chanye*). However, while debates ensued about separation of functions, it was not until the framing of the 12th Five-Year Plan in 2009 that system reform became directly linked to soft power, which as mentioned above had emerged as a national slogan in the HU Jintao period. In 2009, the State Council released its Plan to Adjust and Reinvigorate the Cultural Industry (*wenhua chanye zhenxing guihua*). While there have been numerous sector-specific policies formulated, including initiatives at city, district and provincial level, this represented the first national plan to target the cultural industry. The plan was subsequently incorporated into the Outline of China's Cultural Reform and Development in the 12th Five-Year Plan Period (2011–15) (*shi er wu wenhua gaige fazhan guihua gangyao*), whereupon the Ministry of Culture (MoC) announced that the cultural sector would transform into a 'pillar industry' by 2015; that is, it would account for 5% of GDP. With this ambitious goal in mind, the MoC promulgated another plan aimed at doubling the annual added value of the nation's cultural industries, signaling an average annual growth rate exceeding 20%.

Ambitious targets are fundamental to socialist planning; as Keane (2011 and 2013) has argued, the perception that China is underperforming in 'soft power competition' (Chua 2012) in comparison with South Korea and Japan pricks a bubble of unease in Beijing's corridors of power. While the nation has become a global economic superpower over the past decade, its cultural and media industries have not followed the same growth trend. Yet there is a belief that application of industrial practices, and specifically applied technology, can fast-track cultural productivity and nurture innovation. The idea that economy and culture are co-dependent is now a key idea among Chinese Communist Party think tanks and other epistemic communities.

In 2012, ZHU Zhixin, deputy director of the National Development and Reform Commission, noted:

> Encouraging the development of the cultural industry is essential to restructuring and stimulating economic growth...It is hard to see a revival in international markets in the short term and against this background China's domestic economy is at risk of declining. The cultural industry is not only energy efficient, but will also largely promote consumption and boost a lot of related industries. (cited in Wei 2012)

Statements such as this demonstrate a shift of focus away from an export-led growth model toward greater reliance on domestic consumption. LI Wuwei, a national policy advisor, vice-chair of the Chinese Peoples' Political Consultative Conference (CPPCC), and author of *How Creativity is Changing China*, puts an even finer point to the argument:

> [t]he fundamental problems (or the contradictions caused by imbalance of internal and external economic structures) that led to the economic downturn, are yet to be solved.... we need to transform and upgrade the economy. Creative industries will stimulate the transformation of the Chinese economy from the export-oriented approach to the innovation driven approach. (Li 2011, p. 36)

Notwithstanding the fact that Li uses the term 'creative industries' in preference to the Ministry of Culture's preferred description, 'cultural industries,' it is evident that policy makers are alert to the role these emerging industries play in driving the growth of related industries such as tourism, finance and logistics. The term 'creative industries' had garnered support from other leading reformers, eager to see China move away from its reliance on heavy industry and low cost manufacturing. In 2009, Premier WEN Jiabao had made an important speech outlining the government's work program. Premier Wen addressed the task of 'actively supporting enterprises in accelerating technological upgrading and develop innovation-based enterprises.' He added:

> We will accelerate development of modern service industries. We will promote development of the banking, insurance, modern logistics,

consulting, software and creative industries, and develop new types of services. We will upgrade traditional service industries. (Wen 2009)

The Outline of China's Cultural Reform and Development in the 12th Five-Year Plan Period (2011–15) stresses the urgent need to 'emancipate and develop cultural productivity to provide a wide range of products and services to people.' This 'emancipation' is a means to address a gap between supply and demand in the domestic market. Strong cultural productivity is important in enhancing international cultural competitiveness, a factor that brings China's 'soft power' ambitions into finer focus. According to a document[10] passed at the 17th CCP Central Committee in 2011 (Wang and Cai 2011), China's capacity to innovate is critical in 'enhancing soft power and the comprehensive competitiveness of a nation's culture.' The solution, according to this document, is through 'the convergence of culture and technology.'

What 'convergence' means in Chinese political language is itself open to interpretation. The contemporary convergence discourse is about bootstrapping China to a new development model. The preferred model is the cross-fertilization of technological innovation and cultural creativity (*keji chuangxin yu wenhua chuangyi ronghe*). Policy makers recognize the role of scientific and technological innovation in driving the growth of cultural and creative industries and the expansion of innovation processes within society. Convergence is believed to be the future development model for China's cultural industries as well as a means to transform economic development.

In this model, information technology has moved closer to culture and the arts. In the 12th Five-Year Plan, a 'new generation' information technology industry was identified as one of the seven emerging sectors of national strategic significance. More specifically, this includes next generation information networks, core electronics, high-end software and new information services. The vision is that these digital technologies will play different roles in different regions to benefit cultural industries. In coastal cities such as Beijing and Shanghai, emerging technologies such as mobile Internet, cloud computing, and big data are driving the 'upgrade' of cultural industries; in effect, this implies that non-performing cultural projects should become more creative and innovative. In the less-developed mid-western regions, policy makers see informatization and digitalization as a way to turn traditional cultural resources into development opportunities, for example in the tourism industry or in cultural heritage preservation. Farther away from the east coast cities, the emphasis is less on creativity and innovation and more on protecting.

In line with the upgrading rhetoric, the state has certified 'national demonstration bases' for combining culture with science and technology. These demonstration bases often integrate existing national high tech parks. The current national list of demonstration bases includes 16 national projects. For example, Zhongguancun Demonstration Base in Beijing which includes the high tech district in Haidian District, Shijingshan Cyber-recreation District further to the west, Yonghe Park in Dongcheng District, and Desheng Science Park in Xicheng District. Similarly, Zhangjiang Demonstration base in Shanghai has identified information industries and embraced opportunities in online games and digital publishing. Digital content and services are therefore important sectors in exploring the convergence of cultural creativity and technological innovation. While visible structures such as bases and parks can be easily constructed in China, the 'less visible' creative and innovation processes are critical to nurturing the sector.

The convergence campaign is introducing new approaches to production, distribution and consumption of creative content. This poses challenges to government in terms of responding to such development, especially when content is decoupled from distribution platforms. While the triple network convergence, namely, the convergence of telecommunication, broadcasting and internet networks, has been on the Chinese government's agenda since the 10th Five-Year Plan proposed at the turn of the 21st century, there has been little progress at the national level, mainly because of conflicting interests between the State Administration of Radio, Film and Television (SARFT) and the Ministry of Industry and Information Technology (MIIT); that is, except for some pilot projects in a number of cities (Wu and Leung 2012). Clearly there is a need for establishing a convergent communications regulator to better implement the triple play policy.

As part of the State Council's institutional reform, the General Administration of Press and Publication (GAPP) and SARFT have merged to deepen the reform of cultural institutions and optimize their resources. The newly formed State Administration of Press, Publication, Radio, Film and Television will supervise the related organizations, the content and quality of their products and manage copyright. Moreover, to accelerate development and make cultural industries a pillar of the national economy, the state aims to 'establish a system of technological innovation in the field of culture in which enterprises play the leading role, the market provides orientation, and the efforts of enterprises, universities and research institutes are integrated.' Again we notice a heavy dose of rhetoric that reflects the state's industrial development agenda and its emphasis on IT as a means to catch up to the advanced 'West' and its own East Asian neighbors (South Korea and Japan). Since 1998, science and technology parks based around universities have witnessed rapid development. Earlier parks were focused on science and technology: some specialized in specific technological fields dominated by a single university while other, more comprehensive, parks were managed by local government and participated in by several universities. Since 2006, moreover, science and technology parks have undergone a 'humanities' turn, with many newly established ones linked to universities with strong research capabilities in the humanities disciplines (Peng 2009).

Indeed, innovation is increasingly happening outside corporate R&D. Sustainable innovation means products and services need to be improved via continuous conversation with various actors. Among these 'actors' are consumers who are assuming growing importance in creative production and innovation. For example, the vibrant growth of user-generated content in the digital domain has had significant social, cultural, economic and political impact in China. While grassroots creativity has largely existed in the informal sector, which is not counted in government statistics, there has been a trend where industry players in the formal sector start to work together with grassroots talents (Zhao and Keane 2013). Some have become talent incubators, aiming to develop and exploit grassroots creativity for their growth, in this way helping enterprises to better capture and respond to the market need.

Despite the attention given to the convergence of technological innovation and cultural creativity, there is no consensus about what a cultural innovation system actually is in China. To date, the emphasis has been on supply rather than demand: a 'build it and they will come' approach. There is no shortage of production bases for media and culture; China has excelled in outsourcing for international design and animation (see Keane 2013). The problem is that the brand reputation of China's cultural sectors is weak. In 2011, the former Chinese President HU Jintao lamented: 'The overall strength of China's culture and its international influence is not commensurate with China's international status. The international culture of the West is strong while we are weak.' (Hu 2012)

In addition to promoting cultural productivity (i.e., doubling output to meet domestic consumer demand) many expect that convergence between the cultural, manufacturing and service industries will spur international competitiveness and in this way drive the reform of the cultural system. There is an ironic twist to this – a potential flip side. When China opened its economy in the 1980s, the 'open door' inadvertently generated widespread imitation of overseas branded goods. With authentic originals either highly priced or unavailable, the boom in exploitative *'shanzhai* culture' (copy culture) provided consumers with cheap alternative products (Keane and Zhao 2012; Wallis and Qiu 2012). In fact, as the IT industry boomed in the 2000s, the copying of digital products such as mobile phones had the effect of accelerating *shanzhai* culture.

As China moves up the value chain from 'made-in-China' to 'created-in-China,' the meaning of *shanzhai* has morphed from pure piracy to value-adding creativity and micro-innovation. This is evident in manufacturing and service sectors. In mobile phone manufacturing industry, for example, local producers started with cloning but soon came up with new features such as dual-sim to suit consumer needs in the domestic market. The same applies to digital content or service industry. Weibo, launched in 2009 as a Twitter-like service, quickly added introduced features like embedded photo and video attachments, multimedia posts, verified accounts, and then evolved into a more or less hybrid of Facebook and Twitter. While trendy applications in Silicon Valley usually find a swarm of copy-to-China versions, incremental innovation takes place when local companies adapt the imported idea to local needs or taste.

Moreover, in responding to the popularity of user-generated content (UGC) and recognizing that China's younger generations are digital natives who are keen to engage with commercial industry players, China Central Television (CCTV) launched China Network Television (CNTV) in December 2009. CNTV is a state administered and funded version of already existing private video websites such as Youku and Tudou, which merged in 2012.

With access to CCTV's huge libraries of content without the outlay of expensive copyright fees, China Network Television has obvious market advantages. Sensing an opportunity to tap into creative communities, China Network Television introduced the Ai Xiyou platform (xiyou.cntv. cn), whereby users can upload and share videos. Clearly it has emulated the strategies of many market players in the sector to capture potential profits in the 'informal economy.' Alternatively, this is a case of the government recognizing that grassroots communities have reached a critical mass, albeit a 'mass' that is at odds with the Chinese Communist Party's depiction of 'masses' (*qunzhong*) waiting to be educated, a dominant theme of cultural policy from the 1940s to the 1980s. The new masses are moving online to search for information and entertainment: they are mobile, unpredictable and ubiquitous.

Aside from engaging with the unpredictable digital masses and competing with private media players, China Network Television aims to tell the world about China's development, progress, history and culture. This is perhaps the most important policy intention behind this platform. According to its website, China Network Television is a 'globalized, multi-linguistic, multi-terminal public service platform'; it aims to 'develop it into an authoritative Internet-based broadcaster in China' (CNTV 2010). Such outward-bound aspirations are closely attached to the slogan of 'soft power' (*ruanshili*). The problem that confronts China in its attempts to develop soft power, however, is a widespread global perception that the Communist regime restricts freedom of speech and human rights. Of course, China Network Television steers clear of political minefields by appearing to be an entertainment-focused medium.

Concluding remarks

We began our discussion with a definition of culture from the late-1980s, one nurtured in the womb of historical materialism and political expediency. This definition has served China's policy makers well. However, its efficacy is diminishing as culture power shifts to grassroots. The destabilization of the top-down model is undermining the historically informed stages-of-growth model of culture: this has implications for reform of the social, technological, manufacturing and education systems, as well as the cultural system.

We have argued that the reform of the cultural system has proceeded in fits and starts, accompanied by periods of openness and rectification, by changes in leadership and by the entry of new slogans into policy language. By the end of the first decade of this millennium, it had become apparent to leading policy makers that China's cultural system needed a new lease of life. Reformers focused attention on the separation of public institutions and private business. The concept of innovation made its way into cultural policy language while 'creativity' merged into culture, albeit playing a supporting role to culture in policy language.

The reform of the cultural system now has to deal with a different kind of development issue. China is innovating in the cultural sector, but as we have argued elsewhere (Keane and Zhao 2012) it is striving to do so through a convergence of manufacturing, service industries and technology. Convergence is articulated in government documents and reports as the next stage of China's economic growth. On the ground, there are attempts to build bases that respond to government aspirations, but these are at an early stage of development. Creativity meanwhile has emerged as an aspiration to make China more competitive in the global economy and nurture soft power. At the market level, creativity is often constrained by institutional bottleneck and regulations. At the grassroots level, there is more flux. The *shanzhai* mode of innovation in particular drives demands for cheaper products; it also releases pressure for China's new breed of 'cultural creatives' to strive for novelty. In effect, as thousands of grassroots entrepreneurs and hackers crack the code, the 'Made in China' model becomes 'Remade in China.'

Perhaps more significantly in terms of challenging the top-down model, the convergence of technology and culture has given rise to a groundswell of participation that brings the amateur sphere closer to the mainstream. LI Wuwei (2011, p. 34) concludes: 'Through this practice, the grassroots creators challenge the mainstream with the marginal, the professional with the amateur.' In China today, the reform of the cultural system is no longer confined to the corridors of power in Beijing.

Notes

1. LI Wuwei is one of China's leading policy advisors. From 2008 to 2012, he was vice-chair of the national Committee of the Chinese Peoples' Political Consultative Conference (CPPCC), the leading think in China on social and economic development. He is the author of many books including *How Creativity is Changing China*.
2. The CPPCC is made up of a variety of inputs, including members of China's 'democratic' parties such as the Revolutionary Guomindang, leading entrepreneurs, People's Liberation Army generals and role models.
3. See Brugger and Kelly, *Chinese Marxism in the Post-Mao Era*.
4. See http://www.prnewswire.com/news-releases-test/alvin-toffler-named-among-chinas-most-influential-foreigners-56959942.html.
5. These ideas were influential in a time (the mid-1980s) when the intellectual classes were called up to lead China's transition to modernization in contrast to the previous decades when the value of intellectual work was downgraded and manual labor was elevated.
6. *wenhua tizhi gaige shidian gongzuo de yijian*.
7. *quebao guojia wenhua anquan*.
8. In 2008 SARFT introduced a large-scale crackdown campaign on peer-to-peer sharing websites in the digital sector (see Zhao and Keane, 2013 forthcoming). This was intended to rein in informal distribution activity.
9. *wenhua tizhi gaige shidian gongzuo de yijian*.
10. The Decision of the CCP Central Committee on Major Issues Pertaining to Deepening Reform of the Cultural System and Promoting the Great Development and Flourishing of Socialist Culture.

References

Barme, G. (1992) 'The Greying of Chinese Culture', in K. Hsin-chi and M. Brosseau (eds), *China Review* (Hong Kong: University of Hong Kong Press).

Barr, M. (2011) *Who's Afraid of China? The Challenge of Chinese Soft Power* (London: Zed Books).

Bell, D. (1989) *Zibenzhuyi wenhua maodun (The Cultural Contradictions of Capitalism)*, translated Zhao Yifan (Beijing: Sanlian shudian).

Brugger, W. and Kelly, D. (1990) *Chinese Marxism in the Post-Mao Era* (California: Stanford University Press).

Chin, Y.C. (2011) 'Policy Process, Policy Learning and the Role of Provincial Media in China', *Media Culture and Society*, 33, 193.

Chu, Y.C. (2013) 'The Politics of Reception: "Made in China" and Western Critique', *International Journal of Cultural Studies* (forthcoming).

Chua, B.H. (2012) *Structure, Audience and Soft Power in East Asian Culture* (Hong Kong: Hong Kong University Press).

Cihai (Sea of Words), Shanghai cihai chubanshe, Shanghai, 1989, 1731.

Craik, J. (2007) *Re-Visioning Arts and Cultural Policy: Current Impasses and Future Directions* (Canberra: ANU Press).

Deng, X.P. (1983) 'Congratulation Speech at the Fourth Congress of China's Workers in Literature and Arts', October 30, 1979, in *Selected Works of Deng Xiaoping*, (Hong Kong: Peoples Publishing House and Joint Publishing Co.)

Deng, X.P. (1984), 'Emancipate the Mind, Seek Truth From Facts and Unite as One in Looking to the Future' (December 13, 1978), *Selected Works of Deng Xiaoping (1975–1982)* (Beijing: Foreign Languages Press).

Gerth, K. (2010) *As China Goes, So Goes the World: How Chinese Consumers are Transforming Everything* (New York: Hill and Wang).

Hu, H.L. (2000) 'National Cultural Security – Policies on the Development of the Cultural Industries in the Face of Economic Globalization (guojia wenhua anquan: jingji quanqiuhua Beijing xia zhongguo wenhua chanye fazhan zhenglun', *Academic Monthly* (Xueshu yuekan), (2), 6.

Hu, J.T. (2007) The 16th CPC Central Committee, 2007b. English version of Report to the Seventeenth National Congress of the Communist Party of China on October 15, 2007 [online].

Hu, J.T. (2012) Full Text of Hu Jintao's Report at 18th Party Congress, http://news.xinhuanet.com/english/special/18cpcnc/2012–11/17/c_131981259_7.htm Beijing: The Communist Party of China.[http://www.china.org.cn/english/congress/229611.html], date accessed April 30 2013.

Hu, K. (2006) 'The Power of Circulation: Digital Technologies and the Online Chinese Fans of Japanese TV Drama', *Inter-Asia Cultural Studies*, 6, 71–186.

Hu, S.Q. and Zhang, P.X. (1991) *Zhongguo wenhua shi (The History of Chinese Culture)* (Beijing: Zhongguo guangbo dianshi chubanshe).

Keane, M. (2001) 'Broadcasting Policy, Creative Compliance and the Myth of Civil Society in China', *Media, Culture and Society*, 23, 783–798.

Keane, M. (2007) *Created in China: The Great New Leap Forward* (London: Routledge).

Keane, M. (2010) 'Re-imagining China's Future: Soft Power, Cultural Presence and the East Asian Media Market', in D. Black, S. Epstein and A. Tokita (eds),

Complicated Currents: Media Flows and Soft Power in East Asia (Melbourne: Monash University ePress).

Keane, M. (2010a). 'Reclaiming China's Former Soft Power', *Journal of the Oriental Society of Australia*, 42, 50–64.

Keane, M. (2010b) 'Keeping Up with the Neighbours: China's Soft Power Ambitions', *Cinema Journal: In Focus*, 49(3), 451–463.

Keane, M. (2011) *China's New Creative Clusters: Governance, Human Capital and Investment* (London: Routledge).

Keane, M. (2013) *Creative Industries in China: Art, Design, Media* (London: Polity).

Keane, M.A. and Zhao, E.J. (2012) 'Renegades On the Frontier of Innovation: The Shanzhai Grassroots Communities of Shenzhen in China's Creative Economy', *Eurasian Geography and Economics*, 53(2), 216–230.

Kraus, R. (1995) 'China's Artists between Plan and Market', in D. Davis, R. Kraus, B. Naughton and E.J. Perry (eds), *Urban Spaces in Contemporary China: The Potential for Autonomy and Community in Post-Mao China* (Cambridge: Cambridge University Press).

Kraus, R. (2004) *The Party and the Arty: the New Politics of Culture* (Lanham, Boulder: Rowman and Littlefield).

Kurlantzick, J. (2007) *Charm Offensive: How China's Soft Power Is Transforming the World* (New Haven: Yale University Press).

Lawrence, S.V. and Martin, M.F. (2012) 'Understanding China's Political System' in *Congressional Research Service*, May 12, 2012, http://www.fas.org/sgp/crs/row/R41007.pdf, date accessed March 21, 2013.

Li, M.J. (2008) 'China Debates Soft Power', *Chinese Journal of International Politics*, 2, 287–308.

Li, W.W. (2011) *Creativity is Changing China*, M. Keane (ed.), M. Keane, H. Li and M. Guo. (trans.), (London: Bloomsbury Academic).

Meng, B.C. (2011) 'From Steamed Bun to Grass Mud Horse: E Gao as Alternative Political Discourse on the Chinese Internet', *Global Media and Communication*, 7, 33–51.

Ministry of Culture (2012) Wenhua Bu 'shi er wu' shiqi wenhua chanye beizeng jihua (MoC Plan to Double the Annual Added Value of the Cultural Industry during the 12th Five-Year-Plan), http://www.mcprc.gov.cn/preview/special/3477/3478/201203/t20120301_231780.html, date accessed March 15, 2013.

Naisbitt, J. and Naisbitt D. (2010) *China's Megatrends: The 8 Pillars of a New Society* (New York: HarperBusiness).

Nye, J. (1990) *Bound to Lead: The Changing Nature of American Power* (New York: Basic Books).

Pang, L.K. (2012) 'Post-socialism and Cultural Policy: The Depolitization of Culture in late 1970s and 1980s China', in N. Otmazgin and E. Ben-Ari (eds), *Popular Culture and the State in East and South-East Asia* (London: Routledge).

Peng, X. (2009) 'Wenhua jia keji dianran jingji xin liangdian' (Culture Plus Science and Technology Light Up the Economy), *China Science & Technology Fortune*, 8, 98–101.

Schell, O. (1995) *Mandate of Heaven: A New Generation of Entrepreneurs, Dissidents, Bohemians and Technocrats Lays Claim to China's Future* (New York: Simon & Schuster).

Sun, Wanning (2010) 'Mission Impossible? Soft Power, Communication Capacity, and the Globalization of Chinese Media', *International Journal of Communication*, 4, 54–72.

Wallis, C. and Qiu, J.L. (2012) 'Shanzhaiji and the Transformation of the Local Mediasphere in Shenzhen', in W. Sun and J. Chio (eds), *Mapping Media in China: Region, Province, Locality*. (London: Routledge).

Wang, J. and Cai, R.H. (2011) *Shenhua wenhua tizhi gaige tuidong shehuizhuyi wenhua dafazhan dafanrong shijiang* (Beijing: Zhonggong zhongyang dangxiao chubanshe).

Wang, S.G. (1995) 'The Politics of Private Time', in D. Davis, R. Kraus, B. Naughton and E.J. Perry (eds), *Urban Spaces in Contemporary China: The Potential for Autonomy and Community in Post-Mao China* (Cambridge: Wilson Press).

Wei, L. (2012) Culture to be Pillar Industry, http://usa.chinadaily.com.cn/business/2012–02/16/content_14624552.htm, date accessed March 15, 2013

Wen, J.B. (2009), Report on the Work of the Government, March 14, http://news.xinhuanet.com/english/2009–03/14/content_11009548_5.htm, date accessed April 30, 2012.

Wu, R.W.S. and Leung, G.L.K. (2012). 'Implementation of Three Network Convergence in China: A New Institutional Analysis', *Telecommunications Policy*, 36(10–11), 955–965.

Zhao, E.J. (2011) 'Social Network Market: Storytelling on a Web 2.0 Original Literature Site', *Convergence: The International Journal of Research into New Media Technologies*, 17, 85–99.

Zhao, E.J. and Keane, M. (2013) 'Between Formal and Informal: The Shakeout in China's Online Video Industry', *Media, Culture and Society*, 35(6), 724–741.

10
Creative Industries, Creative Clusters and Cultural Policy in Shanghai
Xin Gu

The last ten years have seen the emergence of Chinese creative industries and creative clusters and accompanying debates in both academic and policy circles. To understand the origin and trajectory of this new policy agenda, we need to understand how most of the assumptions of Western[1] cultural policy and theory – which underpinned cultural and creative industries in that region – were rejected by Chinese communist ideology. Although MAO's socialist members program has been slowly replaced by a more market-oriented democratic program, it is impossible for us to ignore that Chinese cultural policy is not simply based on the Western notion of culture as a 'whole way of life' outside of the state power (Williams 1958) or the state's intention to promote wider participation in civic society as part of liberal governmentality (Bennett 2012). Nor can we reduce it to a 'neo-liberalism' that is seen to pervade the creative industries agenda, especially in Anglo-Saxon countries (Banks and O'Connor 2009). Indeed, Chinese cultural policy presents an alternative both to the art-centric model and the market-centric model, making it a unique case through which to view possible new directions for cultural policy outside the West.

The concept of creative industries, first outlined in the UK in 1998 (DCMS 1998) is a development of a prior notion of the cultural industries, which in turn can be seen as part of longer dialogue within cultural theory and policy that began at the end of the 19th century and the beginning of the 20th century. It raises fundamental questions regarding the relationship between culture and economy that have been at the heart of Western culture at least since the 18th century and which have intensified with the growth of industrial cities and mass reproduction technologies (O'Connor 2010; Hesmondhalgh 2013). The subsequent rise of the term 'cultural and creative industries' can be viewed as a constant rewriting of the paradigms established by culture and economy.[2] Since the 1980s, cultural policy has bifurcated between providing access to arts and culture to ever-wider publics, on the one hand, and becoming more focused on cultural/ creative industries as a growth sector with large economic potential on the other. Debates tend to happen around which of these should be primary, whether they are incompatible and opposed, or if some synergy can be found between them (Hesmondhalgh and Pratt 2005).

But are these accounts of the relationship between culture and economy useful in the Chinese context? If not, what kind of new theoretical frameworks and policy rhetorics might be found that are able to explain Chinese cultural policies – especially those regarding the development of creative industries and creative clusters? What might they tell us about the reconfigured relationship between culture and economy in China? This chapter tries to answer these questions through China's best-known creative city: Shanghai.

Cultural policy – a project of 'Shanghai Modern'

In order to promote itself as the new Asian metropolis, Shanghai has mobilized its earlier modern cultural heritage from the 1920s and 1930s in its modernization and global branding strategies. The built fabric of 'Shanghai Modern' has powered a wider real estate boom and has combined heritage and hyper-modernity in confusing ways (Abbas 2002; O'Connor 2012; O'Connor and Gu 2006, 2012a).

Cultural infrastructure was expanded in the city and re-oriented towards a global gaze. The growth of museums, galleries and concert halls as part of a concerted attempt to construct this modern cultural infrastructure intersected with the revival of a popular nostalgia for the past amongst global actors. These official strategies were accompanied by bottom-up processes. Architects, artists, musicians and other creative entrepreneurs all began to circulate within and transform the local spaces of Shanghai (Gu 2012). The unofficial cultural spaces – cosmopolitan nightscapes, music venues, new media production and the proliferation of online spaces – all came to challenge the protocol and authority of the state in the cultural sphere. How does Shanghai's cultural policy allow for the organization of a new kind of urban cultural economy in a strictly regulated market? What does this 'top down' or macro perspective say about cultural policy in Shanghai (and, with caution, China)?

In the following part, I look at creative industries development policy in Shanghai and assess how this specific kind of policy has continuities and discontinuities with the Western discourses. Next, I assess cluster development policy through a case study of a well-known state enterprise – 'Shanghaitex.' Policies aimed at promoting creative industries clusters have a tendency to shape cultural markets in favor of these state enterprises, mainly through the various entry barriers and protocols established in an attempt to maintain state control over national assets. This allows me to address the wider question of the specific application of policy agendas developed in and adapted from very different contexts.

The formation of cultural policy in Shanghai

It is not hard to understand that the evolution of 'cultural policy' in China was bound to be accompanied by major political and ideological ramifications. Whenever there is a major political change of direction, we can observe a re-structuration of the cultural realm. The open door policy in 1978 gave local cities more freedom in maneuvering its resources based on local know-how. This was influential for cultural policy through its de-centralization of cultural infrastructures and policy development – the two key stepping stones for the transition from a planned economy to the market economy for cultural industries.

Cultural infrastructures that were managed by the nation state now became assets of the local governments. Until the 1950s, Chinese cities received limited investment in cultural infrastructures. Provincial capitals acted as the dissemination loci for centralized cultural policies. These cities had priority over non-provincial cities in cultural development because of well-established culture infrastructures. Shanghai became the film and popular music capital of China based on the private film and recording companies established during the 1920s and 1930s. The nationalization of these cultural infrastructures allowed the merger of previously separated entities to form cultural conglomerates. The Shanghai film production house in particular was one of those mega institutions in the film industry producing more than half of the films commissioned by the state during this period. De-centralization has allowed more innovative use of these infrastructures, and they were a key component of creative clusters in Shanghai.

The formation of local cultural policy is not as straightforward as inheriting cultural infrastructure. It relies not only on local know-how but also on its own vision of what the modern city might be (O'Connor and Gu 2006). This cannot be established overnight. Many Chinese cities, after shutting down from the rest of the world for so long, found it hard to grasp the challenge of 'being modern.' Many regions and cities started to resume their connection with the west in an attempt to be modern. The success of Guangdong's music industry was owed to influences from the highly market driven approaches prevailing in Hong Kong, Japan and Taiwan. These new market trends speeded up the process of commercialization in Guangdong's music industry (Liao 2003).

Shanghai was rather behind in cultural development in this era – awakening from the Cultural Revolution, the city was uncertain about its future and what might happen down the track (Schilbach 2010). In contrast to Beijing's national cultural renaissance and Guangdong's cultural commercialization, Shanghai hesitated to follow either path. A large part of the cultural infrastructure of the city was dysfunctional after the Cultural Revolution, and there were few resources available for rebuilding them. The market connections present in a place like Guangdong didn't exist in Shanghai. Contemporary art probably was the most interesting cultural sector at the time. Artists started to move out of public institutions and experimented with new forms of self-organization while developing new connections with the market. 'Organic' art clusters emerged in the city during this period, operating in a strange limbo between state recognition and discovery by the art market.

Further developing culture in the market economy and promoting cultural affairs suited for an ideology of 'socialism with Chinese characteristics' have been the key policies since 1990s. Although the word 'cultural industries' or 'creative industries' didn't appear in any official document until 2000 in the 10th Five Year Plan, the commercialization of culture was well underway.[3] Beijing took advantage of the concentration of media companies (such as CCTV) to further consolidate its monopoly of the media industry. In comparison, the early risers such as Guangdong lost their advantage because of the lack of market coordination and support by national and local governments. Fierce competition and lack of intellectual property protection backfired (Liao 2003). Cultural policy in this period of re-structuration allocated massive resources to develop cultural infrastructure in sectors that were prioritized by the national state and in cities with strategic economic importance to that state. This created a completely new cultural landscape with limited connection to what was already there (Sun 2003).

Shanghai started to form a rather advanced creative industries policy with a strategy to connect with the 1930s' version of modernity that the city was famously known for (O'Connor 2012). This was clearly articulated in its cultural policy vision statement – from 'made in China' to 'designed in China.' It opened up the complex negotiation of power between state and market that was to follow. In contrast, Beijing's from 'made in China' to 'created in China' vision statement lingers on the role of culture in advancing contemporary Chinese ideology, asserting its 'soft power' (Nye 2005) on the world stage. The concept of 'cultural industries' was strongly established by 2002. Although the national government had concerns over the market takeover of culture, at the local level, there was a widespread enthusiasm to promote the market potential of culture (Xu 2011). Shanghai was the first city to adopt the term 'creative industries,' made voguish by the UK government in 1998 and adopted enthusiastically by the Hong Kong government. Creative clusters were firmly associated with this new idea of 'creative industries' (O'Connor and Gu 2012b). From 2006 to 2010, the number of official creative clusters grew from 12 to over 100 in Shanghai.

Creative industries and creative clusters

Shanghai has the second largest creative industries sector in China. Unlike many other cities, where cultural policy agencies were responsible for 'creating' creative industries, Shanghai's policy in this area has developed alongside the relatively organic growth of local creative industries and has worked through a process of 'normalization': moving from deliberate exclusion, to attempting to understand their needs, to working in partnership and, more recently, directly managing them.

Creative cluster development policy in Shanghai was part of its ambition to be the new Asian metropolis, based on its unique culture and history as the first site of Chinese modernization – in terms of the urban fabric and the new forms of economic and cultural activity to which it gave rise. This more positive image of Shanghai as a site of incipient modernity, long buried under its reputation as base camp of Western imperialism and capitalism, was initially rediscovered through the acknowledgement of the urban heritage of 'old Shanghai.' Many of the creative clusters are restored heritage buildings owned by the city. Not only did the city start building and preserving the urban fabric, it also mobilized its past as a resource for the future (Abbas 2002). In this sense, Shanghai's creative cluster development policy is closer to that developed in the West under the rubric of culture-led urban regeneration. Studying creative cluster development policy in Shanghai thus allows us to assess the process of the negotiation of power between the state and market, acknowledging the complex urban context within which creative industries thrive (O'Connor and Gu 2012).

Despite the absence of major Chinese designer brands, Shanghai's definition of the creative industries focused on individual creativity and their potential commercial outputs as in the UK definition: 'those industries which have their origin in creativity, skill and advanced technologies and clustering of talents and which have a potential for value add in production and consumption, wealth and job creation through their creativities.'[4]

Shanghai's adoption of the term in 2005 was later than other neighboring cities in Asia, hence it has also borrowed some of the policy approaches in the region. Five subsectors were identified, including R&D design, architecture design, culture communication, consultancy and fashion. Instead of focusing on the traditional arts and cultural sectors, this suggested a strong interest in intellectual property and high-tech industries – similar to approaches in Hong Kong and Singapore. Design was placed highest on the agenda because Shanghai was aiming to become a UNESCO's City of Design, part of the Creative Cities network (which was granted in 2011). It was also the case that, ideologically speaking, design was a 'safe' creative industry compared to others – such as literature for example.[5] In many ways, Shanghai's creative industries policy was an update of the existing high-tech industries strategy, promoted through the development of many science parks across the city (Ross 2009). The government was so used to managing large-scale industries ('control the big, let go the small,' was a key strategic slogan of the restricting process (Huang 2010)) that it moved quickly to familiar strategies that would boost economic growth measured in fairly traditional terms. This was very much against the principle of creative industries policy developed in the West, with the emphasis on small or start-up businesses and creative milieu (social networks, informal clustering, soft infrastructure and so on). These elements, fairly central in Western policy discourse and practice, were deliberately ignored in Shanghai (He and Wu 2005).

Shanghai's creative industries development policy also has to face the political test – how can the adoption of 'creative industries' be justified within the largely ideological framework of the national cultural policy? As O'Connor (2010) argued with regard to the replacement of 'cultural' by 'creative' industries, more was at stake than just the tactical benefits of using a (then) more 'sexy' terminology. The term 'creative industries' in the West has walked a tightrope between claims for a new 'democratization of culture' (everyday creativity, individual access to markets through the internet and so on) and the relentless over-commercialization of cultural policy.

The Chinese debate, in contrast, involved three-way re-negotiation between culture, economy *and* politics. The triangular relationship expresses the double requirement of culture as described above. Culture has to be good for economy and abide by current political ideology. This double requirement has deeply influenced Shanghai's creative industries policy. On the one hand, it has led to a strong emphasis on economic outputs for the 'safe' creative industries. On the other hand, more sensitive 'cultural sectors' such as music and publishing, are subject to more control while being deemed to have outputs other than the purely economic. For example, live music venues – deemed to be potential sites of unruly gathering – are tightly controlled in Shanghai. Publishing is heavily subsidized – as are the State-owned Xinhua Bookstores – and foreign capital investment is restricted. As a result, it is the economic development committee that is primarily responsible for creative industries policy, with some input from the cultural committee in Shanghai. This is different from many other provinces and cities. For example, Beijing's creative industries are still under the control of the cultural committee (Hui 2006).

Creative industries policy in Shanghai highlights the ambiguity of Chinese cultural policy caught between economic development and politics. In this case, the adoption of the term 'creative industries' was more than the literal translation of an item of 'fast policy' (Peck 2005, p. 767). What appeared to be an act of 'copying' induces a complex, multi-leveled process of negotiation and re-interpretation. Its complexity was observed by Jonathon Friedmann (2005) who used the term 'amphibian institutions' to describe the ambiguity of the role of local governments in order to negotiate public and private duties and interests. This was clearly the case in the creative cluster development policy – one of the key incentives for local authorities to develop creative industries.

From the surface, Western observers might interpret Shanghai's creative cluster policy as a form of culture-led urban regeneration; that is, as the development of a post-industrial urban cultural economy in what was for a century China's leading manufacturing city (Wang 2009; Zhong 2009). But the role of policymakers in this case is beyond that of facilitators and initiators of local energy (Huang 2008). In many cases, the government owns the land and leases it to private investors who have close affiliation with the government. In other cases, industrial land assigned to state companies is co-managed by the government and the state enterprise. In the latter case, the government will be involved in a series of public and private roles including assisting the privatization of the state company; making sure that the new venture meets the demand for state pensions for displaced workers; promoting local industries and monitoring 'sensitive' cultural content production; brokering relations between the state company and private investors in the renovation of creative clusters; developing adjacent areas of creative clusters in partnership with private investors; and preserving historical buildings. During this process, different levels of negotiation between state power and the market were played out, and it is for this reason that I will be studying this model in more detail in the following section.

I do not wish to deny any similarities between Western creative industries policy and that of Shanghai. The need to introduce 'innovation' to the wider economy, and the restructuring of State management in order to facilitate this process, are both important in understanding creative industries development policy in Shanghai. But rather than foregrounding the role of SMEs in the process of 'innovation' and 'creativity,' creative industries development policy in China tends to marginalize SMEs while continuing to assert the primacy of State direction. This is not to deny the importance of SMEs; rather their activities are incorporated in order to benefit State enterprises. That is, innovation is linked more to State than to market. This is the rationale behind the development of creative clusters and strongly marks the implementation process. That is, the key objective is to establish the boundaries and protocols within which SMEs and independent actors can experiment and innovate; then developing ways to pass these early effects intellectual capital, networks, soft infrastructure and image – onto state enterprises.

Creative clusters development policy – the case of 'Shanghaitex'

Shanghaitex Group Ltd. was established in May 1995, formed from the merger of Shanghai Textile Industrial Bureau (STIB) and Shanghai Textile National Equity Management Company (STNEMC). The former has over 50 textile manufacturing factories under its administration, most of which have ceased manufacturing: some closed down and were vacated, some have merged with other factories, some have been converted into other types of industries, and some have been rented out to a mixture of different private businesses. The sites operating under the last model became attractive to SMEs in creative industries.

The best-known and longest established creative cluster in Shanghai is *M50*, previously Shanghai Chunming Cotton Mill. Leased out to local artists since 1999 when the factory ceased production, *M50* now hosts over 100 art studios, galleries and other creative companies. *M50*, along with a dozen textile factories on the banks of Suzhou River, used to form the largest cluster of textile mills in China. With the rising cost of land (a result of Shanghai's global city aspirations), most of the textile factories have been relocated to the cheaper provinces to the west of the country, leaving behind many old industrial sites (Wu 2004). STNEMC was setup as the temporary agency in order to manage the vast equities that had been left unoccupied. This restructured entity eventually became Shanghaitex Group – a trading company with an estimated market value of 10 billion USD, and listed as one of the top 500 companies in China. Although the newly formed company tried to cling onto its old identity as a textile producer, the reality has been that its main source of income now comes from real estate development, investment and property management – all of which have been learned from its knowledge of dealing with small creative industries that emerged 'organically' in its factories.

When, in 1999, the first group of artists approached *M50* about renting studio space, the factory manager had mixed feelings. On the one hand, it was good to generate income from the old premises. On the other hand, it was uncertain whether this was going to be a legitimate development model, with culture being such a sensitive topic. As a result, contracts between the landlord and the tenants were often temporary and many were based on verbal agreements. During this process, the factory manager became manager of the creative cluster, and displaced workers were reemployed to be part of the everyday operation of the cluster. The lack of policy guidance had many impacts on this first wave of creative clusters in Shanghai (Wu 2007).

The first problem concerned the use of industrial land for commercial purposes (cf. Liu 2007). All warehouses owned by Shanghaitex Group are on industrial land, and factories are not allowed by Chinese law to be leased out for commercial uses. Was it possible to appropriate creative clusters for the use by creative industries without infringing this principle? Second, there was the constant change of ownership of these creative clusters. Due to the scale and complexity of asset restructuring within Shanghaitex, old warehouses and factories were constantly changing hands from one management company to another. This caused confusion amongst tenants regarding their rights in the use of these buildings. This resulted in a clear lack of enthusiasm for refurbishing the spaces. The built infrastructure of many clusters was extremely rundown prior to 2005. The third problem was to do with finance. Most of the clusters started on ad hoc revenue and expenditure models – meaning the factories would pass on all the rental income to Shanghaitex and receive operational costs, including salaries of staff, in return. This model is akin to the old state planned economy and tended to discourage active intervention in the creative clusters (which in some cases meant benign neglect). For example, the management companies were not very interested in improving services and infrastructures within clusters as their performance was not measured on this, nor were they rewarded for it.

This precarious status of creative clusters carried on until 2005, when the launch of Shanghai Creative Industries Centre (SCCI) by the Shanghai Economic Committee marked out clear policy instructions on the development of creative clusters: 'Three No Changes' and 'Five Changes.' The 'Three No Changes' were: no change is made to the property ownership; no change is made to the use of land; and no change made to the structure of the building. These are clearly inherited from the national cultural heritage agenda. The 'Five Changes' were those allowed in areas of industrial structure, employment structure, management model, company composition and corporate culture. They are largely about economic restructuring and development. This policy has in many ways 'normalized' the ad hoc arrangements that were already in place by establishing protocols for private investment and joint ventures in cluster development. The introduction of this policy, as I will explain below, had three aims: to ensure state control, to create better infrastructure by incorporating private investment, and to prepare for the development of state conglomerates in creative industries.

The SCCI acts as a gatekeeper for local government through its creative cluster nomination and assessment program. Only SCCI approved creative clusters are allowed to advertise and rent industrial land out for use by creative clusters. In this way, local government gets to control how land is used and managed. Every year these official creative clusters will be assessed, based on local government criteria including occupancy and tax return. Creative clusters have to have over 70% of creative businesses in order to maintain their 'official' status. This policy was seen as favoring the big state companies, who through their affiliation with governments find it easier to acquire the official status in comparison to privately owned clusters. The tendering process is not transparent, and many private cluster management companies are not allowed to participate. Private companies are marginalized in many other highly regulated processes for receiving state benefits including tax breaks.

This policy further privileges state companies by introducing non-market rules while all creative clusters have been until then operating on the market principle. A good example was the rule that all creative clusters have to re-employ redundant workers from the old factories. It is difficult for many private companies to comply – redundant workers are more likely to opt for working for state enterprise anticipating higher-level pension schemes when they retire. The state enterprises are clearly privileged through these protocols. In some ways, we could read it as the benefit of the 'socialist model' – after all, creative industries have provided jobs to the city (although they are not direct creative jobs) and in some cases, these figures are significant and are important in helping bringing forward the wider industrial restructuring in Shanghai. However, a key problem prevails. Unlike private cluster companies often run by creative entrepreneurs, state run companies are managed by the old factory bosses who have little knowledge of creative industries. This is most obvious in the restoration process of clusters when state management companies – not understanding issues of atmosphere and aesthetic capital – demand a standard modern office look and deny the right for creative businesses within to modify the space.

Both of these 'odd' protocols have been formalized by local government. It is according to the 'Five Changes' that factories were expected to generate revenues to meet the demand of pensions of displaced workers and contribute tax income to the local government. And it is the 'Three No Changes' that specifies that there are many restrictions on the modification of the physical space in clusters. What is worth noting here is that these policies were slowly implemented. It's a learning process for the government that wants to develop state conglomerates in this sector. The result is very clear: from 2005 to 2013, the ratio of public/ private companies in the investment of creative clusters has changed from 1:2 to 21:1. And many remaining independent companies have already partnered with the state company in order to maintain their 'official' cluster status as well as receive tax breaks. The state conglomerates are a 'cluster of clusters' and Shanghaitex is one of them. Shanghaitex developed two main investment models consequent on the introduction of creative cluster policy. One is through direct investment by Shanghaitex's offshoot companies. Such is the cases with *M50* and Shanghai Loft as can be seen in the following illustration.

These clusters have already developed a high profile, and they are also the star projects for the local district governments. This guarantees clusters such as *M50* will receive more local incentives, including local tax breaks on top of the city level tax breaks. According to the manager of *M50*, in the year 2011 alone, *M50* has received enough government subsidies to cover its entire operational cost with profit. Such privileged proposition has attracted many private investors to join forces with

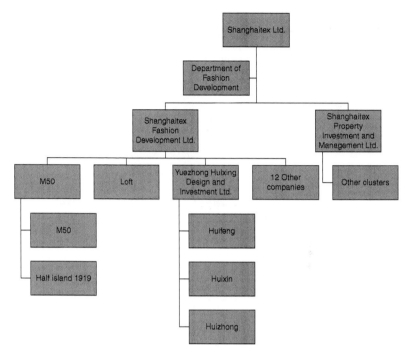

Figure 10.1 Company structure of Shanghaitex Limited

these star projects. And through private investment, the star projects are more likely to improve infrastructures, developing appropriate market strategies and brand the services. In 2011, *M50* received significant private investment to branch out to enter another cluster development opportunity – *Taopu: M50 Stage 2*. The other investment model is based on asset leasing. Factories will lease out them to private developers for a lower than market price rate. In return, the factories will own shares in the newly formed property development company. Most of the less successful clusters are developed based on this model in order to shed risk from directly investing in infrastructures.

In order to coordinate activities and accounts of these clusters, in 2010, Shanghaitex regrouped all its creative cluster management companies that had formed on the two models. The first step was to set up a specialized Fashion Development branch with two new companies under it – 'Shanghaitex Fashion Development Company' (STFDC) and 'Shanghaitex Property Investment and Management Company' (STPIMC). The former were to run the star projects, and the latter for the less successful ones.

Both groups have been given 'official' status by SCCI and contributed collectively to the rebranding of Shanghaitex and its transition from a textile manufacturing company to that of a real estate development company. More market oriented management measures were introduced. These companies are now allowed to manage their own finance and contribute certain percentage of their income to Shanghaitex.

The knowledge and connections developed within the flagship creative cluster projects were essential in Shanghaitex's exploration of other emergent development opportunities. In most of its joint ventures, Shanghaitex gets land lease deals through its connection with other state enterprises, and private investors will supply funds for renovation as well as deal with marketing and business plans. Although private companies have invested the majority of the capital (and will receive the majority of the rental profit from the project), Shanghaitex group has to own majority of the shares in the company in order to retain state ownership as written in the official cluster development policy. It might seem that Shanghaitex has used cluster development as an opportunity for social development. But the underlying intention of Shanghaitex is to use private money to develop public cultural infrastructures, and the social agenda is really the by-product.

This situation might be contrasted with what is happening in the West. Here, creative clusters that were formed 'organically' and received symbolic investment by the creative community frequently face problems of gentrification and rental hikes that undermine their initial creative ambition. In these cases, gentrification comes down as a result of the state's inability to intervene in the market process. The Shanghai case seems promising in preserving creative industries in the city in the sense that the Chinese state has significant influence on the market condition (He and Wu 2005). But if the Shanghaitex model is to work effectively for local creative industries, it is essential for the state to rethink how it should position itself in relation to the market, in particular, its relationship to SMEs and local community.

My own survey conducted during 2011–2012 suggested that SMEs are more likely to thrive in Shanghaitex's star projects than in clusters operated through the other investment model. The reasons are the low rent and the ambition on the part of the management company to keep 'authentic' creative industries. The star projects suggest evidence of a sustainable cluster development model involving proactive state involvement. This could be a viable lesson for cluster development elsewhere in creative industries policy where the state might have other roles to play. However, the survey also shows a tendency to decrease the number of SMEs in the star group. Many creative businesses felt it was increasingly difficult for SMEs to meet the requirement to stay in the 'Star' group. Business success was measured purely in economic terms, and SMEs are not successful businesses, according to these measurements. Here it seems to me a step too far on the part of the state to try to play the role of a market operator.

The alignment of cultural policy with economic development policy was aimed at creating urban spectacles to contribute to a positive global image. The underlying danger of equating culture with development is the over-commercialization of a cultural sector where the only measurement of success for culture is how much GDP it contributes. Shanghai has the most spectacular creative clusters in China, and it also has the most commercially driven culture sector. The saying in China, 'To sell art, go to Shanghai, to make art, stay in Beijing,' is essential to understanding the relationship between culture and development as well as the spatial arrangements of cultural activities. Creative clusters in China are not about making culture as in the Western understanding of urban milieu. They are about success, fame and money, which many argue strongly represent the current status of contemporary Chinese art. Art galleries moving into creative clusters are an example of this as they seek to become part of the global cultural trade.

The question is what impact will the economic rationale now taken-for-granted both by government and by the creative community in Shanghai have on the development of creative industries in the longer term. It has become a trend for artists to leave Shanghai to pursue aesthetic enlightenment for a few months and only to come back when there is an exhibition or other business to be dealt with. Shanghai has increasingly become a node of international cultural trade without the development of creative milieu.

This brings us back to the culture and economic argument outlined earlier. It has been observed that since the introduction to creative industries by the DCMS, there is a tendency for a 'neo-liberal' approach to culture (Banks and O'Connor 2009) in the West. Although the social and political context is different in China, it is equally important for cultural development in China not to fall into the 'neo-liberal' trap by developing its own balanced structure within which the power relation between culture, market and state can be understood and negotiated. This includes the acknowledgement of the organic process of creative development – for the state to learn not to interfere too much. At the same time, more fair play is needed through the state attending to the needs of the SMEs as well as the large corporations.

Conclusion

Can a global city such as Shanghai stand out from a nation state of the size and power of the People's Republic of China? The current narrative promoted by Shanghai is one where 1949 to 1978 (or 1992, when DENG Xiaoping gave it the green light) acts as an interruption of the city's path to global modernity. However, the relation of culture and economy under the dominance of communist politics is crucial in understanding the subsequent policy reforms regarding cultural development. There is no doubt that the communist period laid many of the foundations upon which the post 1978 reforms were built. The reform of cultural policy in recent years still has close relation to the founding ideology of the CCP in its continued reference to culture *as* ideology. Looking at cultural policy in Shanghai, beneath the glitter of the global metropolis, shows how it continues to be affected by the powerful nation state (Lee et al. 2007). Despite the rhetoric of creativity, we can see the institutionalization of organically emerged creative clusters and the integration of privately developed clusters within a state system. Behind the adoption of creative industries is an assertion of national and local state control and an enlargement of the scale of creative industries development which deliberately ignored the needs of SMEs. There is no mention of SMEs in any policy document concerning their importance as outlined in the Western scenario. Not only was their entry to the clusters restricted, they were refused tax incentives and other economic benefits because of the policy makers' inability to comprehend social and cultural benefit these SMEs have brought into the local creative sector.

However, there were also discontinuities with previous policy settings as market competition was introduced and began to grow. There was a privatization and commodification of culture. The adoption first of 'cultural' then 'creative industries' allowed for market competition and pricing and moved the boundaries between culture as a 'sensitive' topic overseen by the state to culture as providing 'profitable' goods (Kraus 2004). This gave a high degree of ambiguity to the role of the local and national state – should this role be about regulation or promotion? The development of cluster policy also demonstrated such ambiguity. On the one hand, the local state tried to use policy to regulate the development of clusters by restricting private investment; on the other hand, the local state has encouraged joint ventures – using private money in the development of creative clusters that will eventually be incorporated by the state enterprises.

Above, we suggested a process of 'normalization' – a loosening of boundaries in order to make space for experiments was followed by a formal policy intervention around these, establishing new protocols between politics, culture and market (Chen and Dickson 2010). We discussed in detail some of the fissures, conflicts and malfunctions of this return of politics-culture-economy through the case study of Shanghaitex. It revealed how the state played a double role as regulator and operator for the benefit of state enterprises. In this case, the state used private investment for public goods that in return generated wealth for state enterprises. We also assessed the formulation of cluster development policy in Shanghai as an amphibian policy in the sense that the development of creative clusters is not just about generating revenues, it is also about institutionalization through a highly regulated market. We also witnessed the construction of a new industry system around large-scale entities similar to that of the rest of the economy for purpose of both ideological *and* economic control by the state. The case of Shanghaitex provides a unique Chinese development model setting the spatial and industrial context for the proliferation of creative clusters in the city. Through looking in detail at the complex policy arrangements between the state enterprise, the local government and private developers, we discovered ways in which a local 'entrepreneurial state' (Huang 2008) worked with development interests to produce cluster agglomerates in a short space of time. We also saw the results in terms of the urban social and cultural fabric and of the growth of the 'creative economy.'

Looking at the glamorous creative clusters in Shanghai, it is easy to overlook the fact that they are not for creative activities. In fact, it has been observed that Shanghai has lost many of its creative talents to Beijing, where the creative atmosphere is less controlled by the state and less oriented towards the market. In this sense, we can argue that Shanghai's cultural policy has created urban spectacles and retail cultures instead of a creative urban milieu.

There are two possibilities for the future of Shanghai's creative industries in the context of the current hype around creative clusters. One possibility is that creative industries will follow the modernization of cultural infrastructure. After all, Chinese entrepreneurs have long been used to operating within the specific context of the PRC. In this scenario the new creative industries will learn their lesson on how to work with both State and Market. Another possibility is that these urban spectacles will fail the market test when the space for 'innovation' becomes increasingly institutionalized and controlled. That is, neither producers nor consumers of culture or creative industries will want to go there. In which case the current disjunct between the city's emphasis on investment in cultural infrastructure as part of its global metropolis ambitions and the reality of its local cultural offer will grow. In this sense, Shanghai's creative clusters, which were predicated on the generation of urban cultural milieus of production and innovation, providing the link with the large-scale infrastructural investments, seem to be headed for failure.

It seems that as in the West, where a post-Global Financial Crisis (GFC) urban cultural landscape has increasingly withdrawn its faith in creative real estate developments and new solutions are sought; in Shanghai, too, new resources of hope are needed. Whether the city's collectivist and industrial past, or perhaps a de-glamorized retrieval of the Chinese modernist ethos of the 1920s and 1930s, can contribute to these resources is hard to say. At present, artists and other creatives remain marginalized in a city that purports to support them and thrive in their company. Perhaps the Shanghai case, as in the post-GFC West, indicates the need to return 'creative industries' back from their insertion into some globalized 'knowledge economy' and rethink them as cultural policy.

Notes

1. In this chapter, I used the term 'Western' to refer to developed economies in North America and Western Europe where policy discourses have been copied by Chinese cities.
2. For a detailed account on the relationship between culture and economy in the West, see Adorno, T. and Horkheimer, M. (1989) *Dialectic of Enlightenment.* NY: Continuum.
3. Key cultural policy documents come out from this period are: CPC Central Committee (1993) Decisions on the development of Socialist Market Economy http://www.china.com.cn/chinese/archive/131747.htm and the 'Proposal of the Central Organization Committee on public institution reforms' http://www.hrbmu.edu.cn/h_zzjg/rsc/faguichaxun/renshizhidugaige/13.htm.
4. The definition of Shanghai's creative industries was first announced in the mayor's speech, see http://www.gov.cn/test/2006–02/07/content_180529. htm. This was made more specific in the 11th Five Year Plan on the Development of Shanghai's Creative Industries, see http://www.sida.org.cn/policy/policy/2010–08–17/407.html.
5. The link between Shanghai's creative industries and local economic development was made clear by policy documents coming out of Shanghai's Economic Development Committee on Creative Industries for example, Shanghai Municipal Development and Reform Commission (2012) Shanghai's creative industries to reach 12% of GDP by 2015. http://www.shdrc.gov.cn/main?main_colid=367&top_id=316&main_artid=19564.

References

Abbas, A. (2002) 'Play it Again Shanghai: Urban Preservation in the Global Era', in M. Gandelsonas (ed.), *Shanghai reflections. Architecture, Urbanism, and the Search for an Alternative Modernity* (New York: Princeton Architectural Press).

Andreas, J. (2010) 'A Shanghai Model?', *New Left Review*, 65, 63–86.

Banks, M. and O'Connor, J. (2009) 'Special Issue: Introduction Creative Industries Ten Years After', *International Journal of Cultural Policy*, 15(4), 365–373.

Bennett, T. (2012) 'Culture, Institution, Conduct: The Perspective of Metaculture', *Creativity and Academic Activism: Instituting Cultural Studies* (Hong Kong: Hong Kong University Press).

Chen, J. and Dickson, B.J. (2010) *Allies of the state: China's Private Entrepreneurs and Democratic Change* (Cambridge, Mass.: Harvard University Press).

Cao, P. (2007) 'Chinese Cultural Institutional Reforms', *Research on Contemporary Chinese History*, 5.

DCMS (1998) *Creative Industries Mapping Document* (London: Department of Culture, Media and Sport).

Friedmann, J. (2005) *China's Urban Transition* (Minneapolis: University of Minnesota Press).

Gu, X. (2012) 'The Art of Re-industrialisation in Shanghai', *Culture Unbound*, 4, 193–211.

He, S. and Wu, F. (2005) 'Property-led Development in Post-reform China: A Case Study of Xintiandi Redevelopment Project in Shanghai', *journal of Urban Affairs*, 27(1), 1–23.

Hesmondhalgh, D. (2013) *The Cultural Industries* (third edition) (Sage Publications Ltd).

Hesmondhalgh, D. and Pratt, A. (2005) 'Cultural Industries and Cultural Policy', *International Journal of Cultural Policy*, 11(1), 1–14.

Huang, Y. (2008) *Capitalism with Chinese Characteristics. Entrepreneurship and the State* (Cambridge, Mass: Cambridge University Press).

Hui, D. (2006) 'From Cultural to Creative Industries. Strategies for Chaoyang District, Beijing', *International Journal of Cultural Studies*, 9(3), 317–331.

Keane, M. (2010) 'Great Adaptations: China's Creative Clusters and the New Social Contract', *Continuum: Journal of Media & Cultural Studies*, 23(2), 221–230.

Kraus, R.C. (2004) *The Party and the Arty. The New Politics of Culture* (Oxford, UK: Roman and Littlefield).

Lee, C-C., Zhou, H. and Huang, Y. (2007) 'Party-market Corporatism, Clientelism, and Media in Shanghai', *The Harvard International Journal of Press/Politics*, 12(3), 21–42.

Liao, X.M. (2003) 'An Analysis of Guangdong's Grassroots Music Industry: Its Rise and Current issues', *Research on Publishing and Broadcasting*, 9.

Liu, J. (2007) 'Industrial Cultural Heritage: Protection and Innovative Use', *Shanxi Architecture*, 33(28).

Nye, J. (2005) 'The Rise of China's Soft Power', *Wall Street Journal Asia*, December 29.

O'Connor, J. (2010) *The Cultural and Creative Industries: A Review of the Literature* (London: Creative Partnerships. Revised edition).

O'Connor, J. (2012) 'Shanghai: Replaying Futures Past', *Culture Unbound*, 4, 15–34.

O'Connor, J. and Gu, X. (2006) 'A New Modernity? The Arrival of "Creative Industries" in China', *International Journal of Cultural Studies*, 9(3), 271–283.

O'Connor, J. and Gu, X. (2012a) 'Shanghai: Image of Modernity', in Y.R. Isar, M. Hoelscher and H. Anheier (eds), *Cities, Cultural Policy and Governance, Cultures and Globalization Series* 5 (London: Sage).

O'Connor, J. and Gu, X. (2012b) 'Creative Industry Clusters in Shanghai: A Success Story?', *International Journal of Cultural Policy*, DOI:10.1080/1028663 2.2012.740025.

Peck, J (2005) 'Struggling with the Creative Class', *International Journal of Urban and Regional Research*, 29(4), 740–770.

Ross, A. (2009) *Fast Boat to China: High-tech Outsourcing and the Consequences of Free Trade: Lessons from Shanghai* (New York: Vintage Press).

Schilbach, T. (2010) 'Cultural Policy in Shanghai: The Politics of Caution in the Global City', *Journal of Policy Research in Tourism, Leisure and Events*, 2(3), 221–235.

Sun, D. (2003) 'Cultural Industries Development in the New Era', *Research on Contemporary Chinese History*, 1.

Wang, J. (2009) '"Art in Capital": Shaping Distinctiveness in a Culture-led Urban Regeneration Project in Red Town, Shanghai', *Cities*, 26, 318–330.

Williams, R. (1958) 'Culture is ordinary' in *Resources of Hope: Culture, Democracy and Socialism* (London: Verso), 3–14.

Wu, H. (2007) 'Problems and Strategies of Chinese Creative Industries', *Contemporary Economics*, 10.

Wu, W. (2004) 'Cultural Strategies in Shanghai: Regenerating Cosmopolitanism in an Era of Globalisation', *Progress in Planning*, 61, 159–180.

Xu, H.M. (2011) 'Private Art Gallery: Its Prosperity and Uncertainty', *People's Daily*, March 17.

Zhong, S. (2009) 'From Fabrics to Fine Arts. Urban Restructuring and the Formation of an Art District in Shanghai', *Critical Planning*, 16, 118–137.

11
Developing the Creative Economy: The Network Approach of the Five Municipalities in Taiwan

Hsiao-Ling Chung

Current cultural and creative industries policy developments in Taiwan

Taiwan's economic strength has been rooted in its manufacturing base and in economies of scale. It started with a labor-intensive manufacturing boom in the 1950s and then progressed rapidly to the technology-intensive sector. The rapid industrialization and growth during the latter half of the 20th century created the 'Taiwan miracle.' In a recent report on global innovation and competitiveness published by the Economist Intelligence Unit in 2012, Taiwan today is ranked sixth globally and second in Asia; its current position is bolstered by a strong entrepreneurial spirit that is transforming Taiwan's economy. However, Taiwan's heavy reliance on the tech sector, which makes up about 40% of its GDP, also makes it vulnerable to global economic downturns and makes it necessary to seek new paths for national competitiveness at various levels.

One of these new paths would unfold from 1995. With the support of cultural experts in Taiwan, the Council of Cultural Affairs (CCA) proposed the concept of 'Culture Industrialization, Industries Culturalization,' a grass-roots approach to generating new economic value from local cultural assets, while improving industrial competitiveness through an appreciation and application of Taiwan's historical and cultural roots.[1] The term 'cultural industries' thus became a cultural policy guideline for involving local authorities and communities developing into an island-wide 'Comprehensive Community Building' plan. This resulted in a new economic model that centered on 'local cultural values' (Yang 2011, pp. 231–250). Subsequently, given the distinct economic contribution of the 'creative industries' recognized by the UK government since 1998, the Taiwanese government adopted the term 'creative industries' and combined it with 'cultural industries' to form the 'Cultural and Creative Industries' (CCI) which would be defined as industries that 'originate from creativity or accumulation of culture which, through the formation and application of intellectual properties, possess potential capacities to create wealth and job opportunities, enhance the citizen's capacity for arts and elevate the citizens' living environment' (CCA 2010).

When the concept of the 'creative city' became another tool for policy-makers and urban planners to enhance the creative economy of cities, this concept was also incorporated into CCI policy, and it has remained a strategically important driving force in Taiwan's urban economic growth and revitalization through the promotion of a renewed sense of the broader 'values' of local culture (i.e., shaping a city's image, retaining talent and generating added value to other industry sectors).

When Taiwan gained formal entrance into the World Trade Organization in 2002, the government introduced Challenge 2008-National Development Plan, a six-year policy plan about how to create new national competitive advantages so as to address the growing economic competition from Mainland China (Executive Yuan 2002). Significantly, among the ten major development plans, CCI was for the first time included in the national development plan, taking their place alongside biotech and digital content sectors. It was hoped that CCI would be able to create added value to other sectors. In 2009, in order to boost CCI development, a four-year national branding campaign named 'Creative Taiwan' was formed to transform Taiwan into a regional cultural and creative hub. Under this project, the government aimed to develop CCI through two major strategies: infrastructure building and flagship industries development. With the action plans outlined, in February 2010, the Law for the Development of the Cultural and Creative Industries was promulgated.

Significantly, having laws in place offered CCI development a clear legal and funding infrastructure and also provided the CCA with a strong foundation on which it could act as a central government agency in charge of the sector's development. In Article 5 of the General Principle of this Law, it is stated that the 'Competent Authority' in charge of CCI development would refer to the CCA in the central government, the municipal government in municipalities, and county governments in counties (CCA 2010, p. 2). This emphasis on local authorities is gener-ally regarded as a decentralizing practice, as it empowers local govern-ments to be responsible for their own CCI development.

Correspondingly, by the end of 2010, five special municipalities were created, as the highest level cities in Taiwan. In the north, there would be

Taipei and New Taipei City, the latter formerly known as Taipei County; in the center of Taiwan, Greater Taichung City was created as the result of a merger of Taichung City and Taichung County and in the south of Taiwan, there would be Greater Tainan and Greater Kaohsiung, both created through the mergers of Tainan City and Tainan County, and Kaohsiung City and Kaohsiung County respectively. As the Taiwanese government sought to strengthen its competitive edge through a redis-covering of local culture, it was hoped that the urban administrative rezoning and the establishment of the five municipalities would serve as a foundation for the implementation of local-level governance and boost Taiwan's economic growth (Chao 2011). These five municipalities had the potential to play an important role in regard to CCI develop-ment, as together they accounted for over 25% of Taiwan's land area and 60% of the overall population, of which 70% was tertiary-educated, contained 72% of the total of CCI enterprises, and generated about 88% of CCI's overall turnover (Annual Report CCI Development 2011).[2]

Despite the fact that CCI is defined as a sector that originates from the 'accumulation of culture ... and is expected to elevate the citizens' living environment,' what actually 'constitutes CCI in Taiwan is an overarching industrial contract that covers the government's ambitious political promises, whilst defining actions across all levels and connecting all sectors' (Chung 2012, p. 342). Given the above, this chapter focuses on the two aforementioned strategies, infrastructure building and devel-oping the flagship industries, to examine CCI development measures in the five municipalities.

Research fieldwork was undertaken in Taiwan between February and August 2012 and empirical material is drawn from in-depth interviews with 6 senior CCI policy planners from the five municipal governments. Interviews were conducted using semi-structured questions and open conversations. In addition, I examined recent official documentation including development strategies, reports and guideline publications regarding their CCI development. The policy implications concerning how to facilitate CCI development from local government level within each city is then identified.

Brief of the five municipal cities

Taipei: becoming a design capital

Historically, the development of Taipei dates back to the Qing Dynasty in the 18th century, when it was heralded as the nexus of Northern Taiwan. Taipei has continually transformed itself since then, playing a key role through the Japanese Colonial Period and the Taiwanese Retrocession.

In 1967, its status as a city was recognized as an Executive Yuan (Cabinet) governed municipality or direct municipality, and remains so to this day, with a population of 2.6 million people. According to the Taipei Yearbook 2011, Taipei, as the capital of Taiwan, can be considered a creative city through successfully hosting international events such as The Flora Expo and International Design Alliance Congress as well as winning the hosting rights for the 2017 Summer Universiade, which has raised the international profile both for the city and Taiwan. Taipei will also be the 2016 World Design Capital.

New Taipei city: a happy city

Surrounding Taipei, New Taipei City started as Taipei County in 1945 after the end of Japanese governance when the Taiwanese government turned Taipei into a provincial administrative municipality while making the rest of the Taipei region into Taipei County. This resulted in independent administrative bodies between these two cities. New Taipei City would develop and prosper due to its location and is today a major commercial city, second to Taipei, yet with the largest population, just over 3.8 million people. It has also become a favored alternative location for citizens and businesses due to the high cost of housing in Taipei. Statistics indicate that 65% of New Taipei City's residents are from elsewhere, which has led to diversity in terms of talent, customs and cuisines, turning it into a culturally diverse and dynamic city. After it became a municipal city, the mayor proposed his vision of transforming the city into a 'happy city' with 'hope and new life,' becoming 'Beautiful New Taipei City' (New Taipei City 2012).

Greater Taichung: a city for creative living

Centrally located in the western half of Taiwan, and literally meaning 'central Taiwan,' Taichung City is the third largest city on the island after New Taipei City and Kaohsiung. It has a population of just over 2.6 million people. Taichung City was established during the Qing Dynasty, but its roots can be traced back to settlement by Taiwanese aborigines before then. The city first emerged as a major political, economic, transportation, and cultural hub due to its railways and shipping port, which were developed during the period of Japanese occupation. The city also retains the original 'chessboard' street plan from the Japanese era, leaving it with abundant parkways and public spaces. The city is now a trade, manufacturing, service, logistics and transportation hub for Central Taiwan, Taiwan and the surrounding Greater China region.

The merger of Taichung City and county has resulted in a land area that is three times the size of Singapore and twice that of Hong Kong. For the mayor, Jason Hu, the creation of Greater Taichung would allow for the 'natural and infrastructural resources of both areas to be consolidated for the development of a stronger foundation and larger stage for the growth of cultural and creative industries' (Taichung City Government 2012). Describing Greater Taichung as a 'cultural, energetic new city,' Hu has declared that the city would use culture as a foundation in which to develop the city economically, and in a recent speech, he highlighted how his government has worked hard to imbue its residents with the opportunities to participate in culture (ibid.).

Greater Tainan: cultural capital, creative city

Tainan is the birthplace of Taiwan and the city with the longest history and earliest cultural roots. Situated in Southern Taiwan, archaeologists have discovered fossils of Hayasaka rhinoceroses and mammoths that date back to the last Ice Age. Neolithic remains have also been found, together with relics from ancient settlements by the Pinghu, Siraya, and Hoanya tribes. The city saw its first Chinese settlement in the late 16th century. The Dutch ruled the city from 1624 to 1662, and used it as a trading base with Japan and China. In 1683, when the Qing Dynasty regained control of Taiwan, Tainan was chosen as the capital and remained the political, cultural and economic center of the island until 1885, when the capital moved to Taipei. The city has thus been able to prosper through its trade markets from the Qing dynasty to the Japanese colonial period. Due to this history, Tainan has the greatest number and highest concentration of cultural assets among the other cities in Taiwan, and with the smallest population – 1.7 million people – among the five municipal cities.

Greater Kaohsiung: an ocean city of creativity

After the Japanese colonial period ended in 1945, Kaohsiung gained city status in 1946, and the city become a special municipality in 1979. Located in southwestern Taiwan and facing the Taiwan Strait in the west, Kaohsiung has grown from being a small trading village in the 17th century into Taiwan's largest industrial and commercial harbor city with one of the world's most important cargo ports. Kaohsiung was the industrial engine behind the 'Taiwan miracle' when the island emerged as a world leader in manufacturing in the 1960s, and it remains as a center of shipbuilding, refining, and light and heavy industries of Taiwan. With a population of over 2.7 million people, it is the second largest city after

New Taipei City. The city entered into a long period of transition and transformation in the 1980s when there was a shift to tech industries. As a result, Kaohsiung is cultivating itself now as a more liveable cosmopolitan city to shake off its image as an industrial city. Following the merger in 2010, Greater Kaohsiung is now Taiwan's largest city in terms of land size and second only to New Taipei City in population.

Infrastructure building: people matter

With an emphasis on the economy, the Infrastructure Building Strategy from the Taiwanese government is focused on financial support, industry integration, market expansion, HR development and park or clustering schemes. While these strategies were criticized as largely reflecting a manufacturing-bound mindset, I would argue that these measures have prompted local governments to improve the public services they offer and determine what is needed to encourage talent in the CCI to thrive. This can be seen in how the hosting of various international events in Taipei has allowed the local government opportunities to train their government officers and transform the image of their city into one that is attractive to creative talent. On being asked about infrastructure building, a government officer in Taipei highlighted these two points by stating how

> 'these events require an international standard (and) we are using these events as the best opportunities to train our government officers ... so as to transform our roles into a one stop service provider ... for creative talents; keeping them happy so that they will be interested in what we are trying to do as well'. (Interview 1)[3]

Another way in which the building of infrastructure can be used to attract creative talent can be seen in the construction of Taipei's CCI Development Double Corridor which would connect existing and emerging cultural infrastructure such as the National Palace Museum Cultural Park and Taipei Concert Hall, the transformation of CCI bases across Eastern and Western Taipei to create services platforms, and an Art Reverberation Space Network to stimulate the regeneration of local communities and promote cultural tourism. These three measures would transform Taipei into an integrated creative city made up of different districts with their own distinct identities that the local government hopes would be attractive to creative talent. As the government officer states,

The development and exploitation of these cultural and creative spots are talent-driven and the development of the ... Corridor follows existing cultural and commercial routes in the city which have grown organically ... we want to promote the idea that the city is an exhibition in itself, in that every area and street in Taipei showcases different stages of the city! We need to ensure that all the districts in Taipei have their own cultural features, based on their own specific historical roots, and that artists and creative talent have the space to stay and live in Taipei. (Interview 1)

Taipei's government's efforts to develop these strategies are triggered by the fact that the city is confronting increasing challenges in retaining creative talent as the recent economic boom in Mainland China and the promotion of CCI in other cities in Taiwan have led to a brain drain. These infrastructure developments have thus induced various changes in regulations, and Taipei's Department of Cultural Affairs has worked with other departments to relax and revise a series of regulations to promote CCI development. This include allowing arts and cultural events to conduct commercial activities, and allowing for greater usage of public spaces at pedestrian malls. The interviewed officer acknowledged that this was a 'cross-departmental collaboration' which is allowing the government to 'explore all possibilities' and 'test (its) limitations' in an attempt to determine what strategies would be the most effective to allow the city to transform itself into a place that was attractive to creative talent (Interview 1).

Greater Kaohsiung also faces the same problem of how to retain and attract creative talent. Their strategies, as their local government officer points out, are a direct approach to creating spaces that are attractive to creative talent, as well as an indirect approach: acting as a facilitator. Through running 'creative markets along the Pier 2 Arts District which has been quite successful in terms of attracting various types of creative producers,' Kaohsiung's local government officer states that the government is hoping that providing venues will 'attract the best talents to create the best value with the spaces' (Interview 5). At the same time, the Greater Kaohsiung government is also facilitating competitions to 'encourage local communities to collaborate and learn from each other' while the government provides advice (Interview 5). It is hoped that both these approaches will provide local residents with a better understanding of what the government seeks to achieve via CCI development, so as to better manage expectations and minimize misunderstandings.

Through my interviews, another key trend identified in infra-structure building was the emphasis on including local communi-ties in these developments through the creation of local districts that promote local culture. This is illustrated with the case of New Taipei City. The city's diversity offered new challenges when the local government was trying to find ways in which to collaborate with local residents. The importance of the 'local' can be seen in the strategies proposed by New Taipei City, which called for building infrastruc-ture of an international quality that would also feature local cultural houses, establish local cultural subjectivity and a sense of mission, enhance the people's recognition of local culture, and integrate devel-opment strategies into the cultural budget. When interviewed about the topic of infrastructure building, the two New Taipei City officers did not talk about infrastructure itself but highlighted the city govern-ment's four-year City Culture Experience Construction Program, that would provide funding for local communities to come up with their own development proposals to cultivate their cultural distinctiveness. In the interview, one of the officers highlighted how the program's aims were to 'strengthen the communities' awareness of their own cultural speciality, traditions and human resources' (Interview 2). For example, some districts are characterized by their higher concentra-tion of natural resources, colonial legacies, antique and classical archi-tecture, traditional businesses, or residents of different ethnicities. It is hoped that through the program, local residents would 'try to partner up with consultants or local experts to discover and re-evaluate their own cultural and historical assets through workshops' (Interview 2). The key role for the government in this program would be to 'provide expert guidance to avoid vicious competition among communities and to encourage mutual learning' (Interview 2). The officer pointed out that the program would allow the government to be involved with local communities so as to be able to gain new ideas and build relationships with local residents. To achieve this goal, New Taipei City government also developed the Directives of the Community Infrastructure Establishment to integrate government and community resources and experiences.

Both interviewed officers also indicated that being able to create cross-district collaborations would prove to be crucial in shaping the future of New Taipei City. In view of this, the government is also launching the New Taipei City's Museums Family Program in the hope that coordina-tion among museums across the city would foster a collective cultural image of the city. New Taipei City possesses more than 32 museums that attract 4 million visitors annually. One of the interviewees mentioned the challenges of creating a coherent city image:

> [d]istricts such as Sansha, Jinshan, Pingxi (in New Taipei City) are already famous tourist destinations; they provide direct cultural images and pictures to tourists and develop their own cultural festivals and merchandise, so people won't say that they have travelled to New Taipei City; they will talk about their experiences using the names of these districts and villages, but not the city. So this museum program hopes to highlight the fact that these unique ancient artefacts and treasures are part of the cultural strength of our city...we need to constantly encourage museums and local cultural houses to get involved to put their programs, information and resources together to collectively market the city! (Interview 2)

What is clear from the government officers from Taipei, Kaohsiung and New Taipei City is that they are acting as agents bridging the external, centrally imposed requirements of the Building Infrastructure strategy with an inward-coordinating role with their local residents. For the officers in Taipei and New Taipei City, there was a concession, albeit reluctantly, that the reality of the strategy was the city governments' eagerness to create commercially driven infrastructure building and a key challenge was how to balance this while not excluding input from local residents. This can also be seen with the efforts from Greater Taichung. After its merger, the Cultural Affairs Bureau of Greater Taichung commissioned a comprehensive survey, Promoting Central Taiwan's CCI, to identify its current clustering conditions so as to be able to develop future CCI strategies. Based on the survey, the Cultural Affairs Bureau released a white paper mapping out 17 development strategies to promote CCI in Greater Taichung. To implement these strategies, a cross-departmental CCI Development Committee was established in 2011, chaired by the Deputy Mayor. This committee would serve as a review, advisory and coordination board. Greater Taichung would seek to develop its cultural economy through incorporating local culture into the creation of events, which would hopefully lead to future commercialization. As the interviewed officer points out, the role of the Cultural Affairs Bureau is to 'provide a small amount of seed funding and space to the local communities, and organize various kinds of competitions...we are acting more as an agent...and we are now teaming up with universities to speed up the commercialization process' (Interview 3).

Economics plays a large part in the development of CCI in Greater Tainan, and their CCI development strategies differ from the other four municipalities, which I would argue is due to the city's past as the first capital of Taiwan. For Greater Tainan, CCI development would mean transforming the city from a historical and cultural capital into a creative city. The Mayor of Tainan stated that he wished to 'reshape Tainan's brand image, so that Tainan could become in much the same way as Kyoto in Japan'.

Four strategies are outlined in Tainan's 'Cultural Capital, Creative City' plan which are (a) Restoring Tainan's Historical Glory, (b) Building a Friendly Arts Capital, (c) Building Tainan Film Centre and (d) Becoming Taiwan's Gourmet City. These plans reveal the city's keen desire to transform itself into a modern, all-inclusive city, while maintaining its historic and cultural richness. Balancing this would be the city's key challenge, as the Greater Tainan government officer stated, 'Tainan is home to Taiwan's extremely large variety of monuments, temples and historical sites...you cannot develop cultural tourism without those assets...but we need to regenerate and modernize the historical city to be able to compete internationally' (Interview 4).

From my interviews seeking the thoughts and opinions of government officers on the Building Infrastructure strategy, I noticed that they answered the questions not only in relation to what the city government hopes to achieve but also reflected upon their own personal and professional experiences as well as their opinions and thoughts on the changes in the city they were working in and the impact on how they worked. Their awareness of a need for greater interdepartmental collaboration between governments, as well as belief that a change in mindset was necessary, along with an understanding of the way in which the development of CCI had to be viewed differently from other forms of infrastructure development, all indicated that, for these officers, their role was to find a balance between two goals: the needs of the creative talent and the management of bureaucracy. Their responses seem to suggest that the former bears increasing weight in their decision-making process.

It is clear with the examples highlighted above that Infrastructure Building concerns not only the construction of new sites and venues, but also the need for people management in terms of greater internal coordination, professional management and networking mechanism to allow city government officers to respond to centrally imposed agendas and external changes. In addition, it is also clear that, at the city government level, there is now an emphasis on moving into a network mode of practices, where the practices of different stakeholders from creative talent to local residents have increased considerably.

Flagship industries development: returning to the community

As a result of the Flagship Industries Development Strategy, the five municipalities decided to identify and nurture their own flagship industries. From the empirical data collected on this strategy, I would argue that city governments have identified that a way to achieve this goal would be to implement holistic, integrated planning and community-based practices. The lack of collaboration can hinder the development of these flagship industries as highlighted by the government officer from Taipei who explained that 'a lack of resource integration and policy coordination in developing those so-called flagship industries' has hindered the identified industries of films, pop music and arts to 'develop and become self-sustaining' (Interview 1).

The attempt by Taipei to become World Design Capital in 2016 was to allow the city to obtain more resources so that it would hopefully be possible to create a more 'holistic CCI friendly environment' (Interview 1). An attempt to create integration between government, industry, academics and communities has been identified by New Taipei City as it hopes to develop its identified flagship industries of animation, comics, games and films. What also emerged from the interviews is a key challenge: how to channel and manage city and county resources in these integrations.

The enormous administrative changes that have occurred with the creation of Greater Taichung, Greater Tainan and Greater Kaohsiung have had an impact on communication across all the offices within the districts in the three municipalities. As the interviewed officer from Greater Taichung explains 'in the past, we only had to take care of the urban city, but now...we need to think of the rural areas which have abundant agricultural, aboriginal and traditional resources' (Interview 3). In response to this situation, Greater Taichung has set up a new Humanity Division in each district to ensure that all the districts are in communication with one another. The need to manage the cultural resources for Greater Taichung plays an important role in their attempt to retain and attract talent and visitors as the city government there hopes to encourage local Taichung city residents to 'realize and recognize the values of (their) own local tourism' so as to encourage them to visit the Greater Taichung area to 'explore the natural resources and vice versa' (Interview 3).

This is similar to the strategies of Greater Tainan, where it has concentrated its efforts and focus on the conservation and regeneration of the historical city. Tainan's flagship industry centers on 'restoring Tainan's historical glory,' where the government hopes that a growth in tourism would serve to attract investment and relocation of businesses and talent to Tainan. Therefore, the strategic policy for the tourism industry serves to provide a link between Tainan's past and future.

The interviewed officer commented on this link by pointing out that while they were dealing with 'old heritage...such as physical buildings' there was also a need to think about how this heritage could be 'presented on mobile phones, the Internet, books' (Interview 4). Once again, a holistic approach is being sought through 'putting together marketing plans for new districts and new ways of marketing' (Interview 4). On the one hand, the attempt of Greater Tainan's government to construct a future-proof plan to promote tourism underscores the significance and difficulties in accommodating the larger landscape of the city. On the other, it also highlights the increasing demands of cultural tourism; while there are various opportunities, there are also increasing challenges in achieving balanced regional development that can bridge the urban-rural divide.

While the interviewed officer from Greater Kaohsiung believed that crossovers between this divide were fundamental in developing its flagship industries, Greater Kaohsiung has also identified another type of crossover that was important: creating collaboration between CCI and the software technology industry. It is hoped that this crossover would be able to promote Kaohsiung as a city for digital content industries and enhance the international profile of Kaohsiung as a center for Taiwan's culture and digital content. However, the issue of retaining and attracting talent remains perennial, and the myriad plans, such as the Kaohsiung CCI Design Talent Return and Settlement Plan, as well as the Pop Music Creative Talent Incubation Plan, have been launched to attract creative talent from the fields of animation, illustration, product design and music. According to the interviewed officer, these strategies would allow the city to 'nurture (its) own seed talent and attract more professionals from other cities' (Interview 5).

Toward a self-organizing network

Based on the above examples and analysis, it can be argued that there is no prescriptive policy-framework for developing CCI, as the economic and cultural conditions vary with each city. However, it is possible to see how decentralization has allowed individual local cultural affairs departments to pursue and develop a locally specific and flexible network approach for CCI development. In particular, the various city governments' attempts to find a future-proof approach in developing CCI underscores the significance of such a network approach. I have shown that culture-led, crossover collaborations are both expected and desired. A network approach provides the starting points for policy planners to act as catalysts within the bureaucracy, allowing them to radiate outwards and across sectors allowing for these collaborations to happen. Through my analysis, there are three key themes that can be discerned from these plans and practices, which I will highlight in this section. I will also provide recommendations for future areas of development.

The first theme is the way the individual officers in these five municipalities work in order to implement strategy. These individual officers act as catalysts in the development of CCI strategy, using not only their personal and professional experiences and resources but work most effectively in capitalizing on their relationships. The networks that they have created through their roles have resulted in an interplay of several different factors, including managing policy ambition and agenda, meeting the aspirations of the creative talent, and working with urban planners and local communities in their cities. Each officer works as a network agent, navigating government bureaucracy while at same time, channeling the diverse needs of creative talent and communities to achieve policy agendas. As a result, a multi-party and multi-directional practice is accepted in the development of CCI and has proven useful and constructive in CCI policy development.

While this has been successful, the process of input and output, from planning to practice, is also becoming increasingly complicated. Interviewees highlight 'personal feelings' and 'job frustration' when talking about their roles in this process. As the key nodes of networks, these officers now play significant roles in the development of CCI and influence the extent into which priorities and resources are allocated. In addition, their roles are now key functions within the department, and working in multiple roles within a network is inevitably more stressful and challenging than operating within a traditional structure. As a result, there is a need to pay attention to the personal and emotional needs of these officers, as their workload is becoming increasingly complicated the further along these strategies progress.

The nature of these individually driven networks means that CCI development has moved from being an inward-focused planning strategy to an outward-directed creative collaboration where key players all have an equally important role. These officers and similar key staff should be considered part of the 'infrastructure' that is allowing the development of CCI within their cities. The knowledge that they have accumulated from their personal and professional experiences should be shared across government so that there is a distribution of knowledge across projects and different departments. The officers have identified that operational inter-connections between government departments provide them with a sense of security and confidence that allows them to pursue further external collaboration. What this calls for is a more flexible way of working that privileges connections and intermediaries to achieve an efficient, well-informed system of decision-making and collaboration.

Such networks function internally as infrastructure, facilitating cross-department collaborations covering a wide range of resources as well as regulations that are related to the preservation, production and promotion of cultural and creative events, spaces and commodities. All these factors shape the economic prospects of the city. Though what actually constitutes a 'creative city' is under debate, the bottom-up and culture-centered practices are now generally acknowledged by policy-makers, creative talents and managers as highly effective. In addition, this way of working via networks has meant that the 'cultural' roles, positions and contributions of the CCI planners are becoming increasingly clear.

The second theme that has emerged from this study is that there is a need to initiate a continual and inseparable planning process from the beginning of the plan to achieve a dynamic balance between bureaucracy, creative talent, commercial businesses and communities. As the five cities have shown, early involvement of the creative talent and local communities is important for the government, as they are now dealing with a wider land area in which there are many regions with which they are not familiar. This is especially important when there is an emphasis from many, if not all five, cities on the importance of promoting local culture. It is also important that all parties share a common goal of cross-departmental collaboration because flagship industries development requires holistic thinking.

As government officers work with their respective city governments and with their local communities and the private sector to achieve this collective goal, the challenge lies not only in acquiring and mobilizing these local resources, but also in finding the right balance between the flexibility and rigidity of policy agendas, the specialization and integration of skills, allowing for the random and the planned to occur, and managing creative talent with the commercial aspects of CCI development. A system needs to be created that would provide officers with information about the global competitive environment, thus assisting them with their work as well as allowing them to enhance and encourage community involvement during the planning process.

At the same time, city governments need to also recognize that there need to be continual adaptation to the changes and requirements brought about by CCI development across all levels. In addition, branding strategies would have to be integrated into these developments, leveraging the existing strengths of the city to promote growth. As the analysis shows, there are differences in each city's economic strengths and cultural assets; however, what was also discovered during the interview process was that there was no significant difference in the way CCI development was planned. Strategies were based on first identifying a plan based on culture, followed by devising a plan to make the best of existing creative talent, so as to attract more talent, and thus further develop CCI. While this plan seems to be favored by city governments, there is also an increasing awareness that greater collaboration needs to be created across all departments of the government. Interviewees revealed that as their strategies are implemented, it is becoming clearer, too, that cultural affair departments are now being asked to meet other policy goals. This might lead to the sidelining of communities and even the key purposes of arts and culture. City transformation, so far, has occurred through bottom-up networks centered on communities; the challenge now is how to maintain these networks while integrating them with top-down government priorities.

Finally, the third theme that has emerged from my analysis is the need for sustainable coordination. Planning strategies for balanced development among the urban, rural and administrative performance in the wider region is now seen as increasingly important. By its very nature, CCI requires new approaches to coordination across all levels of government. The 'bridging' between urban and rural has placed an emphasis on rediscovering original historical and cultural resources; therefore, integration between cultural and economic development is needed in both the urban and rural. Coordination between the city and district offices and cultural organizations is required. This is especially significant if community involvements is important, as greater coordination can only leverage and extend the impact of bottom-up led initiatives.

At a macro level, the recent changes within the city landscape and CCI policy development provide an explanation of how industries in Taiwan are changing and shed light on current planning and practices of city governments. At a micro-level, however, interviews with government officers illustrate how CCI development strategy is a result of networks driven by individuals, and approaches have been created from a bottom-up process through the involvement of local communities. The five municipalities have shown that becoming larger in terms of size is helpful for CCI development, as they now have easier access to resources and key stakeholders, which is useful in such a network-dependent process. In the near future, what will become crucial is how city governments are able to act as bridges between central government and their cities, so as to maintain their local cultural values and dynamics.

Notes

1. The cabinet-level Council for Cultural Affairs (CCA) was founded in 1982, representing the nation's highest central institution for planning and overseeing the country's cultural establishments. It was promoted to ministry status in 2012, becoming the Ministry of Culture.
2. New Taipei City's population is the largest at 3.84 million. This is followed by Greater Kaohsiung at 2.77 million, Great Taichung's population at 2.62 million, Taipei's population at 2.61 million and Greater Tainan's population at 1.87 million.
3. Interview 1: Department of Cultural Affairs, Taipei Government (May 14, 2012); Interview 2: Cultural Affairs Department, New Taipei City Government (May 21, 2012); Interview 3: Cultural Affairs Bureau, Taichung City Government (May 23, 2012); Interview 4: Cultural Affairs Bureau, Tainan City Government (June 5, 2012); Interview 5: Bureau of Cultural Affairs, Kaohsiung City Government (June 13, 2012).

References

Acs, Z.J. and Megyesi, M.I. (2007) 'Creativity and Industrial Cities: A Case Study of Baltimore', *Entrepreneurship & Regional Development. An International Journal*, 21(4), 421–439.

American Chamber of Commerce in Taipei (2011) 2011 Taiwan White Paper. Available from: http://www.amcham.com.tw/white-papers-2/cat_view/158-white-paper/283–2011/284–2011-white-paper-english, date accessed June 22, 2011.

Banks, M. and Hesmondhalgh, D. (2009) 'Looking for Work in Creative Industries Policy', *International Journal of Cultural Policy*, 15(4), 415–430.

Chao Y.M. (2011) 'Rezoning Taiwan', in *Taiwan Review*. Available from http://taiwanreview.nat.gov.tw/ct.asp?xItem=142515&CtNode=1337&mp=1, date accessed February 16, 2012.

Chen, L.M. (2010) A Report on Cultural, Creative Industries, Economy and Tourism Development after the Taichung City-County Merger. Taichung City Government Research Report.

Chun, A. (1994) 'From Nationalism to Nationalizing: Cultural Imagination and State Formation in Postwar Taiwan', *The Australian Journal of Chinese Affairs*, 31, January, 49–69.

Chung, H.L. (2012) 'Rebooting the Dragon at the Crossroads? Divergence and Convergence of Cultural Policy in Taiwan', *International Journal of Cultural Policy*, 18(3), 340–355.

Council of Cultural Affairs (2010) Law for the Development of the Cultural and Creative Industries. Available from: http:// www.cca.gov.tw/ccaImages/ laws/247/1–0-5.pdf, date accessed March 4, 2011.

Council of Cultural Affairs (2009) Creative Taiwan-Cultural and Creative Industries Development Project-Action Plan. Available from http://www.cci.org.tw/cci/ upload/law/20100604104150–8dd3d038610f19c0bd08739c496f4052.pdf, date accessed January 17, 2011.

Council for Cultural Affairs (2004) The White Paper on Cultural Policy. Available from: http://english.cca.gov.tw/ct.asp?xItem=12192&ctNode=4063, date accessed January 19, 2011.

Executive Yuan, Taiwan (2002) Challenge 2008: Six-Year National Development Plan, Available from: http://www.gio.gov.tw/taiwan-website/4-oa/20020521/ 2002052101.html, date accessed March 12, 2011.

Florida, R. (2005) *Cities and the Creative Class*. (London: Routledge).

Taichung City Government (2012) Mayor Hu: A Cultural, Energetic New City. Available from http://eng.taichung.gov.tw/ct.aspx?xItem=12212&ctNode=182 9&mp=18, date accessed November 15, 2012.

Jayne, M. (2005) 'Creative Industries: The Regional Dimension?', *Environment and Planning C: Government and Policy*, 23(4), 537–556.

Landry, C. (2000) *The Creative City: A Toolkit for Urban Innovators*. (London: Earthscan).

Miles, S. and Paddison, R. (2005) 'The Rise and Rise of Culture-led Urban Regeneration', *Urban Studies* 42(5/6), 833–839.

New Taipei City Official Website Introduction (2012) Available from http:// foreigner.ntpc.gov.tw/_file/2968/SG/44813/D.html, date accessed December 11, 2012

Ponzini, D. and Rossi, U. (2010) 'Becoming a Creative City: The Entrepreneurial Mayor, Network Politics, and the Promise of an Urban Renaissance', *Urban Studies* 47(10), 1037–1057.

Scott, A.J. (2000) *The Cultural Economy of Cities*. (London: Sage).

Scott, A.J. (2006) 'Creative Cities: Conceptual Issues and Policy Questions', *Journal of Urban Affairs* 28(1), 1–17.

Taipei City Government (2012) Taipei Yearbook 2011. Available from http:// tcgwww.taipei.gov.tw/mp.asp?mp=100095, date accessed November 9, 2012.

Yang, M.C. (2011) Promote the Central Taiwan CCI- CCI Fundamental Research Project, Commissioned Research by the Taichung City Government.

12

The Film Industry in Japan – Prospering without Active Support from the State?

Nobuko Kawashima

The Film Festival of Cannes in 2013 was remarkable for Japanese film-makers, as the Jury Prize was won by a Japanese independent film (*Soshite Chichi ni Naru [Like Father, Like Son]*, dir. Hirokazu KORE-EDA 2013) while Naomi KAWASE, a Japanese woman director, served on the 2014 jury, reflecting her international reputation. A few years earlier, the Japanese film *Okuribito* (*Departures*, dir. Yojiro TAKITA 2008) was awarded the Academy Award for Foreign Language Film in 2009. Based on these and other pieces of evidence, it may not be an exaggeration to say that Japanese national cinema is in full swing. It is not only such aesthetic successes of independent films that are notable but also the success of Japanese film production as a commercial business within the domestic market. For Hollywood, which increasingly depends on sales from territories outside North America, Japan is one of the most important markets for export. The globally marketed, blockbuster films from Hollywood are indeed popular in Japan like elsewhere, but the Japanese market has gained vigor over the last five to ten years, with domestic films occupying more than half of the box office. This is in contrast to Europe, where Hollywood movies tend to dominate the box office despite large numbers of locally produced films (see Table 12.1).

It must be noted that in fact some of the other countries discussed in this volume, namely South Korea (and China to a lesser extent), also show similar features of cinema admissions where local films are strong in the market (Jin 2006; Gao 2009). The success of the local for the latter group, however, derives very much from their government policies of cultural control and protectionism as well as from the recent economic policy for the creative industries, whereas the Japanese film

Table 12.1   Share of national films in the respective domestic markets in 2012 (%)

North America	India	South Korea	China	Japan	France	UK
91.1	91.5	58.8	48.5	65.7	40.2	31.9

Source: FOCUS 2013, European Audiovisual Observatory.

industry, as this chapter will show, thrives with very little state support or intervention. Research in national film policy has generally assumed that the major purpose of film policy is to protect and nurture national cinema against the flood of super-commercial Hollywood movies into their markets by providing subsidies for local productions, supporting schemes of expertise development in film production, and giving grants for film education to widen consumer taste. None of these has had any significant degree of presence in the cultural policy of Japan. How, then, has the Japanese film industry experienced growth, both commercially and aesthetically, in recent years? This chapter will show that changes in production financing, the collapse of vertical integration, and the change in consumers' tastes in the last ten years or so have been major contributing factors. The chapter will analyze the process through which Japanese films have resurged from a decline experienced in the 1970s and 1980s and will discuss its future.

For such purposes, the chapter is structured in the following way. The first section will briefly describe the historical development of the Japanese cinema from pre-war years to the present with a focus on the industry size and structure. The second section will introduce the basics of Japanese cultural policy and discuss film policy, or the lack of it. The third section will then examine the reasons for the recent upsurge of Japanese films in the domestic market. Finally, the concluding section will critically examine whether the film industry of Japan will be sustainable in its current state and without government support.

The Film industry in Japan – from the 1920s to the present

In discussing the recent resurgence of the Japanese cinema, it is necessary to provide a brief, historical account of the industry. The Japanese film industry is one of the oldest in the world, and was on a par with the American and European movie industries in size in the early years, experiencing its first 'Golden Age' during the 1920s and the 1930s. Based on the so-called studio system, whereby major directors, scriptwriters and actors would work exclusively for the companies to which they were contracted, the major studios continuously supplied films. Within this production system, the first Golden Age saw the blossoming of talented directors such as Kenji MIZOGUCHI and Yasujiro OZU, whose aesthetics contributed to the definition of Japanese film narratives and styles.

As Japan entered the Second World War, however, new legislation allowed the government to censor film works. Permission of the government was also required to distribute and exhibit these films. The film sector as a whole was thus put under the control of the government, which encouraged the production of films to boost the morale of soldiers and the nation. With the sheer paucity of resources for film production and less leisure time for people, the number of films released decreased dramatically from about 500 per year in the early 1940s to 26 in 1945 (Yomota 2000, p. 96). The censorship and intervention into film content by the ruling authority continued during the American Occupation era (1945–1952), when values of liberty and democracy were propagated, replacing those of fascism and patriotism promoted during the war period.

With the end of the censorship undertaken by the General Headquarters (namely, the American Occupation), the film industry started to experience a boom in the 1950s, known as the second Golden Age. While some films nostalgically depicted the war experiences of the Japanese without serious engagement with regard to the vices of the state, films that conveyed social realism and messages increasingly appeared. Period drama, or *jidaigeki*, which was virtually banned during the Occupation, returned to the screens, satisfying a huge mass of fans.

According to the data provided by the Motion Picture Producers Association of Japan, the year 1958 saw the apex of admissions reaching 1.1 billion, meaning every single person went to the cinema 13.4 times per year on average. Directors such as Akira KUROSAWA were applauded at international film festivals, while other directors contributed to the development of diverse genres. The number of films released in 1960 was, stunningly, 547, making this period the second Golden Age of Japanese Cinema. Although the majority were so-called 'program pictures,' which were made to accompany fully fledged, major films, the sheer volume of production had a positive impact on developing the skills and techniques of filmmaking. The following years saw the emergence of a New Wave in the socially turbulent context of massive political protests against the US-Japan Security Treaty. Despite such developments in film culture, however, the industry rapidly declined within a decade for social and economic reasons familiar to the US and European nations, including the development of television broadcast, an increase in the variety of leisure options for people and overproduction by the studios. In only ten years, admissions fell from the 1.1 billion of 1958 (the peak year mentioned earlier) to less than one third of that figure (313 million in 1968).

Unlike the US, where Hollywood studios entered the production sector of television programs, the Japanese film industry generally failed to have a mutually productive relationship with television during this period. Some major studios went bankrupt, while the remaining ones sold their production facilities or stopped producing films. Directors who went independent produced films with foreign capital or worked in television and commercials. Some worked in a newly defined genre of soft core porn to maintain their jobs, where they at least had some freedom to try innovative techniques and expressions. Unlike the US, where the Supreme Court ruling of 1954 had disintegrated the vertically integrated structure of the film industry, namely to prevent the same company from controlling the sectors of production, distribution and exhibition, in order to allow competition in each sector, the Japanese film industry during the late 1960s through the early 1980s kept the integrated structure. As the studio system was defunct, production was largely outsourced, but the majors controlled distribution and exhibition. As a result, the market stayed stagnant, attracting very few viewers to the surviving genres such as *yakuza* and pink movies, with the box office hits dominated by Hollywood films (see Table 12.2).

Table 12.2   Japanese film market, 1955–1995

Year	Number of local films released	Number of foreign films released	Total admissions (thousands)	Share of local films (%)
1955	423	193	858,912	65.8
1960	547	216	1,014,364	78.3
1965	487	264	372,676	66.7
1970	423	236	254,799	59.4
1975	333	225	174,020	44.4
1980	320	209	164,422	55.0
1985	319	284	155,130	50.9
1990	239	465	148,000	41.4
1995	289	321	157,885	37.0

Source: Data compiled from Motion Picture Producers Association of Japan (Eiren) website.

The late 1980s and early 1990s saw a big change, which was a prelude to a transformation to come in the 2000s, with the participation of Kadokawa Publishing House in the filmmaking sector. Kadokawa Publishing has been one of the major companies in popular literature (and later in other media), with good access to literary properties that had the potential for adaptation to film, particularly in the horror genre. The initial interest and purpose of making a movie was to promote the novel series on which the movies were based, but the reverse has become a successful model of business for Kadokawa. It then became Kadokawa's distinctive style that movies, novels, and music used in the films would be promoted together with massive advertisement, creating synergistic effects. Kadokawa would produce a film by actually using one of the remaining majors, contract another major for distribution, and then another major for exhibition. With the strong legacy of vertical integration, such cross-company contracts of filmmaking and marketing were unusual but effective for commercial gains. Although Kadokawa's move did not go so far as to completely destroy the vertical structure of the majors, the old film industry was refreshed by the challenge posed by the business firm from outside. Initially, critics were critical about Kadokawa for its heavy use of advertising and commercialism, but in fact Kadokawa did provide opportunities to emerging, talented directors and started to produce critically acclaimed works, too. Kadokawa Publishing House continued the merger and acquisitions of companies specializing in different media platforms, resulting in a major media and entertainment conglomerate.

The change in the film industry has been furthered with television network companies since the 1990s. Terrestrial television broadcasting in Japan has been relatively large for the last six decades. There is a public broadcaster, NHK, for two channels along with five national networks in the commercial sector. The major broadcasters in Japan may contract actual program production out, but would mostly retain the copyright to the finished products. They are thus more than 'networks' and very powerful content providers in the mass media and entertainment in many ways, rarely threatened by challenges from outside, although highly competitive for ratings between themselves. With the technological development of broadcasting and communications since the 1980s, more slots for programs have become available or have to be filled by the broadcasters, but the license fees from Hollywood and premium sport content have escalated in response to the same demands for content in many deregulated markets in the world.

Under such circumstances, major broadcasters strategically started to invest in filmmaking. *Nankyoku Monogarati* (*Tale of the Arctic*, dir. Koreyoshi KURAHARA 1983) was one of the early examples, involving Fuji Television, which turned out to be a mega-hit, earning 5.9 billion yen (approx. US$59 million)[1] (Calculated by distribution revenue, as opposed to by box office revenue).[2] If this particular movie project for Fuji TV was purely a financial investment with little relation to its television business except that it acquired the rights to broadcast, the following years have seen the rise of integration between film projects and television drama series. The same actors as well as directors and crew would work on the feature film project as if it is only an extension of drama shooting.

Another mega-hit of this kind was made by Fuji TV, when it released *Odoru Daisosasen* (*Bayside Shakedown*) in 1998, as a sequel to the TV series of the same title aired in early 1997. The box office revenue for this movie was more than 10.1 billion yen (US$101 million), one of the highest grossing films of all-time in the Japanese market including Japanese and non-Japanese films (except animations). The *Bayside Shakedown* franchise had three following films released in 2003, 2010 and 2012, as well as spin-off movies focusing on some of the protagonists in the series, each of which was a box office success. The franchise has included extended versions of television series for broadcasting, music CDs of soundtracks, small programs for mobile phones, novelized works and accompanying booklets as well as a theatre play. With this blockbuster series, the producer Chihiro KAMEYAMA from Fuji TV (who became the CEO of the company in 2013) has set the norm for others to follow.

As production budgets rose, and in order to spread the risk inherent in filmmaking, not only television companies but also other players have been brought in to form consortia for production, or 'production committees.' Now an established form of film financing in Japan, a production committee would typically include stakeholders such as major advertising agencies who have expertise in marketing communications to consumers, video/DVD distributors as well as retailers and merchandizers for tie-in promotions. In return for investment, each committee member would control the relevant rights to the film. The presence of a television company is absolutely crucial for any production committee, as it promises free and massive PR on television when the film is close to release. One might even suggest that the traditional majors in film business such as Toei and Shochiku are almost subcontractors of the committees led by television companies.

Table 12.3 Japanese film market, 2000–2012

Year	Number of local films released	Number of foreign films released	Total admissions (thousands)	Share of local films (%)
2000	282	362	135,390	31.8
2001	281	349	163,280	39.0
2002	293	347	160,767	27.1
2003	287	335	162,347	33.0
2004	310	339	170,092	37.5
2005	355	375	160,453	41.3
2006	417	404	164,585	53.2
2007	407	403	163,193	47.7
2008	418	388	160,491	59.5
2009	448	314	182,297	56.9
2010	409	308	174,358	53.6
2011	441	358	144,726	54.9
2012	554	429	155,159	65.7

Source: Data compiled from Motion Picture Producers Association of Japan (Eiren) website.

With these changes since the 1990s onwards described above, the share of Japanese films in the market has gradually increased from a low of 30.2% in 1998 to the first instance of overtaking foreign imports in 2006. The trend still continues, with the result for 2012 as 65.7% for Japanese films (see Table 12.3). It must be noted that most of the Japanese live-action films are consumed only within the country. Thus, Hollywood obviously remains dominant in the global context, but its low penetration rate into one of the largest markets must cause concern and frustration to the Hollywood majors.

Film policy of Japan

Is the recent upsurge of Japanese films, then, the result of concerted efforts made by the cultural policy of Japan in order to protect and revitalize her national cinema culture? The short answer is 'No,' as there has been no policy of that kind, and public intervention, if any, has been *ad hoc* and fragmented. The following will investigate the cultural policy of Japan in relation to film.

A very short summary of cultural policy in Japan, to start with, is that it has been very limited in scale. Until the early 1990s, the Japanese Government has had very little interest in cultural matters, letting the arts and culture operate solely within the market economy. In advanced nations outside Japan, arts and culture such as symphony orchestras and theaters may well be publicly supported, for they cannot survive in the market alone; because their non-economic – cultural, educational or social – values cannot be fully captured, government intervention is required. This line of thinking has never taken root in Japanese policy-making. It is not that Japanese people disregard the importance of, or no one has interest in, culture and the arts altogether, but these activities have long been considered as the personal hobbies of those involved in creation or in consumption, with little significance to society at large.

To better understand the above, it is useful to refer to the basic political and economic features of Japan. Japan is a unitary country with strong authority and power given to central government. After the loss of World War II, it has been a liberal democratic country with a capitalistic economy. It is one of the earliest examples of so-called 'developmental states,' which characterize most of the countries in East Asia discussed in this book (Vogel 1991; Johnson 1999); in a developmental state, industries with strategic importance such as the automobile or electronics industries are identified, and the country's economic development is strongly driven by support measures to help advance these industries. Distinct from socialist economies, however, a developmental state still operates within the structure of free market.

The developmental state of Japan, perhaps weaker in retrospect than her followers in East Asia, with stronger leadership of top politicians and stricter market controls, has worked well in expanding the country's economy until the 1980s. The national preoccupation was first and foremost with economic development – to raise the standard of living for citizens by increasing the national wealth and by building the necessary infrastructure for transport, energy production and transmission, communications, and much more.

Among welfare state measures, education, housing and healthcare were given sufficient attention as they would improve the quality of the labor force necessary for economic development. However, support for the arts and culture was never on the agenda of policy-makers. Quality of life, distinct from the standard of living that suggests physical conditions rather than personal happiness and well-being, has come to receive attention only in the late 1980s in Japan when the nation acquired confidence and satisfaction with her economic achievements.

Taiwan, South Korea and Singapore may have had similar paths, giving economic objectives a high priority, supplemented by state welfare only to the extent necessary to achieve these objectives. These countries, however, have had the problem of national identity for reasons of their colonial pasts and/or mixed ethnicity and the need to build unified nations, often leading to strong cultural policies. For Japan, such a need is relatively weak. Moreover – and this is perhaps more important as a reason for Japan's weak cultural policy – unlike Taiwan, South Korea and Singapore, any hint of patriotism had to be avoided in Japan in an effort to eradicate the remains of the authoritarian rule of the pre- and inter-war years and build a liberal, democratic and free country.

Indeed, this was the theme of nation building in the 1950s and 1960s. Thus, whereas the government of Singapore still has measures to monitor the 'appropriateness' of citizens' culture (Lim 2012) and retains censorship, Japan has had no hesitation in signing up to American or more broadly Western ideals and values such as freedom of expression. With little perceived danger of cultural imperialism from the West, Japan has also had the basic attitude of *laissez-faire* for the sphere of culture, a factor that in fact contributed to the weak basis of cultural policy development in the following decades.

To return to the description of cultural policy *per se*, the Agency for Cultural Affairs (ACA), a ministerial department in the Ministry of Education, was created at the national level in the 1960s with the major mission of preserving the national heritage. It has expanded its area of responsibility to include language policy and copyright policy as well as support for the arts and culture more generally. Its budget has seen a constant rise since the 1990s, a surprise considering the difficulty of the Japanese economy in the last twenty years and fiscal restraint exercised by the Treasury. Nonetheless, the total budget is still about 100 billion yen (US$1 bil), occupying only 0.11% of total public spending. This is well below that of European nations (for example, 1.06% for France) and of South Korea (0.81%) in 2010 (calculated only by the budget of the national cultural ministry or agency) (ACA, n.d.). In short, public or philanthropic funding for the arts and culture is fairly limited by any standard in Japan.

Cultural spending of local authorities as a whole has always (at least in the recent decades since the statistics have been collected) surpassed that of ACA (366 billion yen, or US$3.7 mil, in 2009, ACA, n.d.). However, the majority of local spending goes to capital projects such as cultural facility development and maintenance expenses, leaving very little for funding artistic and cultural activities. At any rate, the total of cultural budgets for all local authorities has declined from over 709 billion yen (US$7.1 bil) in 1996–1997 to 274 billion yen (US$2.7 bil) in 2010–2011 (ACA 2012, pp. 19–20). I have written elsewhere on the significance and distinctiveness of corporate support for the arts and culture in Japan much as a positive evaluation, but its contribution in spending is limited compared to public expenditure (Kawashima 2012).

Considering that even non-commercial art forms and culture that are usually subsidized outside Japan receive limited support in national and local cultural policy, it should be no surprise that film has stayed outside the domain of cultural policy. Cultural policy for film, if any, was that of censorship in the inter-war years. That, however, finished with the end of the American Occupation, as censorship is strictly prohibited by the newly-adopted constitutional law. In addition, there has never been any screen quota for Japanese films for the purpose of protecting national cinema unlike in South Korea.

Within such a context of policy in Japan, no one in the film industry had any thought of asking the government for help, even during the period of decline, as it did not occur to them that film might deserve public support. This is changing, as will be explained shortly, but unfortunately film has never attained the status of 'the arts' above mere entertainment. A change in mindset could have occurred when cultural policy as a whole gained momentum in the late 1980s through the 1990s in an effort to improve Japan's national image in the international arena, changing from an aggressive economic nation to a respectable people with a sophisticated culture and tradition. Although first-class, flagship facilities for culture such as museums and arts centers for multiple purposes have been constructed all over the country in these two decades; film screening facilities have not been incorporated in these buildings. Cinemas have largely remained commercial theaters operated by national chains. Independent films are screened at art house cinemas or film festivals by cinephiles dedicated to the introduction of diverse film culture to the Japanese public with little or no support from public authorities. It is only in the last ten years or so that people engaged in screening independent films have come to realize that what they are doing should receive government support and public recognition, and created a 'community cinema center' to represent a cultural sector. Filmmakers, however, have not formed a similar alliance to argue for their public value, even though their works have started to receive prestigious awards at international film festivals.

Most illustrative of my discussion above, Japan has had no public organization dedicated to film policy, like the French CNC (Centre national du cinéma et de l'image animée) or the (previous) UK Film Council and the British Film Institute. Funding for the film industry is almost negligible and the film archive is maintained on a tight budget by one of the national museums. In recent years, there have been some, albeit limited in scale, efforts to help film from two perspectives. One is a small budget from the ACA designated for Japanese films since 2003. This particular budget is about 800 million yen (US$8 mil) in 2013, to be spent on feature and documentary film production, the promotion of international co-productions, and support for Japanese film promotion overseas. The fact that film funding is now earmarked may well be good, but the amount is pitifully small, equivalent to less than 1% of the annual budget of CNC in France (770.36 million euros in 2012, [CNC 2012, p. 173]). Other items in the ACA budget may well benefit films, such as the development fund for the 'media arts' (including animation, manga and video games), but the total is only around 2 billion yen (US$20 million) at most. There are other available pots of money that can be used for promoting Japanese films abroad, for example, by the Japan Foundation, which is a cultural diplomacy institution, but the total is insignificant.

Since the 2000s, the cultural policies of the East Asian nations have latched onto the creative industries. This is not surprising, considering the transition of their economic bases from manufacturing and service to value-added, knowledge creation sectors. Interest in the notion of the creative economy, creative cities and the creative industries has equally been shown in the policy discourse of these countries. Japanese cultural policy has also been following this trend in recent years, but compared to other countries in East Asia, Japan is perhaps the least committed. The government of Japan has recognized the potential of the creative industries with regard to their contribution to the national economy and export and in relation to the side effects of their activities such as attracting tourists and producing positive images of the country. Japan has undoubtedly been successful in animation, comic books and video game industries on a global scale. *Animé*, the Japanese shorthand of the English word 'animation,' has already become established as an English word in its own right, as is *manga* when referring to comic books. Japanese media products, like TV dramas, have also been very popular in East Asia, where popular series would now be officially broadcast within a week from the broadcast of the program in Japan.

However, when it comes to concrete policy for the creative industries, these industries are generally outside the jurisdiction of the central ACA whose responsibility is for the non-commercial arts and cultural heritage. The economic and industrial promotion of the cultural industries has thus largely fallen into the realm of the Ministry of Economy, Trade and Industry (METI) and to a smaller extent among other ministries and departments for local governance, communications, tourism and the Cabinet Office. Although this is a new area for METI, it has swiftly come to understand the economic features of the creative industries and identified issues for long-term development. For example, the lack of good business managers with expertise in financing, knowledge of legal matters and skills in global marketing have been identified as key issues. However, most of such issues can only be tackled in the long-term and are not necessarily amenable to the short-term nature of policy intervention.

One measure specifically for the film industry, created with a supplementary budget for 2013 especially made by the efforts of METI (together with the Ministry for Internal Affairs dealing with communications), is a fund of 15.5 billion yen (US$155 mil) that will subsidize localization and promotion of Japanese media content for export (METI 2013). For example, audiovisual products such as feature films, animation films and television programs need to be subtitled or dubbed for export; half of this expense may be financed by this newly created fund. When these products are to be marketed overseas, similarly the expenses may be subsidized. While this is big news for the industry, again the total amount is limited and the duration of the fund is only for one fiscal year. Although METI's grasp of the issues involved in the development of the creative industries is generally sound and good, Japanese policy for the creative industries remains devoid of sustained commitment.

Reasons for resurgence

Given the lack of public support for film, one is bound to ask how the film industry in Japan has revitalized itself, as can be seen in the following statistics: number of films released per year, the share of Japanese films in the total box office of Japan (both in Table 12.3) and number of films given prestigious awards at international film festivals mentioned at the beginning of this chapter.

As was mentioned earlier, the commercial success in recent years of Japanese films owes much to television stations. Their investment in films, however, should not be misunderstood as similar to the legally defined collaboration between the film and television industries in Europe. In France, tax on the sales of television stations comprises a major revenue source for CNC, the national institution for film funding. This financial scheme is based on the logic that television stations benefit from broadcasting films that attract audiences, hence they should pay some monies back to film production. In the case of Japan, it is only because television stations saw commercial opportunities in this area;

most of the stations now produce several works per year, including extended versions of their own television dramas as well as adaptations of major hits in novels, manga and video games.

The impact of television on the film industry is not confined to the new financing method but extends to the introduction of different styles and cultures of filmmaking when compared to those of the previous era. Even after the second Golden Age, Japanese films were based on auteurism with directors not obsessed with commercial appeal, whereas the producer KAMEYAMA and his followers have taken an unashamedly populist approach to filmmaking. It can be said that the 'light' and quick style of film shooting has in fact attracted consumers who were alienated by the 'heaviness' of previous Japanese movies. There is a *zeitgeist* that film going can be fun and cool for the general public.

Other factors have also helped create a favorable environment for the film industry. One is the success of Japanese anime not only in Japan but also in the global market. Studio Ghibli has been a major hit maker since 1984. *Sen to Chihiro no Kamikakushi* (*Spirited Away*, dir. Hayao MIYAZAKI 2001, winner of an Academy Award in 2003) is still the top of the all-time box office in Japan at the time of writing (30.4 billion yen, or US$304 mil), more than double the revenue of *Avatar* in the Japanese market. While Ghibli films have been a huge success worldwide both commercially and critically, due to the humanistic fantasies and meticulously made, beautiful artwork, other animation films specifically targeting children such as *Pokémon* and *Doraémon* have also made enormous profits. Together with other innovative works, for example, those of Katsuhiro OTOMO in science fiction and Makoto SHINKAI in poetic stories, Japanese anime has been firmly established as a film genre in its own right in the eyes of global audiences and critics (Napier 2011, p. 226).

The second factor is the fall of vertical integration between distributors and exhibitors. This disintegration was not a result of competition law as in the US but a natural and gradual development, initiated by Kadokawa and furthered by the penetration into the Japanese exhibition market by Warner Inc. in 1993, which then extended multiplexes around the country. This has allowed newcomers into the film business, creating competitiveness among exhibitors, who now enjoy more freedom to choose programs that they think will sell. This has created a positively competitive, commercially oriented environment for film production and distribution.

Finally, it is worth mentioning that Hollywood movies have become spectacles with a heavy use of computer graphics, thinner stories to tell, and less reliance on stars. Those films do have commercial appeal to the Japanese public, who however, would increasingly prefer films with scenarios and local idols they feel more relevant to (Kakeo 2012, pp. 171–174). During the 1960s and 1970s, people were generally keen to learn American and European cultures, and young people would read about foreign films to understand them. Such time-consuming activities, whether undertaken seriously or as a snobbish pretention, are no longer considered 'cool' among the younger generations of today. They are said to be less keen on non-Japanese music, less interested in Hollywood movies while being enthusiastic about Japanese anime, manga and video games. The spectacular characteristics of recent Hollywood films has certainly turned some of the film fans away, whose unsatisfied demands for cultural products have been met by medium- to small-scale, yet not too demanding, movies of Japan.

Conclusion – the future of the Japanese film industry

This chapter has discussed the lack of government's film policy in Japan and the resurgence of Japanese films in the domestic box office nevertheless. One major landmark was the release of *Bayside Shakedown* made by Fuji Television in 1997, which has led to a flood of entertainment films produced by the major broadcasters following the same business strategy. The remaining part of this chapter will critically discuss the future perspective of the Japanese film industry both in economic and cultural respects.

Firstly, it is doubtful whether the current state of the film industry in Japan is in good shape and will be sustainable for the years to come. I have so far discussed the recent success of the film sector in terms of the total number of productions and domestic share of the market, as they are the benchmarks often employed in the discussion of this topic both in academic and industry literature. But in fact, the size of the Japanese market is largely due to the size of the economy and, more particularly, to the high level of ticket prices in Japan. In a recent report of the European Audiovisual Observatory (2013) on the world market of films, the average price per ticket in 2012 was US$15.8 in Japan, while it was US$8.9 in the European Union and US$8.0 in North America. The average number of admissions per capita in Japan is very low, only 1.2, whereas it is 4.0 in the US, 3.2 in France and 3.9 in South Korea. As can be seen in Tables 12.2 and 12.3, the total size of film audience in fact has not increased since the 1970s, but the growth of the market has been made possible by the increase in ticket price, which masks the stagnant state of the film market.

In the meantime, actual growth, namely the enlargement of the cinema-going public, has not occurred, whereas it has been witnessed in countries like China and South Korea, Japan's two important neighbors. With the shrinkage of the film market in Japan in the foreseeable future inevitably caused by an aging population, it is becoming increasingly important for the industry to go global, or at least be more proactive in co-productions with China and South Korea (Kakeo 2012). It is known that Japanese live-action movies do not travel abroad well, except for some highly acclaimed art house films, and the best the industry has been able to achieve is to license Japanese films for adaptation by Hollywood. The 2000s have seen a boom of Japanese horrors, called 'J-horrors,' now recognized as a genre internationally (see Davis and Yeh 2008), starting with the success of *Ringu* (dir. Hideo NAKTA 1998) remade as *The Ring* (dir. Gore Verbinski 2002) starring Naomi Watts.

It would be necessary for the industry, furthermore, to work on international co-productions. Chinese and Korean directors have had these experiences already, but the Japanese have largely been reticent. So far this aloofness or exclusivist attitude is not a big problem, as the size of the Japanese market can sustain the inward-looking industry, but this sustainability is already much in doubt. Government funding, albeit on a small-scale, is trying to facilitate co-productions, but there has been no official co-production treaty with any country, nor has there been any tax incentive for inward investment in film production in Japan. There are numerous film commissions that try to attract location shooting across the country, but without fiscal incentives, international producers are not interested in coming to Japan where labor and other costs are very high.

The second critical comment on the future of the Japanese film industry comes from cultural concerns. The blame typically leveled at TV station-made films in general is that, while it may well be all right to have commercial, entertaining films to an extent that they have raised the profile of Japanese films, they have had negative impacts on the development of quality and diversity in films. The critics allege that because audiences have become used to easy-to-understand films, their taste is becoming narrower, more homogeneous and increasingly close-minded to socially or aesthetically challenging works. Internationally awarded works may well attract the attention of the media and the general public for a short while, but that is insufficient to sustain independent film culture. Indeed, one may argue that the recent recovery has been a matter of luck with Hollywood driving Japanese consumers to local entertainment, but without market expansion or taste widening.

As a further piece of evidence, art house cinemas are failing to attract enough audiences, leading some venues to close down.

While the producer KAMEYAMA suggests that commercial films generate money and creativity into the industry that would then nurture independent films (Nihon eiga senmon channel [ed.] 2010, pp. 241–242), the details for the vitality of such an ecosystem are not clear. The diversity of films produced and consumed needs to be supported by conscious measures of cultural policy (see Jäckel 2007 for details of French cultural policy in this regard), but such efforts have not been made in Japan. The establishment of a specialist agency for film culture and industry could make a big difference, but that is unlikely to happen in the foreseeable future. Without a comprehensive policy for film as a cultural form – ranging from the policy to encourage production and screening of diverse films, to develop human resources, to promote Japanese films to international markets, to the policy of facilitating film education to help the public appreciate different narratives and imageries of world cinemas – the government's intervention in the industry is going to be heavily skewed toward economic aims: that is, the promotion of Japanese audiovisual production on the basis of economic potential alone by the creative industries policy pursued by METI. Before Japan realizes that no policy for film is better, the industry itself must reflect on the past, assess its current state and determine strategies of development.

Notes

1. Throughout the chapter, 100 yen is equivalent to one US dollar to reflect the approximate exchange rate.
2. The record was broken fourteen years later by the Ghibli studio with its *Mononoke hime* (*Princess Mononoke*, dir. Hayao Miyazaki 1997), which earned 19.3 billion yen (US$193 million) in Japan alone.

References

Agency for Cultural Affairs (2012) *Chihou ni okeru Bunka Gyosei no jyokyo ni tuite* (Report on Cultural Administration of Local Authorities), Agency for Cultural Affairs (in Japanese).

Agency for Cultural Affairs (n.d.) *Bunka Geijutsu Kanren Deta Shu* (Selected Data on the Arts and Culture), unpublished, Agency for Cultural Affairs (in Japanese).

Davis, D.W. and Yeh, E.Y-Y. (2008) *East Asian Screen Industries*. (London: British Film Institute).

European Audiovisual Observatory (2013) *Focus 2013. Marché du Film* (Strasbourg: European Audiovisual Observatory).

Gao, Z. (2009) 'Serving a Stir-fry of Market, Culture and Politics – On Globalization and Film Policy in Greater China', *Policy Studies*, 30(4), 423–438.

Jäckel, A. (2007) 'The Inter/Nationalism of French Film Policy', *Modern & Contemporary France*, 15(1), 21–36.

Jin, D- Y. (2006) 'Cultural Politics in Korea's Contemporary Films under Neoliberal Globalization', *Media, Culture, and Society*, 28(1), 5–23.

Johnson, C. (1999) 'The Developmental State: Odyssey of a Concept', in M. Woo-Cumings (ed.), *The Developmental State* (Cornell, CA: Cornell University Press).

Kakeo, Y. (2012) *Nihon Eiga no Sekai Shinshutsu* (Japanese Films toward the Global Market). (Tokyo: Kinema Junpo (in Japanese)).

Kawashima, N. (2012) 'Corporate Support for the Arts in Japan—Beyond the Emulation of the Western Models', *International Journal of Cultural Policy*, 18(3), 295–307.

Lim, L. (2012) 'Constructing Habitus: Promoting an International Arts Trend at the Singapore Arts Festival', *International Journal of Cultural Policy*, 18(3), 308–322.

Ministry of Economy, Industry and Trade (2013), *Press Release*, March 19, 2013.

Motion Picture Producers Association of Japan, Inc. Available from http://www.eiren.org/toukei/data.html, date accessed November 19, 2013.

Napier, S. (2011), 'Manga and Anime: Entertainment, Big Business, and Art in Japan', in V.L. Bestor and T.C. Bestor, with A. Yamagata (eds), *Routledge Handbook of Japanese Culture and Society* (London: Routledge), 226–237.

Nihon eiga senmon channel (ed.) (2010) *Odoru Daisosasen ha nihon eiga no nani wo kaetanoka* (What Has Been the Impact of Bayside Shakedown on Japanese Cinema?) (Tokyo: Gentosha (in Japanese)).

Vogel, Ezra F. (1991) *The Four Little Dragons: The Spread of Industrialization in East Asia* (Cambridge, Massachusetts: Harvard University Press).

Yomota, Inuhiko (2000) *Nihon eigashi 100 nen* (*A History of Japanese Cinema Over the Century*) (Tokyo: Shueisha) (in Japanese).

Index

Printed in Great Britain
by Amazon